Reading Bridal Magazines from a Critical Discursive Perspective

Reading Bridal Magazines from a Critical Discursive Perspective

Ewa Glapka

First published 2014 by
PALGRAVE MACMILLAN

Palgrave Macmillan in the UK is an imprint of Macmillan Publishers Limited, registered in England, company number 785998, of Houndmills, Basingstoke, Hampshire RG21 6XS.

Palgrave Macmillan in the US is a division of St Martin's Press LLC, 175 Fifth Avenue, New York, NY 10010.

Palgrave Macmillan is the global academic imprint of the above companies and has companies and representatives throughout the world.

Palgrave® and Macmillan® are registered trademarks in the United States, the United Kingdom, Europe and other countries

ISBN: 978–1–137–33357–5

A catalogue record for this book is available from the British Library.

A catalog record for this book is available from the Library of Congress.

Transferred to Digital Printing in 2014

To my parents and sister, for all your love and support

Contents

Acknowledgments

There are many people whom I would like to thank for their support. It would be difficult to mention all of them personally, but there are a few to whom I would like to give special credit. I am very grateful to the women who kindly agreed to talk to me – I appreciate their time as well as their readiness to share with me their own experiences and opinions. I am indebted to Prof. Małgorzata Fabiszak, who both encouraged me to undertake the work and provided support during the process. I am thankful to Prof. Michał Krzyżanowski, whom I also owe a deep debt of gratitude for all his advice and constructive criticism. I would like to thank the authors who provided me with their works on which I relied in my study, as well as the editors who allowed me to use and reuse some of my interview data. Last but not least, I would like to thank my editors at Palgrave Macmillan for their support throughout the process of publication.

Notes on Transcription

[	point of overlap onset
]	point at which utterance terminates
=	no gap between utterances (latching utterances)
,	short pause in the flow of talk
.	full stop, stopping fall in tone, not necessarily end of sentence
...	longer silence
–	a dash marks a sharp cut-off of a word or sound
<u>word</u>	underline indicates speaker's emphasis
LOUD	capitals mark talk that is noticeably louder than the surrounding speech
!	animated and emphatic tone
?	rising intonation, not necessarily a question
:	prolongation of immediately prior sound
°	relatively quieter than surrounding talk
< >	bracketing an utterance indicating speeding up
(( ))	transcriber's descriptions rather than or in addition to transcriptions
( )	inability to hear what was said
(word)	dubious hearings or speaker identification
mm	I agree a lot/yes, go on
[...]	material omitted by the author

[Adapted from Heritage (1984) and
Hutchby and Wooffit (1998)]

Introduction

Gender and media

This book has its origins in my interest in the relations between language and people's sense of self and the world. The underlying idea of the volume is that language mediates reality by enabling and constraining individuals' understandings of the reality, as well as the actions which follow from them. The awareness of the relations is accompanied by my concern with language itself – its meaning-mediating mechanisms and capabilities. Added to this curiosity, there is another vital object of the current exploration – gender. Much of what people think and do is connected to the ways in which they see themselves as women and men. Pertinent to both the language that individuals use and the notion of gender they develop is their exposure to media, especially given the media's overbearing presence in the contemporary world. Because of their pervasiveness, the media accompany people's everyday lives unheeded, similarly to language, which mediates human thoughts and actions basically unnoticed, and similarly to the gender binaries, which are taken for granted as the axiomatic categories of human ontology. It is usually seen as obvious that we use language, we are born men and women (and live accordingly), and that we are accompanied by a continuous stream of media-generated information and stimulation.

At the same time, as witnesses to the arrival of late modernity, more and more people make many of the once self-evident issues the objects of doubt and intense reflection. The devaluation of tradition and the all-pervading sense of uncertainty have uprooted the established models of gender and sexuality. The fact that the voices criticizing the socio-cultural dominance of heterosexuality are more and more audible in the public discourse is one indication of that. The wide currency which the notion of the 'crisis of masculinity' has gained is another such symptom, suggesting that the established masculine paradigm has been unsettled. The rigidity of the patriarchal definition of femininity has also been loosened with women taking advantage of this, for instance by negating wedding conventions and making a clear case for this in bridal magazines:

> Wearing a big, white frock dress for a second wedding might have been frowned upon years ago, but times have changed. ...Jennifer Lopez has worn traditional white dress for all three of her weddings. ...'I thought my husband deserved to marry a bride in white', says Joanne Sluzny, 33. (*Brides* 7–8/2008)

Not so long ago, it would never occur to people to deliberate on the color of the wedding gown, in the same way the bride's virginity, which it has symbolized, was taken for granted. But, as stated, the times have changed and the emergence of brides who do not observe wedding conventions is a clear indication of the influence of the sociocultural transformation on gender. As can be seen in the excerpt above, apart from being given the freedom of choice, women are also provided with the sites where these issues are freely discussed. Media (magazines, television, movies etc.) have become the space where the 'post-traditional' thaw in the once-established gender relations is celebrated.

Nevertheless, very much in the spirit of late modernity, this book assumes the position of doubt and calls in question both the thaw in the traditional gender order and the media's relation to it. So as not to either acknowledge or deny its factuality without proper justification, and to substantiate the study's concern with language as the medium of social meanings, this book sets its focus on the ways in which discourse may either reinforce or impede the actual changes in the traditional model of gender. With this aim in mind, the object of the current study is the discourse of wedding magazines – as an example of the media genre which has its every reason to guard the longstanding gender conventions but at the same time, as the excerpt above implies, responds to the sociocultural transformations within the contemporary wedding culture.

To briefly illustrate the critical perspective from which discourse is approached in this study, apart from what has already been noted about the magazine excerpt, it is possible to put an entirely different interpretation on it by observing how it reinforces some entrenched gender notions. For instance, one may ask, why should a woman state that her husband "deserves to marry a bride in white"? What does the color then represent that makes men 'deserve' or desire it? Why is the woman concerned with the husband's opinion when choosing her dress? Does it mean that the woman considers the bride's appearance as something that she 'presents' the groom with? Is that how she thinks of her appearance on an everyday basis? Finally, if gender conventions have indeed become so relaxed, why is the right of all women to wear a white wedding dress still made the object of a media debate? After all, the assertions of the bride's freedom to choose any gown she fancies are based on the presumption of this not being indubitable at all.

In the light of the above, does the excerpt still sound so revolutionary? Not to my critical linguist's eye, nor to me as a woman.

Nonetheless, so as not to rely solely on my own academic and personal standpoint in the study, I decided to complement my insights with those of other women – non-linguists. The inclusion of their voices in this research was considered as vital for two chief reasons. For one thing, as women who were either married or were about to get married, the interviewees added a perspective that I would not have provided as a single woman. For another, they added to the overall picture the insights of people to whom media are not the object of study but something that accompanies them in their everyday lives. Such a configuration of the two perspectives is what animates this piece of research. The spoken accounts of the women's relation to the media discourse and of their lived experience have a vital role in the book's exploration of the social circulation of gender discourses.

The content of the book

Conceptually, the book has been divided into three theoretical chapters through the lens of which the relations between discourse and gender are approached empirically in two other chapters of the volume. Importantly, accompanying the pursuit of the discursive mediation of femininity, there is the second major object of the book's concern – the analytical tools available for exploring the gender-mediating processes. Therefore, in each chapter more and less extensive consideration is given to the methodological solutions selected for the purpose of the current investigation.

Chapter 1 delineates the view of discourse on which the study is premised. The key notions discussed set the parameters of the exploration; they include both purely theoretical concepts and the concepts which serve the double role of theoretical and analytical units. It is an underlying premise of this book that the linguistic and the social (the discursive and the extra-discursive) are in a dialectic relation; both theoretical and methodological implications arising from this view are briefly discussed. The chapter provides a brief overview of Critical Discourse Analysis (CDA), which is one of three formal models of discourse studies informing this piece of research. While outlining CDA's programmatic preoccupations, the appraisal of its assumptions and goals is offered and attention is paid to the controversies aroused by the methodologies applied within the paradigm. Another substantial feature of the chapter is the review of the theories of power. The notion is given an extended scrutiny in order to explain in what sense wedding magazines are regarded here as a media genre which reproduces power relations by perpetuating normative discourses of gender.

While the theory of discourse and power advanced in Chapter 1 may compel the picture of the world being a realm of flowing ideas and secret power operations navigated by some undisclosed forces, Chapter 2 is supposed to counterbalance the view by elaborating on and providing a few critical comments to the previous part. Premised on the insights from poststructuralism, Chapter 2 attends to the individual level of discourse and gender practices, and underscores the human ability of independent sense- and self-making. The discussion deals with the main tenets of feminist poststructuralism. Feminist Poststructuralist Discourse Analysis (FPDA) is introduced as the second formal approach to discourse and it is contextualized within the research project. First, the incompatibility of FPDA and CDA is contested but part of the FPDA's critique of CDA's program is upheld. Next, the key concepts of subjectivity, identity, and gender are introduced and clarified. The understanding of the latter, briefly outlined in Chapter 1, is specified and the conventional notion of gender socialization is challenged. The constructive and interpretative nature of gender is noted and the role of language in the production of gender subjectivities underscored.

So as to deny the book's subscription to the poststructuralist 'negative paradigm of subject formation' (McNay 2000), FPDA's belief in the possibilities of powerful positioning is highlighted, which belief is informed in the study by two other frameworks introduced in Chapter 2 – the theory of textually mediated femininity and feminist standpoint theory. They are included in the discussion to compel thinking about media and gender practices in terms of individuals' lived experience and lifeworld knowledge. In this way, the study seeks to avoid neglecting the forms of agency and reflexivity which may come to surface in these practices. Once it is acknowledged that individuals can be reflexive agents, the discussion briefly outlines the ways in which their role in reception processes has been conceptualized and investigated so far. The examples of the approaches applied to date are briefly reviewed to spell out the book's contribution to the field of media reception research. As can already be seen, the driving force of the volume has been to explore media reception in a way that the forms of subjection and constraint are recognized but some room for individual agency is also allowed for.

In Chapter 3, the media constructions of gender are subject to an extended inquiry as the study narrows its focus onto the discourse of British bridal magazines. The exploration begins with a brief outline of the media genre which the magazines represent. They are recognized as an integral part of the contemporary wedding market connected with wider systems of sociocultural and economic relations. Emphasis is put on situating the magazines in the sociocultural reality of late modernity as one of the major results of the analysis was to identify numerous traces of late modernity in the magazines' texts. Informed by the theory of discourse and power elaborated in the first two chapters, the examination of wedding magazines concentrates on the workings of the discursively mediated power which positions their recipients firmly within the nexus of the dominant discourses of traditional femininity and consumerism. The underlying reflection of the analysis is, then, how women need to consent to think of themselves to read texts in the magazines as coherent, relevant, and informative.

The subject positions into which the magazines interpellate women are explored by means of the analytical units most of which are introduced in Chapters 1 and 2. Such an organization of the discussion is supposed to enable readers an informed insight into the analyst's engagement with language data and to make her arguments easier to follow. As will be underscored in the volume, the analysis of the language data is conducted with the adequate reflexivity of the polysemic nature of texts. On this basis, readers' right to disagree with the author's inferences is emphasized more than once in this book, so is the impossibility of making insights into the 'actual' intentions behind any discourse use. Chapter 3 concludes with the note of the magazines' reliance on the conventional meaning-making resources, but the magazines' capability of generating their own socio-semiotic inventory is also observed. The possible social implications of that are briefly discussed.

The chief aim of Chapter 4 is to briefly introduce Critical Discursive Psychology (CDP) – the third of the three formally established models of discourse analysis endorsed in the study. As explained in the volume, this model of discourse analysis takes the 'synthetic approach' to discourse and identity, which this book finds coherent with its view of subjectivity, and which it considers as applicable in the exploration of media reception.

As has been stated, the second stage of discourse analysis presented in Chapter 5 consisted in the interviews during which women were asked about their reception of one prompt magazine and their own wedding experience. The bottom-up perspective was taken to pay heed to the role of individual sense-making and self-making practices in the circulation of sociocultural meanings and in the ensuing formation of the consensual understandings of gender. What the interviewees said as regards media discourse is loosely divided into their general attitudes and their references to specific articles in the prompt magazine. The discussion of the latter body of data includes cross-references to the articles analyzed in Chapter 3. Because the interviews were semi-structured and the participants were asked not only text-based questions, a substantial volume of the data is not directly related with the media texts. As it yields insight into the women's own experience of getting married, the book has taken the opportunity of presenting the media-based picture of weddings side by side with the accounts of lived wedding experience. It will also be demonstrated how the talk which is not directly related with the media frame may be found enriching in the analysis which takes an interpretative, contextual approach to media reception.

Introduced and discussed one by one in Chapter 5, in Chapter 6 the interviews are summarized and overall patterns of media reception and gender positioning are distinguished. They are discussed in reference to the arguments advanced in the volume. The confrontation of individual lifeworld perspectives with the same media frame was meant to probe the questions of the polysemic nature of media texts and of the role of one's lived experience in the practices of text interpretation. Such an approach was supposed to allow this study to follow its participants in their situated textual encounters, as they negotiate their subjectivities (of women, readers, brides etc.). Another line of confrontation proposed in Chapter 6 is one between the women's personal relation to the discourse of the magazines and the analyst's interpretation of the discourse. The results of this configuration of subject positions are presented and some methodological implications are discussed.

1
Discourse and Power

Critical Discourse Analysis

As outlined in the introduction, the primary consideration in this volume is that societies are organized first and foremost by texts. Language regulates social life in ways that people are usually unaware of. This viewpoint requires a conceptual framework informed by the theories of both discourse and power. Because this book is centrally involved with the media-based reproduction of the consensual understanding(s) of femininity, specific questions that follow from this interest should be addressed by means of this framework as well. The aim of the current chapter is to briefly introduce the basic theoretical tenets of this study and to explain reasons behind applying specific analytical concepts. As will be seen from the discussion below, in its explorations of the intricate connections between discourse and gender, this volume draws centrally on the theory of discourse developed within Critical Discourse Analysis (CDA).

Recognizing the theoretical and methodological diversity of the extended field of discourse analysis, Litosseliti and Sunderland (2002: 18–19) make an emphatic distinction between critical discourse analysis (that is, adopting a critical disposition to language) and "doing Critical Discourse Analysis". This distinction enunciates the general agreement among linguists to consider CDA as a specific school of language. At the same time, although 'formalized' as an already established and self-recognized program of discourse analysis, CDA continues to develop and include new methodological solutions. In keeping with its transdisciplinarity (see Kellner 1989; Chiapello and Fairclough 2002; Fairclough 2005a; van Leeuwen 2005b), CDA has remained open also to other, not necessarily purely linguistic, ideas to strengthen its exploratory and explanatory potential.

The underlying aim of CDA-based studies has been to explore the "non-obvious ways in which language is involved in social relations of power and domination" (Fairclough [2001] 2009: 229). The role of a careful, linguistically informed analysis is to expose the opacity and intricacy of the relations:

> Language indexes power, expresses power, and is involved where there is contention over and a challenge to power. Power does not derive from language, but language can be used to challenge power, to subvert it, to alter distributions of power in the short and long term. (Wodak and Busch 2004: 109)

Consequently, despite its linguistic character, Fairclough (2001: 229) emphasizes that "[t]he starting point for CDA is social issues and problems". Following van Dijk (1993: 280), CDA is "primarily interested and motivated by pressing social issues, which it hopes to better understand through discourse analysis". This social and political engagement is clearly manifested in CDA's research agenda, which has so far included racism and nationalism (van Leeuwen 1996; van Dijk 1997; van Leeuwen and Wodak 1999; Arnott 2010), mass media (Fairclough 1995b; Flanagan 2010; Marling 2010; Shirazi 2013), education (Lee 1997; Ivanic 1998; Lemke 2003; Lim 2014), and institutional and workplace discourse (Sarangi and Slembrouck 1996; Iedema and Wodak 1999; Krzyżanowski 2010). Gender issues have also been pursued within CDA (Caldas-Coulthard 1993, 1996; Wodak 1997; Litosseliti and Sunderland 2002; Cameron 2003, 2005; Lazar 2005; Jeffries 2007; Annandale and Hammarström 2010; Chinwe and Osakwe 2013). Gender has become one of the objects of CDA research because it has been regarded within the paradigm as "an idea, or set of ideas, articulated in and as discourse" (Sunderland 2004: 18). Clearly, if mediated by discourse, of which CDA is fundamentally mistrustful, gender needs to be scrutinized for its potential involvement in power relations.

The programmatic engagement with the issues of power means that research steps necessary in any critical project may be reproached as value-laden. Therefore, such investigations require more than any other that analysts "take an explicit sociopolitical stance: they spell out their point of view, perspective, principles and aims, both within their discipline and within society at large" (van Dijk 1993: 252; see also Jeffries 2007: 16). When outlining the theoretical assumptions informing this piece of research, I will thus also seek to explain why the discursive mediation of bridal femininity is explored here as potentially involved in the reproduction of specific ideologies. At the same time, because CDA is not the only model of discourse analysis informing this project, the formulation of its theoretical premises and 'sociopolitical stance' will have been completed upon the end of the subsequent chapter.

Discourse, language and text

CDA has been engaged with both analyzing and conceptualizing language. Critical discourse analysts share an interest in the linguistic surface of social phenomena and present their own, but usually alike, understandings of 'discourse' and of its relation to the concept of 'language'.[1] Discourse, in very basic terms, means language used in context. As Gouveia (2003: 51) notes:

> CDA may well prove to be the catalyser of a new model of understanding what happens when one uses language. In order to understand this, language has to be seen as a set of multilevelled layers of meaning in interconnection, which may only be defined by the interconnections they establish with yet other interconnections. As in physics, linguistic events do not occur according to deterministic laws but according to a set of probabilities in different dimensions.

Based on that, discourse can be more specifically defined as socially embedded and socially meaningful uses of language. For example, Jäger, following Link (1983: 60), regards discourse as "an institutionally consolidated concept of speech inasmuch as it determines and consolidates action and thus already exercises power" (Jäger 2001: 34). Wodak proposes to see discourse as "a complex bundle of simultaneous and sequential interrelated linguistic acts, which manifest themselves within and across the social fields of action as thematically interrelated semiotic, oral or written tokens, very often as 'texts', that belong to specific semiotic types, i.e. genres" (Wodak 2001a: 66). Chouliaraki and Fairclough (1999: 38) refer to 'discourse' as "semiotic elements of social practices. Discourse therefore includes language (written and spoken and in combination with other semiotics, for example, with music in singing), nonverbal communication (facial expressions, body movements, gestures, etc.) and visual images (for instance, photographs, film)."

In the same way CDA analysts share their basic understanding of discourse, they seem unanimous in allowing for a broad and inclusive definition of 'text'. In contrast to the popular notion of 'text', they point out not only its written but also oral forms, as well as its increasingly multisemiotic nature. The visual analysis in the book's exploration of bridal magazines demonstrates that, indeed, texts (although primarily linguistic) blend with other semiotic forms in ways that necessitate methodologies which respond to those other forms. Vitally, while text is usually defined in rather broad terms within CDA, it has been guided by a particularly specific understanding of textual analysis as one that is centrally involved with 'texture'. The "textural properties of texts", Fairclough (1995a: 4) explains, are valuable indices of the sociocultural contexts in which they originate. Both the linguistic and intertextual features of texts are therefore no less important for CDA researchers than their content.

Constructivist structuralism

Acknowledging the intricately social nature of language, this book considers it to be both socially constructive and socially constricting. This logic has been incorporated into CDA from *structuration theory* (Giddens 1984) and *constructivist structuralism* (Bourdieu and Wacquant 1992). When proposing his understanding of the dialectic between structure and agency, Bourdieu resuscitated the philosophical concept of *habitus* and conceptualized it as embodied ideology (Bourdieu 1990). People, he suggested, act by relying on mental, internalized schemes. These dispositions to action and thinking are standardized within a given social field and structured by the field's fixed properties. Accordingly, habitus can be understood as the routine sense- and self-making practices, what people take for granted, the lifeworld experience in which individuals follow what they consider natural and most sensible. Importantly, however, although structured by the local conditions of living, habitus is not determined by them. Likewise, Giddens (1984: 25, 169) proposes that structure is "always both constraining and enabling".[2]

Clearly, this book distinguishes between the discursive and the social practices by treating them as distinct parts of the socio-semiotic dialectic. Language use leads to either construction or reproduction of discourses, with specific social implications; the production of language is however conditioned by social structures and practices. An important caveat as regards the 'structures and practices' is added here from the poststructuralist tradition of discourse analysis (see Chapter 2). Namely, this volume considers 'reality' as available in the form of multiple realities – subjective, emerging from contexts, mediated by socially located discourses. In other words, both the social structures and the changes made within them by social agents are part of individuals' subjective experiences. This does not mean that the extra-discursive is denied in this study. Following the *critical realist* epistemology (Bhaskar 1986; Archer 1995; Archer et al. 1998; Sayer 2000; Fairclough 2005b), the study acknowledges that any knowledge about the extra-discursive depends on the researcher's position but interest in the material level of discursive practices is nonetheless maintained in this book.

This understanding of the relations between the discursive and the social is elaborated on in reference to the book's view of identity. The book regards discourse as "an array of enabling potentials...[and] a set of constraining boundaries beyond which selves cannot be easily made" (Shotter and Gergen 1989: ix). In other words, although people's creative and self-determining abilities are not denied, their thoughts and actions are shaped by the objective structures of society, culture and language, that is, the socioculturally available discourses. Following the constructivist-structuralist perspective, this volume seeks to address these socio-semiotic intricacies empirically in the investigation of the public and private discourses of gender, as found in British bridal magazines and in women's talk about them. The analysis of the magazines is intended to give some insight into "the way we are spoken about" (Jaworski and Coupland 1999: 412), while the interviews with magazine readers present "the way we speak both to and about others" (and, in the current investigation, about ourselves) (Jaworski and Coupland 1999: 412). The former concerns "various private and institutional discourses [that] are constitutive of us (and others) as social subjects" (Jaworski and Coupland 1999: 412–3). The latter is related to the practices by which people negotiate their identities, or subject positions. In these practices, the book considers, individuals are capable of shaping their social realities.

Struggle over meaning

In this book's elaboration of its critical perspective on language, it proposes to see language as the site of 'struggle over meaning'. While language is the site of the struggle, and meaning is at stake, the struggle takes place during the practices of discourse. Following Bakhtin ([1935] 1981: 272), discourses operate centrifugally and centripetally:

> Every concrete utterance of a speaking subject serves as a point where centrifugal and centripetal forces as brought to bear. The processes

of centralization and decentralization, of unification and disunification, intersect in utterance.

Centripetal forces are the normalizing, stabilizing and prescriptive pressures to subject language to arbitrary conventions. They "produce the authoritative, fixed, inflexible discourses of religious dogma, scientific truth, and the political and moral status quo" (Maybin [2001] 2009: 65). Centrifugal forces represent the opposite directions by pulling language to diversity and creativity, and making it a vehicle of resistance. A discourse that emerges from this dynamic is "open and provisional in the way it produces knowledge and is often swayed by other people's inwardly persuasive discourses and by the authoritative discourses which frame people's everyday actions" (Maybin 2009: 65).

This underlying dynamic of language explains why gender, which is understood here as 'set of ideas articulated in discourse', needs to be scrutinized in terms of power hidden behind the relations of meaning. Both femininity and masculinity are centrally involved in the processes discussed here because the formation and contestation of gender takes place in the practices of discourse – what it means to be a woman or a man is usually the effect of some form of 'struggle'. As will be demonstrated in this volume, the media discourses of gender propose definitions of femininity that they subsequently normalize and stabilize through, for instance, repetitions, consensual tone, stylistic coherence, modality and genres. However, these apparently conventional and non-negotiable meaning structures can be challenged. They can be undermined or subverted by the centrifugally organized 'private discourses' in which people articulate their lived experience. Accordingly, in terms of Bakhtin's insights, research presented in this volume confronts the normalizing media discourses of gender with the potentially subversive, 'inwardly persuasive' discourses of embodied speakers.

Explanatory critique

CDA has been recognized in the field of discourse studies as a research tradition that "openly professes strong commitments to change, empowerment, and practice-orientedness" (Blommaert and Bulcaen 2000: 449). Namely, apart from exposing the indirect links between language and power, a critical discourse study is supposed to provide "the basis for political action to bring about radical and emancipatory social change" (Hammersley 1997: 238). From the very beginnings of CDA, its main theorists and practitioners have underscored the importance of providing people with the knowledge of the power-related processes, that is, 'critical language awareness' (Fairclough 1995a: 217ff.). CDA's *explanatory critique* (Bhaskar 1986) is intended to play an auxiliary role in identifying the power relations and proposing the discursive resources for resistance.

Following Smith (1992: 93), this book considers that "in ... contemporary societies, the functions of organization and control are increasingly vested in distinct, specialized, and (to some extent) autonomic forms of organization and relations mediated by texts". The 'relations of ruling', as Smith calls the textually mediated regulation of social life, reproduce specific understandings of gender. The 'explanatory critique' that this volume hopes to offer is its contribution to a better understanding of the ways in which the prevailing conceptions of femininity circulate in media discourse. Nevertheless, neither it is this study's goal to 'prove' that popular media (such as wedding magazines) inferiorize women by presenting them with depreciative definitions of femininity, nor does it assume that women do not have their own ways of contesting hegemonic discourses. Firstly, the aim of this book is to analytically connect the mechanisms of meaning construction and the ideologically or economically motivated processes behind them. Secondly, this study seeks to explore the dynamic between the media and the reader by looking into how the predominant understandings of bridal femininity are negotiated in women's encounters with media texts.

Regarding the latter, although this piece of research takes an openly critical approach to discourse and believes that media discourses reproduce gender-based inequality, it does not claim that women are completely unaware of it. Such an assumption, this book posits, implies ignoring the "knowledgeability of social actors" (Giddens 1984: xxxvii). Even though this does not necessarily mean patronizing them as unthinking and passive recipients of media content, the appearances of such a presumptive approach, I propose, might emerge from the investigation of media discourse reduced to one (academic, feminist) perspective. Far from denying the value of CDA's approach to media discourse, this book will take the opportunity to enrich the critical examination of bridal magazines with interviews in which readers individually related to the magazines' discourses. In its critical engagement with interview data, the study will explore how the women's identities were encoded in their language use. The texture of the spoken data is intended to cast some light on the dynamic between the reader, media texts and, perhaps, on how those texts tap into her sense- and self-making practices.

Analysis

Because of the undeniable complexity of the processes of meaning construction, any arbitrary conventions of data analysis would unnecessarily decrease the research potential of critical discourse studies. As van Leeuwen (1996: 33) cogently explains, "[t]here is no neat fit between sociological and linguistic categories, and if Critical Discourse Analysis ... ties itself too closely to specific linguistic operations or categories, many relevant instances of agency might be overlooked". This very way that CDA addresses the complexity of social reality has been has been criticized by some linguists. For example, according to Widdowson (2004: 97), it makes research a "random enterprise" in which methodological choices are based on analysts' subjective judgments. Nevertheless, as this book posits, preparing 'catalogues' of acceptable methodologies would be counterproductive, mainly because CDA has traditionally pursued dynamically changing areas of sociocultural life as well as contexts whose 'reality' is difficult to predict.

Therefore, following the principles of *conceptual pragmatism*, this book considers that social theory's "major task [is] to clarify conceptual tools and to construct new ones by following criteria of utility rather than truth" (Mouzelis 1995: 9). Variation in the methods of analyzing discourse, the volume posits, is particularly worthwhile for dealing with complex objects of study. Apart from allowing analysts to pursue diverse topics (by providing a wider range of relevant concepts), it can help them to formulate specific research question. Of course, such a pragmatic approach can be a productive way of exploring discourse on the condition that analytical tools are carefully chosen and consistently implemented, and as long as the choices are firmly grounded in the nature of data. For example, originally in this project no extended scrutiny of the visual modality was planned. It was included upon my recognition of the extent to which bridal magazines rely on the use of images in the construction of a coherent discourse of gender.

Studies conducted under the rubric of CDA have been criticized not only for lack of a consistent methodology of data analysis, but also for the critical interpretations that they render (see Blommaert 2005; Schegloff 1998). It has been argued that CDA's engagement with uncovering implicit relations of power is not accompanied by sufficiently thorough analyses of language. In turn, critics claim, this model of research fails to provide unambiguous, verifiable links between data examined and the ideological interpretation of the material. Consequently, this piece of research may be questioned on two premises – not only may my application of specific methodologies be found unjustified, but also the results of my critical engagement with the data may be challenged as shaped by the study's ideological position.

However, in continuity with the general position of critical discourse analysts, it is noted here that discourse data are open to multiple interpretations. Thus, if results of the critical analysis of discourse are at variance with the results of an analysis that claims 'sociological neutrality', CDA's sociopolitical program may not be the only reason behind this. As Jeffries (2007: 14) contends, any investigation of language can be found to be slanted because there are no direct relations between meaning and form that could systematically validate a given way of interpretation:

The lack of straightforward mapping of meaning onto form, then, is one of the factors that militate against any purely objective analysis, since a case may have to be made for the analysis offered, rather than being an automated procedure.

Therefore, because of the perplexity of relations between linguistic and social categories, all findings presented in this volume need to be regarded as but one possible way of interpretation. A disclaimer for those readers who consider the analysis as dogmatic in 'revealing' the ideological encodings of discourse comes from Fairclough (1992: 75):

The meaning potential of a form is generally heterogeneous, ... texts are usually highly ambivalent and open to multiple interpretations. ... Providing we bear in mind this dependence of meaning in interpretation, we can use 'meaning' both for the potential forms, and for the meanings ascribed in interpretation.[3]

Following Thompson's (1990: 133) line of argumentation, this book comes to terms with the potentiality of multiple readings and sees any analysis as a form of "synthetic construction" whereby theoretical and analytical units, as well as they ways in which they are deployed, are tapped into what is presented as the results of the analysis. Hence, this study openly denies that it is value-free, not only because it represents research tradition that has been ostensibly involved with ideological critiques, but also because any possibility of conducting value-free, 'objective' research is doubted here.

Another vital way of reducing the ambiguity of the object of critical discourse studies is by the *triangulation* (Cicourel 1969) of data.[4] The triangulating method adopted in this investigation, apart from merging multiple disciplines "in the analysis of a specific discursive occasion" (Weiss and Wodak 2003: 22; see also S. Scollon 2003: 172), consists of relying on more than one way of data collection in the investigation of the same problem (Taylor [2001] 2009: 322). Accordingly, in this book the media reproduction of gender is explored at its two vital sites – production and reception. The intention behind this organization of research was to see how the two parts of the examination inform one another by generating themes and insights that would have otherwise been imported by the analyst.

By drawing on more than one methodological paradigm, this book posits, after Baxter (2010: 132), that "[w]ithin linguistics, there is much value to be gained from a multiperspectival approach that combines different methodological tools in a pragmatic way as befits the task in hand". Such a pragmatic approach to the construction of relevant frameworks seems even more reasonable if we consider that many problems pursued within the CDA framework may not have occurred to linguists when formal linguistic categories and principles were developed. Because of that, this volume suggests that, imposing any formal requirements on the selection of conceptual units could weaken analysts' explanatory potential, and hence undermine the overall aim of increasing critical language awareness in society.

Finally, as noted, the current investigation is not a purely linguistic undertaking. It is accompanied by a critical appraisal of relevant insights from sociology and feminist theory. For one thing, the exploration of the social, along with the semiotic, is compelled by the dialectic perspective endorsed here. For another, as Sparkes (1992: 48) argues, "if one voice, or paradigm, dominates then there is real danger that we end up just speaking to ourselves. This can lead to a form of tunnel vision whereby some problems are explored exhaustively while others are not even perceived." In that sense, including insights from social sciences can be considered as the analyst's pragmatic choice to "transcend the purely linguistic dimension" (Wodak 2008: 12) of research in order to enhance its analytical capacities, as well as to open new possibilities of the transdisciplinary exchange of ideas and observations. Therefore, drawing on multiple perspectives is, the book suggests, not a 'random enterprise' but an asset of the transdisciplinary approach allowed by CDA.

Intertextuality

To understand the CDA's concept of the socio-semiotic intricacy it is crucial to consider 'discourse' as the circulation of texts in society. This means seeing discourse in terms of the connections between texts and discourses that are established on a socio-cognitive (Fairclough 1989, 1995a) and a sociocultural (Fairclough 1992, 1995a) level. As Litosseliti and Sunderland (2002: 12–13) argue, "[d]iscourse analysis necessarily involves analysis of the text as a product, but if the ultimate concern is language in a social context, such analysis alone can only ever be of limited value. Is there even such a thing as 'a text' (alone)?" Likewise, Hodge and Kress (1996: 181) notice that although texts are commonly seen as concrete units, their unity is arbitrary and misleading: "Texts are constantly recycled, appearing in an endless succession of text-about-texts, readings of readings."

This conception is by no means CDA's original contribution. It can be traced back to Foucault's concept of 'discursive unity' (Foucault 1972) and to Bakhtin's ([1953] 1986) notion of dialogical connections between texts. Relating directly to the latter conception, Fairclough (2009: 233) points out that "any text is explicitly or implicitly 'in dialogue with' other texts...which constitute its 'intertexts'." These meaningful connections generate coherence which, in turn, allows discourses to be formed: "The meanings that they [readers] construct are therefore not precisely 'in' the text....These meanings are realized in other texts which readers produce,...which are never transparent, never produced in social isolation" (Hodge and Kress 1996: 175). Moreover, when advancing his understanding of intertextuality, Fairclough posits its text-transforming capacities. In doing so, he elaborates on Bakhtin's (1973) notion of *double-voicing*, namely, the idea that a word is the site of struggle waged over its meaning between two voices. Based on that, Fairclough et al. (2011: 361) note that when one text refers to another, the meaning of the original text is often changed: "Any text is a link in a chain of texts, reacting to...and transforming other texts."

Understandably, intertextuality is an indispensable object of study in the investigation of media discourse. Apart from the obviously poly-glossic elements, wherein, for instance, journalists explicitly draw on their interviewees' or experts' words, the discourses circulating in the media form a variety of hardly discernible connections. The systems of connections are vital objects of any critically inclined study because they allow forging the unrecognizable relations between meanings.

Decentralization of text

The text-transforming capacity of intertextuality raises questions about the authorship of meaning. While it is commonly assumed that words are given meanings at the moment they are used by a given speaker or writer, Hodge and Kress (1996) challenge this view. Rejecting the unity and autonomy of texts, they advance the metaphor of 'fissures' that split texts and make authorship of meaning more problematic than it usually seems to be. Texts constitute intricate networks within which the voices of their authors are dispersed. Their autonomy and agency are hence problematized:

> The text (any given text) ceases to be a self-evident unity, but appears as a relatively accidental site.... Producers (authors, speakers) likewise lose the semblance of unity, and become channels through which various authors and agencies speak and act – the fissured authors of fissured texts. (Hodge and Kress 1996: 181)

Similarly to how the idea of 'fissured' texts undermines the autonomy of specific texts, the idea of the 'fissured' authorship tells us to doubt and interrogate the actual autonomy and agency of discourse users. Therefore, whether people speak their own voices or echo voices once heard will be a recurrent question in this piece of research.

Furthermore, meanings are shared by not only the original and the subsequent ('new') authors of texts. As observed by Vološinov ([1929] 1973: 86), a word "is precisely the product of the reciprocal relationship between speaker and listener, addresser and addressee.... A word is territory shared by both addresser and addressee". Yet, unlike Barthes' (1986) metaphor of "death of the author", the idea of 'fissured' authorship implies a shared, intersubjective mode of meaning construction. As Hodge and Kress (1996: 174) explain, "[m]eaning does not exist unless there are people who make it happen, in a process where those who receive texts (readers, listeners, viewers) engage in an activity which produces its distinctive kinds of meaning".

All these considerations provide a strong rationale for the 'decentralization of text' (Wodak and Busch 2004: 106). In line with this major reorientation, critical discourse analysts approach meanings as constituted in extended contexts (Wodak and Busch 2004: 106). Apart from the chain relations between texts and discourses, researchers consider also the social contexts of meaning-making processes:

> A fully 'critical' account of discourse would... require a theorization and description of the social processes and structures which give rise to the production of a text, and of the social structures and processes within which individuals or groups as social historical

subjects, create meanings in their interactions with texts. (Wodak
2001b: 3)

In the present analysis it is thus regarded that the authorship of media
texts disperses in the intertextual connections established in the wider
contexts of media consumption. While interpreting media texts, readers
negotiate their meanings with the authors, and they draw on the memory
of other texts ('intertexts'). Moreover, how texts are made meaningful
depends both "on the receivers and on the settings" (Wodak and Busch
2004: 106). For instance, in the current study, the social context needs
to be understood in terms of the local dynamic between the reader and
the text, and between the interviewer and the interviewee. Additionally,
each of the local encounters with media text is situated at the macro-
level of social institutions, norms, ideologies, etc.

The 'decentralized' view of text is presented here not only for the
sole purpose of theorizing about language but also to lay a theoretical
ground for data analysis. The notion of 'fissures' informs the study in
a number of ways. Firstly, it reminds us of the need to account for how
meanings are negotiated between interactants (rather than enunciated
by speakers and writers). Secondly, because of the intersubjective nature
of meaning construction, when expressing themselves, people consider
how their "text will itself be read by its proposed readers" (Hodge and
Kress 1996: 175). The current exploration takes this as a reminder of
people's rhetorical orientation to talk. This in in turn means that what
they say should not be assumed to directly express their thoughts and
experience. Finally, as has been noted, analysts cannot abstract the
textual and intertextual processes of meaning construction from the
larger social context.

Interdiscursivity

Elaborating on Bakhtin's notion of intertextuality, Fairclough (1992)
distinguishes between "manifest intertextuality" and "constitutive intertextuality". While the former occurs when specific words from one text
are explicitly put in another (Fairclough 1992: 104), the latter (which
Fairclough terms as *interdiscursivity*) consists in the "combination of
elements of orders of discourse" (Fairclough 1992: 118). Interdiscursivity
is definitely less discernible because discourse orders are not constituted
by specific texts. They are the configurations of discourses and genres
that render socioculturally constructed norms of expression and interaction "available to use" (Chouliaraki 2002: 105). In addition to their own

ways of using language, discourse orders have "diverse representations of social life which are inherently positioned" (Fairclough 2009: 235). In other words, the meanings that are used within specific discourse orders are always in some way valued, marked by their intrinsic moral or ideological dispositions.

Therefore, the notion of 'discourse order' allows a better understanding of CDA's belief in the social implications of language or, more specifically, in the reciprocal relations between the social and the semiotic. Language use, which is implicitly suggestive of (moral or ideological) values and which regulates interactions between people, does not merely 'reflect' reality. Although it is constrained by the existing social conditions, it also has the capacity to affect them. For example, even though used by people who are bound by some social rules, it can be used by them to change the rules.

This renders a purely theoretical model. Yet, one of the main reasons for which the current volume draws so extensively on CDA is that CDA's conceptual apparatus allows the exploration of the mechanisms outlined above directly, as they emerge from data. As will be seen in the empirical part of this volume, the idea of the socially constructive potential of interdiscursivity is a telling example in that regard. Still, if not justified, the claim of the socially transformative power of interdiscursivity may leave readers skeptical of the analysis presented in Chapters 3 and 5, where the idea is presented as self-evident. To avoid that, some brief explanation is now provided as regards the theory of discourse from which this idea follows.

To begin with, similarly to texts, discourses "have no objective beginning and no clearly defined end" (Wodak 1997: 6). They usually form interdependent configurations of two or more discourses (or genres), which have commonly been termed *hybrids*. As Jaworski and Coupland (1999: 99) posit, "most texts are not 'pure' reflections of single discourses" and the continual changes make language fluid and creative. As such, hybridity can be seen in terms of *affordances* (Gibson 1979) that allow a continuous introduction of new meanings into society (van Leeuwen 2005a: 5; see also Chouliaraki 2002).

Importantly for the dialectical perspective, "[i]nterdiscursivity, which ensures discourses' continuing fluidity, may be key to both discoursal *and* social progress, and can also be seen as dialectically ... 'transforming' texts through encouraging a rethinking of their meanings" (Sunderland 2004: 30). In other words, texts people read may compel them to rethink specific meanings, sometimes leading to change in their social actions. In particular, some discourses present us with social practices that are *recontextualized*, that is, moved from one discourse order to another (Chouliaraki and Fairclough 1999: 110). The meanings of the practices may be reconsidered because when the practices are put in different orders of discourse, relations between them are reconfigured – the practices are consequently rearranged and reconstructed. For instance, in Chapter 3 this process will be addressed with reference to the recontextualization of consumption in media discourse. It will be seen that moved to the discourse order of the media, where it is presented as a social practice related with wedding experience (rather than a purely economic and commercial practice), consumption is dealt with in new terms and its understanding can be established anew. This example illustrates the implicit mode of controlling social practices and thus of wielding power in a culture regulated by the conditions of neoliberal economy.

As can be seen, the socially constructive power of discourse which has been postulated in the present chapter means that instead of putting it bluntly to people that 'you are what you have', the media can recontextualize the practices of consumption in ways that make people arrive at this conclusion on their own. Noting this, the current study adopts Berstein's view that ideologies are not supposed to be explored by looking into "content but a way in which relationships are made and realized" (Bernstein 1996: 31). Similarly to Bernstein, Chouliaraki and Fairclough (1999: 109) specify that the role of recontextualization is to establish the relationships in ways such that "practices or subjects are ideologically constructed as unproblematically real". The implicit mode of the reconstructive work is highlighted also by van Leeuwen (2008: 12–13) when he claims that recontextualization

is rarely transparent to the participants of the recontextualizing practice, and is usually embedded in their common sense, in their habits of relating to each other, in what they take the purposes of the recontextualizing practice to be – all those things which form the usually tacit know-how of experienced participants of the recontextualizing social practice.

Briefly, recontextualization enables the distortion of the represented reality. According to Bernstein (1996: 24), "every time a discourse moves, there is a place for ideology to play". With this in mind, in this volume the mixing of discourses and genres in wedding magazines is examined with an accompanying consideration of their covert power of regulating readers' social practices.

Transdisciplinary approach to discourse and power

The dialectic perspective on the relations between language and power requires a framework that attends to both the discursive and extra-discursive mechanisms involved in those relations. Therefore, the discussion below will proceed to review concepts that are not directly derived from linguistics but cast a vital sidelight on the issues that are pursued in this book (and have been weaved into the transdisciplinary program of CDA). The theories explored below share an interest in the decentralized power. Although some of the individual models differ as regards their ontological and epistemological premises, they present a relatively coherent view of the dispersed forms power. The brief reappraisal of the models enumerates what distinct qualities of the power they highlight; to demonstrate how they inform discourse researchers is a further intention of the discussion.

Interpellative power of discourse

One of the theories that draw on the idea of discursive mediation of power is Althusser's (1971) concept of *Ideological State Apparatuses* (ISAs), which are dispersed, yet organized forms of control such as family, art, systems of religion and education. Conversely to the *Repressive State Apparatuses* (RSAs) (such as government and police), ISAs reproduce power indirectly.[5] They compel submission to specific ideologies in the processes of *interpellation* (hailing),[6] that is, through calling individuals into specific subject positions:

> ideology "acts" or "functions" in such a way that it "recruits" subjects among the individuals...or "transforms" the individuals into subjects...by that very precise operation...called interpellation or hailing, and which can be imagined along the lines of the most commonplace everyday police (or other) hailing: "Hey, you there!" ... [T]he hailed individual will turn around [and] by this mere one-hundred-and-eighty-degree physical conversion, he becomes a subject. (Althusser 1971: 174)

To link this view to the subject matter of the current volume, it can be said that a woman who sees a bridal magazine on a newsagent's shelf and buys it, is hailed similarly to the individual stopped by a police officer. Following logic proposed by Althusser, she apparently accepts the media's ideologically laden distinction between the female and male audiences, whose interests are presumed to revolve around, for example, beauty and sports respectively. This, in turn, may imply even more as regards her submission to the dichotomous gender order because the same ideology that informs the 'gendered' organization of the contemporary media market justifies the patriarchal organization of society. However, it is suggested in this volume that this now classic metaphor, though compelling, implies an arguably reductive logic. As will be demonstrated, to be hailed into the position of a female media consumer does not necessarily tell much about one's involvement with the hegemonic discourses that the media perpetuate.

The concept of interpellation lends itself to this study because media discourses are approached here in terms of reader positioning. Because subject positions that are made available in media texts imply specific identities of text recipients, they indicate what media producers assume about the recipients. If the latter indeed read the texts from the positions provided, media interpellations become self-fulfilling prophecies. This puts the media in the powerful position of creating social reality (rather than merely representing it):

> the subordination of the subject takes place through language, as the effect of the authoritative voice that hails the individual.... [A] policeman hails a passer-by on the street and the passer-by turns and recognizes himself as the one who is hailed. In the exchange... interpellation – the discursive production of the social subject – takes place. (Butler 1997: 5)

It will be demonstrated in the book that interpellation consists in various uses of language (see Bardin 1977), ranging from direct address (such as in the simple illustration of hailing by a police officer) to more implicit forms, such as presuppositions and implicatures. As regards the implicit forms, it can be noted that the interpellative mode of power would not be possible if it were not for the intertextuality of language. According to Fairclough (1992: 134), texts "interpellate interpreting subjects who are 'capable' of making relevant assumptions, and of making the connections which yield coherent readings". In other words, the ability to use 'intertexts' may indicate one's knowledge and acceptance of a given discourse, and hence of its underlying ideology. For this reason it has already been proposed in the discussion, after Jaworski and Coupland (1999: 412–3), that "various private and institutional discourses are constitutive of us (and others) as social subjects".

Regimes of truth

The regularity with which 'meaning' recurs in CDA's theory of power (as constructed, negotiated, contested, etc.) stems from the idea that the decentralized power is enacted through the production and organization of knowledge. Following Foucault's structuralist view of power, CDA considers discourses as productive of the objects of which they speak within successively added 'epistemes' (Foucault [1966] 2001). The successive layers of the systems of knowledge (epistemes) define what is possible at a given time and place. Although he was not concerned with the linguistic minutiae of the process, Foucault acknowledged its linguistic nature by approaching discourse as "the production of knowledge through language" (S. Hall 1992: 291). He elaborated on this by developing the notion of the *regimes of truth*:

> Truth...induces regular effects of power. Each society has its regime of truth, its 'general politics' of truth; that is, the types of discourse which it accepts and makes function as true, the mechanisms and instances which enable one to distinguish true and false statements. (Foucault 1980: 31)

Clearly, then, CDA's research (exploring the "non-obvious ways in which language is involved in social relations of power" (Fairclough 2009: 229)) has been driven by the logic of the 'archeological' study of the production of knowledge. According to Foucault, the 'regimes of truth' are created and managed through the construction and organization of specific modes of understanding and seeing.[7] Hence, his theory

> allows us to understand how meaning is produced not at the will of a unitary humanist subject, not as a quality of a linguistic system..., but rather through a range of power/knowledge systems that organize texts, create the conditions of possibility for different language acts, and are embedded in social institutions. (Pennycook 1994: 128)

The functioning of social institutions is regulated through the *microtechniques of power* (Foucault 1981). This is a decentralized mode of power because, although enacted within institutions, the 'microtechniques' are enforced by individuals, after they submit to a given 'regime'. Thus, Foucault (1981: 94) claimed, "[p]ower comes from below...there is no binary and all-encompassing opposition between rulers and ruled at the root of power relations".

All this offers a convenient perspective for considering the role of media in social life. The media can be regarded as one of the major vehicles of the decentralized power in late modern societies because of the extent to which its public and private realms have become mediatized (see Giddens 1991; Couldry 2000; Bennett and Entman 2001; Hepp et al. 2008). Media discourses generate bodies of knowledge that are later embodied in social practices. Giving a full account of this process is beyond the scope of this book. What this volume seeks to explore is whether/how media discourse can be used to produce coherent systems of knowledge (in other words, the appearances of 'truth') and whether media recipients consent to consider the media-popularized knowledge as 'true'. Finally, the concept of individuals who internalize ideologies and become 'docile' subjects (Foucault 1977) lends itself to the examination of the sociocultural construction and management of gender order. Although gender analyses influenced by Foucault (see de Lauretis 1989; Bartky 1990; Bordo 1999; Thorpe 2008) draw on his conceptual framework, the methodologies that they apply differ. By the same token, the current project is informed by Foucault's theory of discourse but it does not follow his methodology of discourse analysis (see Carabine [2001] 2009).

Hegemony

The media's capability to regulate social life in the way described above stems from its hegemonic position. *Hegemony*, in the sense proposed by Gramsci (1971), is another key concept in the conceptualization of power advanced in this volume. According to Gramsci, holding a dominant position does not require coercive or repressive forms of influence – power can be enacted consensually. Emphatically, 'hegemony' is not simply 'domination' but the ability to win the approval of a given ideology by impressing its 'commonsensicality'. The consensus about the legitimacy and naturalness of hegemony is accomplished discursively in a "series of cultural, political and ideological practices" (Hargreaves and MacDonald 2000: 49), and the forms of leadership hence effected are contestable.

Gramsci's emphasis on the contestability of hegemony (and ideologies legitimating it) resonates with the notion of discourse presented above in this chapter. In the discussion of Bakhtin's view of language, it was proposed to consider language as a site of a continual struggle over meaning that renders meanings "open and provisional" (Maybin 2009: 65). The struggle, it was explained, takes place in the practices of discourse. Laclau and Mouffe (1985) see struggle for power in terms of 'bids for meaning closures'. This, they posit, takes the form of *articulations*, which they define as "any practice establishing a relation among elements such that their identity is modified as a result of the articulatory practice" (Laclau and Mouffe 1985: 105). Because none of the 'meaning closures' is likely to be sustained, the hegemonic arrangements (which are legitimated by means of meaning relations) are instable, in the way it was proposed by Gramsci and Foucault (see Pringle 2005). Based on that, in the current book, this view of hegemony is considered as a rationale for exploring the construction of power in terms of recontextualization and hybridization processes. Because gender order is organized in the way Gramsci understood hegemony, his concept has been applied by Connell (1995: 77) in her notion of *hegemonic masculinity*, that is, "the configuration of gender practice which embodies the currently accepted answer to the problem of the legitimacy of patriarchy".

The dominant gender paradigm, based on the axiom of binary sexes, is sustained because most people accept it as natural and reproduce it in day-to-day practices. Therefore, in contemporary Western societies, no overt persuasion is necessary to naturalize essentialist masculinity and femininity:

> Gender is embedded so thoroughly in our institutions, our actions, our beliefs, and our desires, that it appears to us to be completely natural. The world swarms with ideas about gender – and these ideas are so commonplace that we take it for granted that they are true, accepting common adage as scientific fact. (Eckert and McConnell-Ginet 2003: 9)

In the absence of any particularly explicit system of reward and punishment for gender compliance and resistance, people rarely experience their gender self as externally imposed, regulated and monitored. This sense of imposition is, however, part of the experience of those who (wish to) live beyond the bisexual, heteronormative paradigm, and those who feel victimized by the established gender norms (such as the division of social life that assigns women and men private and public realms respectively).

One's internalization of the dominant gender order is hence a form of 'subliminal pedagogy' (Bem 1993), whereby the commonsense knowledge about femininity and masculinity is gained, not enforced. For instance, even as girls, women are provided with a narrow scope of socially ratified feminine roles – mainly pleasing and attracting. Consequently, they are socialized into 'emphasized femininity' (Connell

1987), that is to say, they internalize the concern to accommodate to the demands and expectations of men (see Pipher 1994).[8] Apparently, the 'subliminal pedagogy' continues throughout women's lives. For example, in the study presented in the current volume, the constructions of emphasized femininity were found to pervade the pages of all wedding magazines examined.

Although this view of gender order is insightful in many ways, it has some deterministic overtones that may render such an understanding of gender hegemony easy to invalidate. To illustrate, applying Connell's concept of hegemonic masculinity in their examination of men's identity work, Wetherell and Edley (1999) found their participants to work up their own, 'non-hegemonic' masculinities. On that basis, Wetherell and Edley (1999: 352) propose to reconsider the hegemonic consensus on gender in terms of versions of reality that are "plural, inconsistent, achieved through discursive work, constantly needing to be brought into being over and over again". The understanding they advance, therefore, chimes with the emphasis put in the discussion above on the contestability of power. Thus, it also corresponds with the book's aim to explore individuals' relationships to the hegemonic constructions of gender (as opposed to 'proving', or 'disproving', the legitimacy of the dominant understandings of femininity and masculinity).

Symbolic power

The idea that social order is reproduced predominantly through meanings and practices rather than force and discipline is key in Bourdieu's theory of *symbolic power* (1991). Similarly to the models discussed above, it concerns the kind of power that is exercised by the 'cultural arbitrary' (Bourdieu and Passeron 1977), that is, those social groups who are in a position to create meanings and reinforce them in ways that lead to the legitimation of the existing status quo.

Clearly, Bourdieu's view of power is another one that can be applied in a critical examination of media discourse. Media are unequivocally in the position of the 'cultural arbitrary' – their power is symbolic because it consists in the construction and organization of the relations of meaning. Moreover, gender is by all means a product of symbolic power. Reality becomes 'gendered' thanks to the mechanisms of symbolic power because the biological differences between men and women are mapped onto other aspects of their lives in ways that manipulate meanings of the differences. As Eckert and McConnell-Ginet (2003: 10) claim, "[g]ender builds on biological sex, it exaggerates biological difference and, indeed, it carries biological difference into domains in which it is completely irrelevant". For instance, can the sex differences between people be a reasonable explanation of why wedding magazines are addressed to women? After all, it takes a woman and a man to get married (as the magazines persist to claim within their heteronormative discourse). Because this book finds no straightforward justification for this, it considers that gender is a construct. The hegemonic social order based on it is hence a sociocultural arrangement that is symbolically reinforced "in the misrecognizable form of relations of meaning" (Calhoun et al. 1993: 21).

Expert systems

The powerful role of media discourse in late modern societies has predominantly been explained in terms of their enhanced mediatization. Although this view is not discounted in the current discussion, the media's remarkable presence in people's everyday lives does not suffice to account for the degree to which the media affect social life.

First of all, media are predominantly seen as a source of information and entertainment. The acknowledgment of the information role is an important note in light of what has been stated above about the key links between power and knowledge. Its weight appears even greater considering how highly valued any relevant and promptly delivered piece of information is nowadays. The late modern pursuit of knowledge involves a "chronic revision in the light of new information or knowledge" (Giddens 1991: 19). Adding to the enhanced amount of information and knowledge, because of their increased accessibility, the media make various events enter our everyday lives rapidly: "'[t]he world'...intrudes into presence via an array of varying channels and sources" (Giddens 1991: 189; see also Grodin and Lindlof 1996). The accumulating images and texts circulating in the media form their own 'hyperreality' (Baudrillard 1988) in which the distinction between 'reality' and the media representations of it is lost. This continuous production and availability of knowledge, one may argue, leads to confusion and makes individuals more vulnerable to manipulation.

Apart from recognizing the value that late modern societies ascribe to knowledge, Giddens (1991: 18) finds them regulated by *expert systems*:

> Expert systems bracket time and space through deploying modes of technical knowledge which have validity independent of the practitioners and clients who use them. Such systems penetrate virtually all

aspects of social life in conditions of modernity – in respect of food we eat, the medicine we take ... and multiplicity of other phenomena. Expert systems are not confined to areas of technological expertise, they extend to social relations themselves and to the intimacies of the self. The doctor, counsellor and therapist are as central to the expert systems of modernity as the scientist, technician or engineer.

The increased pursuit of knowledge that expert systems thrive on is the result of the late modern crisis of tradition. Because of people's "incredulity towards metanarratives" (Lyotard 1984: xxiv) – that is, disbelief in the universal, traditional forms of knowledge – all assumptions about science, literature, art, etc. are now doubted and interrogated. For lack of a stable system of knowledge and beliefs, individuals search for 'constructed certitudes' (Beck 1992) that are supposed to provide a new frame of reference. Consequently, on the one hand, the traditional certitudes no longer neither cap people's imagination nor do they constrain individuals' understanding of the world. On the other, the incredulity generates the sense of uncertainty about self. For example, referring to contemporary times as "liquid modernity", Bauman (2004: 32) notes that the identities that emerge from it are "the most acute, the most deeply felt and the most troublesome incarnations of ambivalence". Troubled by the emergent "tribulations of the self" (Giddens 1991: 189ff.), individuals consider their identities as a project which needs to be accomplished, or simply, something they need to 'work out' for themselves. As Giddens argues, because identity is no longer given or imposed, and has become a 'reflexive project of the self' (Giddens 1991), it is now accomplished through an intended and systematic search for coherence.[9]

The overall confusion accompanying the increased reflexivity is a rich soil for those who are in a position to provide relevant information. Because media are among them, they are turned to as one of the expert systems. The media evidently take advantage of it by presenting themselves as a valuable source of lifestyle information (Giddens 1991: 199). As will be evident from the study, in doing so the media are likely to impress on their audiences the need for self-work in a variety of ways (apparently, wedding preparation may also be one of them). Providing individuals with the "methodology of life-planning", the media insist on the importance of becoming the "capable individual", that is to say, capable of developing a full self-understanding and control of life (Giddens 1991: 180). In this way, it can be argued, media consumers become involved in the 'microtechniques of power'. Encouraged to self-work by the media's expert knowledge, they commit themselves to what

Foucault termed as the 'technologies of self' (Foucault 1986, 1988). The technologies consist in individuals' practices of personal self-actualization and transformation, which they consider as self-chosen but which are in fact related with the macro-politics of decentralized power.

Conclusion

This chapter has attempted to outline the theory of discourse underpinning the whole volume. The book's theoretical framework includes concepts that it considers as key in the critical inquiries into the discursive mediation of femininity. Some of the concepts discussed here are purely theoretical constructs, others serve in this volume as both theoretical insights and as units of analysis. The latter have been endorsed because of the direct relation they establish between the analyst's epistemological position and her engagement with data. The former have been addressed for how they contribute to the development of a comprehensive and coherent picture of the discourse-based reproduction of gender that this book presents.

Meaning relations are understood here in terms of 'struggle over meaning'. The notion was highlighted in the chapter more than once. First, it was noted that this metaphor refers to the internal dynamic of language; next, it was found related with the ways in which language is implicated in the mechanisms of power. The dialectical relations between society and discourse were elaborated on in the discussion of intertextuality and interdiscursivity, which will be important analytical concepts in the empirical parts of the volume (i.e. Chapters 3 and 5). In the further chapters of the book the processes of forming and reproducing the consensual knowledge about gender will be considered in terms of the intertextual and interdiscursive processes of establishing relations between social practices. To complement this book's view of the discursive regulation of social life, this chapter provided a synthesis of ideas concerning the decentralized forms of power – although they are not immediately relevant to language-based research, they are vital in the current project in which the social and the semiotic are seen as intricately connected.

CDA was also introduced in the chapter by a brief discussion of what CDA researchers mean by discourse, language and text. As explained, while numerous understandings thereof have been advanced to date, they all agreeably point to the social nature of language, which CDA sees apparent in discourse practices and their materializations, that is, (written and spoken) texts. Based on that, in the analysis presented in this book I will investigate the socially meaningful uses of language – (written) media texts, textually mediated images (as other semiotic forms which CDA includes in its understanding of a comprehensive textual analysis), and, finally, (spoken) texts produced during interviews.

The connections between language and society, which were formulated in this chapter under the concept the socio-semiotic dialectic, imply that an analysis of discourse needs to be conducted with the appropriate reflexivity of the social context of the discourse practices under study. While CDA has usually been regarded as interested in the wider social contexts, this piece of research seeks to combine the macro- and micro-level layers of analysis. Namely, in line with CDA's decentralized view of text and due to its interest in power relations, this book will retain the focus on the socioculturally and historically available discourses. This will be supplemented with the micro-level investigation of how the discourses are drawn upon both in the construction of media texts and in the local contexts of text interpretation.

Finally, the purpose of this chapter was to provide a CDA-based view of the relations between discourse and power with the specific focus on the issues of gender. According to Walsh (2001: 27), "a number of approaches to CDA, including that of Fairclough, marginalize the importance of specifically gendered identities and the social inequalities to which these contribute" (see also Cameron 1998). The current piece of research seeks to demonstrate that even though gender identities are not at the top of CDA's research agenda, the framework is applicable to the investigation of the discursive mediation of femininity. The covert relations of power with which it has been preoccupied centrally concern gender. At same time, as I signaled in the discussion, the notions that have so far been included in the book's conceptual framework do not render a full view of discursively mediated femininity proposed in the current study, neither are they endorsed here without reservations. These will be elaborated on in the following chapter where another perspective is explored to illuminate those aspects of the discursive mediation of gender that are underplayed in the paradigms presented above.

2
Women as Subjects of Discourse

Critical Discourse Analysis and (Feminist) Poststructuralist Discourse Analysis

The central point made in this volume is that the study of the media-based reproduction of gender requires two plains of analysis. One of them concerns the macro-level of grand discourses that seek to enforce and legitimate specific relations of power. The other is preoccupied with the micro-level of lifeworld practices, where the power relations become part of people's lived experience. The former level was attended to in the previous chapter in the discussion informed by the Critical Discourse Analysis (CDA) theory of language. The latter is the subject matter of the current chapter and it will be discussed here primarily from the perspective of Feminist Poststructuralist Discourse Analysis (FPDA).

In this book, these two models are integrated within the framework of a single study because they are considered here as both complementary and compatible. As for the former, it was stated above that FPDA and CDA pay more attention to the micro and macro facets of exploration respectively. As regards their compatibility, FPDA, like CDA, asserts its central focus on language and its interest in the covert relations of power. In so doing, it is informed by the wider poststructuralist perspective:

> For poststructuralist theory, the common factor in the analysis of social organization, social meanings, power and individual consciousness is language. Language is the place where actual and possible forms of social organization and their likely social and political consequences are defined and contested. (Weedon 1997: 21)

Engaged with the study of the "great anonymous murmur of discourses" (Foucault 1989: 27), both CDA and FPDA make it their programmatic aim to break the anonymity.

Still, integrating CDA and FPDA within one research project might be problematic because of the differences that their programs are seen to render. To begin with, subscribing to the Poststructuralist Discourse Analysis (PDA), Baxter (2002: 830) rejects the idea of discourses being both constitutive and constituted (see also Baxter 2003). She follows Foucault in seeing discourse purely in the former ('constitutive') sense and ascribing it with "the capacity to produce what it names" (Butler 1994: 33). Referring to PDA's engagement with the role of discourse in people's experience of self, Baxter (2002: 830) emphatically asserts that their identities are "continuously reconstructed and open to redefinition *through* discourse, not outside it".

Conversely, this book rejects the relativist perspective and, as stated in Chapter 1, endorses a dialectical view of language. Maintaining this study's interest in both the discursive and the extra-discursive, the current chapter turns to the investigation of the textual mediation of femininity and takes it from D. Smith (1992: 92) to understand text as "the bridge between the actual and the discursive". In doing so, this work seeks to show that the consideration of the extra-discursive ('the extra-discursive' is preferred here over Smith's conception of 'the actual') is an important inclusion in the investigation of the local, subjective experience of power. Crucially for the current discussion, proposing this the work additionally seeks to prove that such a perspective does not contradict its belief in the constructive capacities of discourse.

With reference to that, in this volume, as explained, people's experience of self, and all other processes described here, are seen from the critical realist perspective. It is considered that reality should not be confused with the perception of it because language is not "an unobtrusive conduit between thoughts or concepts and things" (Shapiro [2001] 2009: 320). The fact that reality cannot be objectively demonstrated, or 'proven', however, is not a sufficient premise upon which to deny its existence. Asserting this, the current study takes it from the Foucauldian tradition not to involve itself with the nuances of truth and falsity but instead to "focus on the production of knowledge through institutions...and on what knowledge is used for without being side-tracked by the participants' concern as to whether the knowledge is true or not" (Potter 1996: 86).

Another line of critique developed by Baxter concerns CDA's emancipatory research ethos. She finds it totalizing as opposed to FPDA's focus on the local configurations of power (Baxter 2002: 830–1, see also Baxter

2008, 2010). Nonetheless, the research position presented in this book is that to attain what Baxter presents as FPDA's chief goal of identifying the local possibilities of resistant positioning, it is indispensable to *first* take the 'totalizing' perspective. What is meant here by this emphatic assertion is basically my partial agreement with Baxter, which I explain below.

Baxter (2002: 831) argues that with its openly deconstructive and emancipatory agenda, CDA has developed its own 'grand narrative', hence undermining the self-reflexive research position that it claims to have. Similarly, the research framework of this project is informed by the doubt that it is possible to pursue the emancipatory agenda by studying discourse solely from the analyst's own, academic (and ideological) positions. On these grounds, in its engagement with how discourses obscure power relations, this study seeks to avoid creating its own discourse that 'forms the objects of which it speaks' (Foucault 1972: 49). Indeed, just to claim the will of moving beyond the confines of one's own sense-making repertoire suggests a naive belief that some degree of 'objectivity' in research can be maintained. Thus, with this assertion I might be exposing myself to the accusation of undermining what I argued in Chapter 1 about the impossibility of value-free research. Still, far from denying the earlier statements about the inherent subjectivity of language and research, by 'avoiding creating one's own discourse' I mean the self-imposed discipline of the social scientist to remain reflexive of one's position and tools and to look for methodologies that facilitate this.

Accordingly, the analysis presented in this book starts from the notion that language, because of its intertextual links, is incomprehensible without allowing for "broader forms of intelligibility" (Wetherell 1998: 403), which include, social, cultural, political and historical circumstances. Therefore, even if researchers pursue the local contexts of power practices, they need to take "a more macroscopic view of the state of hegemonic relations and hegemonic struggle in the orders of discourse" (Fairclough 1995a: 229). After all, a sound understanding of historical, political or sociocultural implications of any discourse use enables a better understanding of how they are made relevant in the situated discourse practices (for example, what common-sense categories, arguments or ideas are employed in the negotiation of power). It is specifically in this way that CDA and FPDA, with their macro- and microscopic foci, are considered here as mutually informing.

Consequently, assuming the combined perspective, this project deconstructs some of the "various private and institutional discourses ... [that]

fabricate our subjectivities" (Jaworski and Coupland 1999: 412–3). Focus on institutions and any formal structures, entails deconstruction of the 'grand' discourses that position people as subjects. How the discourses 'fabricate our subjectivities' will be examined in this volume in the analysis of the media discourse of wedding magazines (the subject positions that they make available to readers). The 'private discourses' that fabricate our subjectivities are attended to when the investigation turns to the micro-level of discourse practice, that is to the analysis of the interviews during which readers negotiated their subjectivities in relation to media discourse in the local context of interaction.

Subjectivity

By approaching gender identity in terms of subjectivity, this book reveals its contribution to the poststructuralist understanding of self as experienced in terms of subject positions. A subject position can be defined as "the ensemble of beliefs through which an individual interprets and responds to her structural positions within a social formation. In this sense, an individual only becomes a social agent insofar as she lives her structural positions through an ensemble of subject positions that makes sense to at least one other person in one other time and place" (A.M. Smith 1998: 58). In this sense, identity is made meaningful by specific discourses. As Butler (1990: 143–5) posits, "to understand identity as a practice, and as a signifying practice, is to understand culturally intelligible subjects as the resulting effects of a rule-bound discourse that inserts itself in the pervasive and signifying acts of linguistic life". Simply, subjectivity is a way of being enabled (or enforced) by discourse and society:

> As we acquire language, we learn to give voice – meaning – to our experience and to understand it according to particular ways of thinking, particular discourses, which pre-date our entry into language. These ways of thinking constitute our consciousness, and the positions with which we identify structure our sense of ourselves, our subjectivity. (Weedon 1997: 32)

Because of the view of self as located in multiple discourses, the poststructuralist engagement with identity has consequently been a study of language, in the variety of approaches that have has taken within the wide scope of poststructuralism (see Butler 1990, 1993; Walkerdine 1990; Davies 1991; Poynton 1993; Thorne 1993; Weedon 1997, 1999; Davies and Harré 1999; Bucholtz and Hall 2005; Winslade 2005; Willig 2007).

Such an understanding of self clearly contends the humanist notion of identity as a distinct, fixed and fully comprehensible product of cognition and socialization which preexists the moment of its expression in language:

> While humanism implies a conscious, unified, and rational subject who stands apart from the text, postmodern poststructuralism posits agency in the linguistic and other signifying systems through which "the subject" is formed. Because identity is experienced as fragmented and conflictual, subjectivity is likewise an unstable site of continual contestation. (Currie 1997: 458–9)

In another insightful clarification, addressing this form of contingency, D. Smith (1988: xxxv) contrasts the notion of 'subject' with the one of 'person'. The former does not refer to an individual agent but to "the series or conglomerate of positions, subject-positions, provisional and not necessarily indefeasible, in which a person is momentarily called by the discourses and the world he/she inhabits". Similarly, drawing on the concept of subjectivity, Davies and Harré ([2001] 2009: 264) argue that "being is not inevitably caught in the subject position that the particular narrative and the related discursive practices might seem to dictate". In other words, although people are constructed by discourses as 'unitary' and 'stable' subjects, their lived experience of self is local – it consists in taking subject positions that are not 'fixed' to individuals but are taken in specific contexts. Bearing this in mind, the investigation presented in this volume is not meant to reveal what kind of media consumers the participants 'are' but to demonstrate how they dealt with dominant discourses circulating in wedding magazines in the specific context of research interviews.

Gender – feminist poststructuralist perspective

The poststructuralist view of subjectivity implies a specific view of gender. In Chapter 1, gender was provisionally defined as "an idea, or set of ideas, articulated in and as discourse" (Sunderland 2004: 18). This conception needs to be specified to make it easier to link with the analytical framework established for the purpose of the current exploration.

In this volume, gender is approached similarly to identity, its "frequent collocate" (Sunderland 2004: 18). Accordingly, femininity is investigated in terms of multiple, dynamic and contradictory forms of subjectivity, rather than taken for granted as a socioculturally constructed category internalized by individuals. The book recognizes the concept of 'gender identity' as problematic for the reductive idea of gender construction it sometimes implies (see Butler 1990; Gal 1995; Bergvall et al. 1996; West 2002; Eckert and McConnell-Ginet 2003; Cameron 2005). Therefore, when the concept is referred to throughout this volume, it is as a set of subject positions made available by discourses. Accordingly, instead of examining media as the agent of the ongoing gender socialization, this research project looks into the media and lifeworld discourses to see how language constructs "conflicting subject positions which become labelled as gender differences" (Simpson 1997: 204).

Based on what has been stated above, investigating gender in terms of subject positions is convenient in the analysis which claims its interest in the power relations hidden in the structures of language. This mode of research on gender is a methodology derived from feminist theory. For poststructuralist feminists – both theorists and discourse researchers – language is involved in ambiguous power practices in the same way it is claimed under the rubric of CDA. As Weedon (1997: 37 emphasis added) claims, "[t]he meaning of the existing structure of social institutions... and the subject positions which they offer their subject, is a site of political struggle waged mainly, though not exclusively, through *language*."

Importantly, in the data analysis, gender will also be discussed in terms of 'indexing' and 'performing'. Although the two concepts stem from different methodologies of language study and thus imply slightly different theoretical perspectives, they are part of the analytical toolkit in this investigation because, like positioning and constructing, they follow from the idea that gender is "precarious, contradictory and in process, constantly being reconstituted in discourse each time we think or speak" (Weedon 1997: 32). Hence, all the notions accommodate the perspective that gender is "a *process*, something that people *orient* to and *do* – including their spoken and written discourse" (Sunderland 2004: 17). In other words, discourses do not construct gender simply by infusing people's words with meanings because it is people who make language meaningful by referring to the preexistent meanings and norms of interpretation. Although the meanings and norms include the "static and exaggerated dualisms" (Thorne 1993: 91) of the dominant essentialist paradigm, this relation is continually negotiated.

Still with regard to the feminist poststructuralist perspective, another concept that recurs in this book is one of 'gendered' positions, ideas and contexts. It is used at those points of the discussion where what is referred to is not intrinsically related to gender but is assigned specific gender qualities. Importantly, however, in the same way gender can be made relevant, the relevance of gender can be negated. For instance, in Chapter 5 it is seen that the analyst's gendered reading of some texts was not confirmed by the interviewees; the data show how the academic, ideologically informed discourse was contested by the participants' life-world discourses.

The feminist poststructuralist understanding of the ways in which gender is implicated in the relations of power is premised on Althusser's logic of interpellation. Applied to gender, his view of power implies that gender order is produced by constructing the obviousness of specific practices and structures. Apart from identifying specific practices as obvious ('natural', commonsensical etc.), the discourses of power hail people to recognize the practices as such by accepting subject positions related to the practices: "Like all obviousness, ... the 'obviousness' that you and I are subjects – and that does not cause any problems – is an ideological effect" (Althusser 1971: 161). Accordingly, "[l]ike Althusserian Marxism, feminist poststructuralism makes the primary assumption that it is language which enables us to think, speak and give meaning to the world around us. Meaning and consciousness do not exist outside language" (Weedon 1997: 31).

Many discourses interpellate people as gendered subjects, but the individuals who accept their 'obviousness' do not tend to perceive this as an arbitrary regulation of their lives. For example, the hegemonic discourses of gender and sexuality construct the naturalness of a nuclear hetero-sexual family. It is the people who do not accept the dominant gender order that see the nuclear family as an arbitrary, artificial construct – to them 'a husband/father' and 'a wife/mother' are thus gendered positions, rather than natural gender roles. The social and psychological implications of one's location in this normative model of society cannot be overestimated, but the curiosity driving the current research project was to see the implications that gendered interpellations may have for the individuals who apparently identify with the dominant gender order.[1] In fact, this research has been born out of interest about whether the dominant discourses of femininity constrain their subjectivities too, but perhaps in less obvious ways.

As regards FPDA's interest in the local possibilities of power negotia-tion, which Baxter contrasts with CDA's pursuit of grand discourses, this book notes that some of the feminist poststructuralist insights are actually still involved predominantly with the 'totalizing' perspective. Namely, they imply a fatalistic view of all-powerful discourse, according to which changes can ever appear only within the limits set by the available discourses. For instance, according to Weedon (1997: 31), "it is language in the form of conflicting discourses which constitutes us as conscious thinking subjects and enables us to give meaning to the world and to act to transform it". Following Althusser's notion of subject pre-positioning, she argues: "If language is the site where meaningful experience is constituted, then language also determines how we perceive possibilities of change" (Weedon 1997: 82). Thus, the possibilities of effecting an actual transformation by the subject are only apparent because one's conception of the transformation is discursively predetermined.

The more empirically minded feminist poststructuralism, rather than slip into the bleak view of the constitutive power of discourse, puts more emphasis on the agentic aspects of identity. For example, A. Jones (1993) claims that educational research needs to be based on feminist poststructuralist methodology, but in so doing she clearly means studies of women's production of powerful subjectivities which will eventually show "more possibilities to develop and use a wider range of practices" (Jones 1993: 164). Similarly, in her study of classroom discourse, Baxter (2002) postulates the need for girls to be institutionally assisted in their pursuits of powerful positioning in public contexts. Importantly, in the same study Baxter observes that girls, although systematically positioned as 'victims' in the discourse of education, do not impassively submit to the position and negotiate their subjectivities in the local context of classroom communication. The current investigation, likewise, follows women in their local discourse practices, driven by the interest in individuals' capabilities of positioning within media discourses otherwise than as their powerless dupes.

It is proposed here, after Weedon (1997: 101), that "the battle for the meaning of gendered identity and the many attempts made by conflicting discourses to fix meaning once and for all are doomed to failure by the very nature of language". As discussed in the previous chapter, language is open to new meanings and continuously produces new 'intertexts'.[2] In regard to individuals' subjectivity, because of the consequent fluidity and contestability of meaning, language enables both the production and contestation of the same ideologies. Simply put, people can contest hegemonic concepts of gender for the same reasons other people seek to impose them – by constructing relations of meaning, and hence discourses and subject positions.

Yet, at this point in the discussion, it is not taken for granted that all individuals are able to take advantage of the possibilities to produce new forms of subjectivity. Therefore, in addition to the discussion that has so far been developed at a thoroughly theoretical and rhetorical level, this volume offers a more empirical approach to the problem. As mentioned above, in the interviews, which are presented in Chapter 5, individuals related to the media discourses of gender. The purpose of the discussion above was to explain the reasons why this context was arranged. As should be clear at this point in the discussion, in the interview data it is explored whether the participants, confronted with the hegemonic media discourses, were indeed capable of the deconstructive readings of media texts and of establishing powerful subjectivities in relation to the discourses that position them as powerless.

Textually mediated femininity

Another perspective from which women's reception of media has been approached in the current study is the theory of *textually mediated femininity* (D. Smith 1990). The theory stems from Smith's dissatisfaction with the essentializing, top-down approaches to gender. Contrasted with 'sex', 'gender' has commonly been regarded as the sociocultural interpretation of biological differences between people and, hence, as the aspect of identity that can be negotiated and contended. Nonetheless, because the interpretation has been based on the socioculturally available, predetermined premises, the meanings that have consequently been attached to masculinity and femininity have been essentialized and taken for granted similarly to the biological categories of masculinity and femininity (D. Smith 1990: 159). This, clearly, means that little space is provided for individuals' own interpretation of who they are as women and men.

Women, in that regard, are in a particularly disadvantaged position because, Smith states, their world has been organized extra-locally – through man-made, abstracted and institutionally grounded forms of knowledge (D. Smith 1990: 6). Their experience, in consequence, has been mediated by externally produced discourses, such as the ones of administration, professional organizations, the media, science, culture, etc. In order to expose and deconstruct what the discourses take for granted, Smith proposes a bottom-up perspective: "[t]aking up 'gender' from within, exploring social relations of women's experience, ... attending to specificities, not gender in the abstract, not as total, but as multiple and sometimes contradictory relations" (D. Smith 1990: 159). The relations are mediated by texts that surround women and enter their daily experience in a number of ways:

In our time to address femininity is to address, directly or indirectly, a textual discourse vested in women's magazines and television, advertisements, the appearance of cosmetic counters, fashion displays and to lesser extent books. These are constituents of the social relations they organize. Discourse also involves the talk women do in relation to texts, the work of producing oneself to realize the textual images. (D. Smith 1990: 163)

Hence, to take the bottom-up approach to the discursive mediation of femininity means to address the contexts of discourse practice where the arbitrary and objectified notions of gender are actualized in an individual's lived experience.

Still, it has been noted, local gender practices are inextricably bound with the wider, socially and culturally established norms and definitions of femininity. One of them is of a particular interest in this study, namely, "the talk women do in relation to texts, the work of producing oneself to realize the textual images" (D. Smith 1990: 163). Therefore, the interest in the situated practices of femininity should not annul the reflexivity of the grand, hegemonic discourses of gender. The media, Smith observes, organize "particular places, persons, and events into generalized and abstracted modes vested in categorical systems, rules, laws, and conceptual practices. The former become subject to an abstracted and universalizing system of ruling mediated by texts" (D. Smith 1988: 108). In this sense, this book proposes that the consumption of specific media (such as 'glossies'), as well as of other commodities, becomes a learnt cultural activity that is conceptualized as gender-specific. Therefore, discourses can be seen to operate across different modalities (as they materialize in various contexts and practices), which is another reason why research needs to be sufficiently contextualized.

Similarly to D. Smith, Weedon (1997: 25) claims that in the contemporary culture, the media-based production and reproduction of global meanings affixed to gender only apparently offers women multiple forms of feminine subjectivity:

A glance at women's magazines ... reveals a range of often competing subject positions offered to women readers, from career woman to romantic heroine, from successful wife and mother to irresistible sexual object. These different positions which magazines construct in their various features, advertising and fiction are part of the battle to determine the day-to-day practices of family life, education, work and leisure.

Following this perspective, the current book regards media discourses of femininity as a form of 'symbolic power' wherein texts are "subordinated to practical [social structural] functions" (Bourdieu 1979: 82) of gender order.

The consumption of the media texts about femininity is bound with the material production of the texts and specific artifacts (cosmetics, clothes, etc.) (D. Smith 1990: 173). The media's regulation of individual practices, such as the consumption of commodities, is rarely immediately recognized by the subjects of the discourses. As will be demonstrated in the study, the media-reinforced power relations between individuals and the market (producers, advertisers, etc.) are made covert in the media texts where consumption is affixed with symbolical meanings in ways that recipients may not notice. Vitally, this book considers that the assumption of the power processes that may be at work in the reception of media discourse requires the analyst's attention to the potential forms of agency of individuals involved in the processes:

> Women aren't just the passive products of socialization; they are active, they create themselves. At the same time, their self-creation [is] coordinated with the market...through print, film, etc. This dialectic between the active and creative subject and the organization of her activity in and by texts coordinating it with the market is captured here using the concept of textually mediated femininity. (D. Smith 1990: 121)

Clearly, "bridging the sociological dichotomy of structure and agency" (Currie 1997: 461), D. Smith emphasizes the agency of subjects in how they actualize texts in their lived experience. This perspective is therefore adopted in the current study along with that of FPDA, even though it is far from FPDA's non-materialist position. After all, similarly to poststructuralist feminists, D. Smith acknowledges the role of power in discourse by considering social relations mediated by the texts as 'the relations of ruling' (D. Smith 1992), and she also emphasizes that the textually mediated power can be locally challenged.

Gender scripts and social texts

Vitally, in the context of the current piece of research, D. Smith's (1990: 215) mode of examining the discourse of femininity contends the narrow textual approach to meaning construction and justifies the 'decentralized' approach to media texts proposed earlier in the volume:

In recognizing how texts function as constituents of social relations...my interest is not in tracing back through a given text to the
determinations of its meaning structure but in explicating discourse as
a social process. This can be seen in my exploration of the discourse
of femininity. It means that investigation cannot be confined to the
text alone, but must take into account the socially organized practices,
including sequences of talk, that are integral to the discursive process.

Given that texts interweave with other texts and thereby mediate social
relations, texts of femininity cannot be explored as separate textual
units, displaced from the local discourse and social practices. Instead,
the texts, for example women's magazines, need to be approached as
continuous with "the talk women do in relation to texts, the work of
producing oneself to realize the textual images" (D. Smith 1990: 163).
In other words, they are not to be understood as 'gender scripts', that is,
universalized, abstracted bodies of knowledge grounded in extra-local
discourses (D. Smith 1990: 167–8, see also Currie 1997: 454). They need
to be seen as 'social texts', whose meanings are contingent on how their
recipients contextualize them in their lifeworld experience. The recipient, accordingly, should be approached as the 'knower' who is "always
situated in the actualities of her experiencing" (D. Smith 1990: 5).

'Subject-in-discourse' and 'subject of one's actions'

Finally, in agreeing with the theory of 'textually mediated femininity', this
book includes the distinction between two major forms of subjectivity
which D. Smith's theory discerns. Accordingly, for one thing, readers of
media texts are seen here as "subjects-in-discourse" (D. Smith 1990: 192),
that is, as prepositioned by socially and culturally shared discourses. For
another, they are approached as the 'subjects of their actions':

> For while the subject-in-discourse is denied agency, there is another
> subject who is here speaking in her capacity as a knowledgeable prac-
> titioner of the discourse of femininity. She is putting her judgement
> that "I don't think...etc."...We come, then, upon this irony. While
> the appearance, the presentation of themselves that women seek
> to create on their bodies, denies and obliterates their heterosexual
> appearance as autonomous subjects, the production of appearance
> calls for thought, planning, exercise in judgement, work, the use of
> resources, skills. Behind the appearance and its interpretation there is
> secreted a subject who is fully an agent. (D. Smith 1990: 192–3)

Clearly, the distinction between the two forms of subjectivities follows from the notion of 'social texts'. Although the media interpellations perpetuate fixed and normative definitions of femininity and assume women's compliance with them, individuals establish their own relations to texts. In so doing, they may defy the hailing power of the media.

As in the quotation above, D. Smith draws a rather implicit boundary between the relations that women establish with discourses of gender in text reception and the ones that follow from the relations and are carried over into their embodied experience of femininity (such as practices of the heterosexual body). Therefore, by approaching women as subjects of their actions this exploration neither implies a definite binary of discourse and actions, nor does it claim that it is in people's 'actual' actions that meanings are made. To the contrary, the book is interested in the women's constructions of their embodied practices (consumption of media texts and commodities, bodily practices, etc.). In accordance with its critical realist premises, by investigating the *constructions* of the practices, this study does not deny the reality of the embodied experience. Yet, it contains an implicit belief that, as any other analyses, it is unable to render the women's 'actual' actions because of their inevitably mediated character. (After all, the actions of interest were mediated by the participants in the immediate context of the interviews and subsequently by the analyst when she recontextualized them in the discourse of academic research.[3])

Finally, D. Smith's idea of women living their lives amidst preconstructed discourses of power resonates with the view that other theorists saw in terms of, for instance, people living 'not in the conditions of their choosing' (Marx [1852] 2000), habitus and social structure (Bourdieu 1992), or in terms of 'accumulating capital in a bank owned by someone else' (Scollon 2003: 186). Proposing the latter metaphor in her discussion of habitus, Scollon notes that Bourdieu underestimated the capacity of individuals to position themselves within the field (see also Calhoun 1995; Mouzelis 2007). By contrast, D. Smith apparently does not. Likewise, the present study is centrally interested in the scope of agency that individuals establish in media text reception as well as in how this experience appears related with the individuals' everyday experience.

Approaches to media reception

Because the overall aim of this book is to address the sociocultural and psychological complexity of individuals' encounters with media texts, the remaining part of the current chapter conceptualizes text reception looking into what has already been claimed with regard to the process. First of all, although text reception has been the object of increasing interest among researchers in various disciplines, it has still not been given enough attention, especially considering how complex and important media reception processes are. The complexity is probably the main reason why analysts have, to date, approached reception from a number of angles and no dominant paradigm of audience research has been developed.[4]

To begin with, text reception research has been initiated in stylistics. Stylistics, however, has traditionally been involved with text itself rather than the reader. Starting from the cognitive poetics of the Constance School (Iser 1978; Jauss 1982), its shift to the 'reader' consisted in turning to a highly abstract concept of the text recipient. Based on the phenomenological analysis of text, it developed an account of the reader "resembling the interests of the analyst...rather than a historically identifiable specific individual" (G. Hall 2009: 332). Nowadays the dominant approaches to text reception, such as Text World Theory (Werth 1999) or cognitive stylistics (Semino and Culperer 2002; Stockwell 2002), do not show much more interest in the social context of reading than the earlier models of text analysis. Often based on fine-grained analyses of text corpora, they render abstract accounts of discourse processing.

As for openly critical approaches to the recipient, diverse methodological solutions have been proposed. For example, the framework that has commonly been associated with a programmatic interest in the recipient emerged as the so-called Frankfurt School (Marcuse 1968; Horkheimer and Adorno [1972] 1993; Adorno 1974). This Marxist tradition of media studies is famous for its approach to popular culture, which invariably turns people into 'passive dupes' susceptible to covert power workings. A similarly reductive account of reader subjectivity can be found in another Marxist framework, the 'screen theory' (MacCabe 1985; Mulvey 1988). Its idea of 'text productivity' implies "the capacity of the text to set the viewer 'in place' in a position of unproblematic identification/ knowledge"' (S. Hall [1980] 1996: 159). Thus, like other text-immanent approaches, this one also renders "an unbridgeable gap between 'real' readers/authors and 'inscribed' ones, constructed and marked in and by the text" (Willemen 1978: 48).

This underlying fallacy was addressed in the analyses associated with the Birmingham Centre for Contemporary Cultural Studies. With its original concept of the 'circuit of culture', wherein circulating meanings are produced in a variety of places, the model undermined the established distinction between media producers and consumers. The blurred line between 'coding' and 'decoding' means that "the social processes involved in encoding the meanings of media texts are not the same as those involved in decoding them, to the extent that we simply cannot assume that the texts 'mean the same' to producers as to audiences" (Talbot 2007: 7). Consequently, critics turned to regard the process of media reception in terms of interpretative practices in which subjects establish their spaces of agency. For instance, Fiske (1986) observed that media texts contain an excess of meaning rendered to multiple interpretations. S. Hall's (1996) encoding/decoding model was drawn on by Morley (1986) who found that interpretations of media messages depend on viewers' social status and their familiarity with the media codes and conventions. The three frames of text interpretation established by Morley and Brunsdon (1999) (dominant, preferred and oppositional) were a groundbreaking contribution to audience studies in that they acknowledged the polysemic potential of texts and audiences' creativity in deriving meanings from the texts.

Approaching reception from a number of angles, the empirical studies on media audience undermine the once taken for granted model of transmission and ideological indoctrination (Carey 1989). Some of the studies point to the class-based differences in both taste and the ideological interpretation of media content (Gray 1992; Thomas 1995). Others challenge the model by falsifying the assumption of the globalizing influence of popular media (see Liebes and Katz 1993; Husband 2000; Miller and Slater 2000; Ross 2001; Sinclair and Cunningham 2001; Downing and Husband 2005). Whether they delve into cultural, national or ethnic identities, they all reveal patterns of active engagement in media reception and the importance of accounting for the local contexts of media practices. An interesting way of exploring the localized media practices consists in investigating how media texts become occasionally situated in their consumers' daily practices. The diverse trajectories of recipients' involvement in talk identified in the analyses also challenge the idea of passive audience, especially by pinpointing continuities between the recipients' interpersonal communication and media-related talk (H. Wood 2005, 2006).

What seems particularly in evidence in Wood's 'text-in-action' approach to media audience is that paying due attention to text enables media reception analysts to bring out the complexity of receptive processes that should be neither taken for granted nor neglected (see also Moores 1990). The pronounced awareness of the "textural properties of texts" (Fairclough 1995a: 4) can also be found in the analyses of situated book talk (see Benwell 2009; Eriksson Barajas and Aronsson 2009;

Benwell et al. 2012). Importantly, in these studies, researchers take care that their accounts of text reception have a sound empirical grounding in the social context of reading. In doing so, they examine text reception as a resource of identity work and, on this premise, approach talk around text in terms of its rhetorical organization.

This book is another attempt to conceptualize and analyze text reception and it tries to shed some new light on it by combining the exploration of the 'textural' and situated properties of the productive and receptive media practices with a critical reflection upon them. In this way, the volume seeks to examine the role of media's ideological encodings without neglecting the affective nature of lived media reception. Clearly, because of its ostensibly critical premises, this study will not provide an ethnographic account of women's reception of magazines. Rather, the goal has been to occasion the intersubjective experience of positioning to the textual reality of a magazine in which the local textual encounters would be investigated as anchored in the macrolevel discourses of gender. In this way, this book seeks not to overestimate the 'active' viewer/reader and not to downplay the sociocultural power of media discourses that intersect in the local contexts of media reception.

Feminine subjectivity in media reception research

In a theory developed with women in mind, differentiating between the subject of discourse and the subject of one's action is not simply a theoretical or analytical distinction but a conception that makes a strong feminist argument. In fact, making a distinction between people's lived experience and the assumptions that are made about them and reproduced by institutionalized and objectified discourses can be universally applied in all kinds of research on discourse. After all, it compels attention to the sufficient contextualization of discourse practices. But, as mentioned in this chapter, this differentiation between the two forms of subjectivity was made by D. Smith with women in mind. It came out of her concern with how research on feminine experience was dominated by masculinist epistemologies.

Accordingly, by incorporating Smith's views into this research project the current volume underscores the importance of attending to media consumption from the perspective of women who function outside the dominant discourses of both media and academic research. In the light of the expanding field of research studies, it would be an exaggeration to claim that researchers do not show any interest in women as one of media's target groups. Rather, this book seeks to highlight the caveat that comes from Smith's line of reasoning that without the proportionate amount of attention on both texts and their readers, research on media and femininity will lead to the "unacknowledged eliticism" of research valorizing the perspective of a feminist critic (Currie 1997: 457).

The increased interest in media reception owes a lot to feminist media studies. The neglect of women's subjectivity has been addressed by many gender and media analysts (see Radway 1984; Frazer 1987; Winship 1987; Ang 1988; Livingstone 1994; Hermes 1995; Currie 1999; Long 2003; Gauntlett 2008).[5] A substantial body of feminist literature addressing that neglect represents a broader turn in media and cultural studies, which gave rise to new audience research (see Corner 1991). The explorations conducted under this rubric were driven by the interest in the uneasy distinction between low and high culture, as well as in the inconclusiveness of the notion of 'media pleasure' and individuals' non-obvious (for example, subversive) strategies of consuming popular culture (see de Certeau 1984; Fiske 1986). Many feminist writers who followed the turn not only postulated an enhanced attention to readers' reflexivity, but also observed the need for analysts to realize their own fallibility.[6]

For example, Modleski (1991: 4) claimed that "the cultural analyst may sometimes be a 'cultural dupe' – which is, after all, an ugly way of saying that we exist inside ideology, that we are all victims...of political and cultural domination". Currie (1999: 146) observed this limitation, arguing that "we hope to enlighten, to open eyes...but our position is never unquestioned". Similarly, in her critique of Radway's assumptive approach to audience pleasure, Ang (1996) insightfully problematized the relationship between the researcher and participant. In doing so, she drew attention to feminists' proclivity to bring into their analyses ideological dogmatism (see also Brunsdon 1993, 2005).

By trying to avoid the academic vanguardism of critical media research and its edifying undertones, this book finds itself at a difficult position of negotiating between its reluctance to take the critic's privileged, infallible position and its will to sustain the study's critical view of discourse. As a way of proposing a reasonable solution to this, the book takes account of *feminist standpoint theory* (Hartstock 1983; D. Smith 1988; Harding 1991; Wylie 2004). As noted earlier in the discussion, D. Smith considers textually mediated femininity as situated between the lifeworld experience of femininity and socioculturally available discourses for articulating it. The object of this study is to account for the richness and complexity of the former without losing track of the latter. As a way of explaining this, the view of the subject implied in Smith's theory can also be found in the standpoint feminist distinction between 'standpoint' and 'location'. The latter is given, while the former is an achieved, reflexive position; it is "earned through critical reflection on power relations and through engaging in the struggle required to construct an oppositional stance" (J. Wood 2009: 56). J. Wood (2009: 85) explains that standpoint "refers not simply to location or experience, but to a critical understanding of location and experience as part of – and shaped by – larger social and political contexts and, specifically, discourses" (see also Intemann 2010).

Consequently, the book posits that any research also needs to be seen in terms of a standpoint that is developed within a given location. This provides a strong premise for repudiating any forms of decontextualized knowledge and argumentation. These, the book claims, need to be foreclosed because they obliterate not only the epistemic differences between researchers on the one hand and participants on the other, but also among individual researchers and among individual participants themselves. Therefore, by recognizing this distinction, the present study acknowledges that in the same way the interviewees' understandings of media texts and media-based discourses were contextualized in the conditions of their living, the study itself is a form of accomplished, contextualized standpoint.

Conclusion

Briefly, poststructuralism has been included in this study as a way of foregrounding the experience of individuals involved in power relations. This, thus, adds a vital plain of analysis to the CDA-based investigation, which takes a top-down view of power. Research informed by feminist poststructuralism examines gender as experienced in various subject positions involved in the relations of power. This perspective precludes the essentialist conception of gender in terms of one stable and coherent identity acquired in the process of socialization. Therefore, whenever in this volume reference is made to 'gender identity', readers need to consider what complex understanding of the concept is meant.

The poststructuralist approach to discourse studies is considered here as instructive in the examination of media reception. Its involvement with the local contexts of power negotiation enables a critical mode of research that takes the mechanistic view of media reception. Accordingly, rejecting the idea that media content is passively absorbed, this study considers media reception as a process in which meanings are negotiated, and in ways that may be related with power.

As noted, it could be argued that weaving FPDA with D. Smith's sociology is not warranted because her interest in the 'subject of one's actions' is in a problematic relation to FPDA's non-materialist perspective. Nonetheless, the book proposes that investigating the discursive mediation of subjectivity does not preclude consideration of individuals' embodied experience. In fact, the proper and systematic attention to lifeworld practices and discourses is regarded here as necessary in the critical studies of gender.

This book is a critical project, hence one which is not a purely ethnomethodological account of embodied media reception. Moreover, it observes that the fault line is addressed by Smith who combines the ethnomethodological engagement with women's micro-level self- and sense-making practices and the Marxist critique of the textually mediated 'ruling relations' of the capitalist system. Similarly, this exploration is interested in the hegemonic discourses of media and gender as well as contextualizes reception of media texts in readers' accounts of their lived experience. As explained, this design of the study reflects its central concern to address the issue of the intricate relations between what is assumed in the media about women and women's accounts of self.

Consequently, this inquiry takes into account the potential differences between women's location amidst public discourses and their personal relationships to them. It is proposed here that the awareness of dominant discourses may not necessarily consist in women's involvement in a feminist polemic, and that this diversity may be found in the interviewees' ways of confronting the dominant discourse of bridal femininity. Claiming its interest in the diversity of women's relationship to the discourses, this book aims to maintain reflexivity of its own standpoint. By making the standpoint transparent to readers, I hope that although this research project is a critical involvement with discourse, it does not give the appearance of crediting itself with the authority to determine what a subversive relationship to the media 'actually' consists in. Therefore, because I have acknowledged my feminist position at the outset of the study, in the analysis of interviews I will seek to draw a line between the interviewees' discourse practices and my own, feminist, interpretation of the practices.

If poststructuralist feminists are right in stating that gender is a site of the discursive battle for subjectivity, the media (through its continuous and strong appeals to women and men) can be considered as one of the major agents in the battle. Therefore, based on the perspective delineated in this chapter, the current book focuses on the production and situated reception of bridal magazines to explore the meaning and power processes empirically. The analysis confronts the media discourses of femininity with the subjectivities that women work up in relation to them as well as in their accounts of lived experience.

3
Bridal Femininity in Wedding Magazines

The study

This chapter provides a critical discourse analysis of bridal magazines. Findings discussed are based on the investigation of a sample of British wedding magazines[1] which was preceded by a more informal analysis of many other bridal magazines available on the market. In line with what has been argued in previous chapters in the book, the broad goal of the investigation was to identify discourses by means of which the magazines address their readers. Also in relation to the theoretical premises of the study, it is expected here that the subject positions that are mediated by the discourses reveal preconstructed gender expectations. The discussion below additionally shows how the hybridization of the existing discourses enables construction of new relations of meaning, the coherence of which may generate the appearances of common sense, truth and obviousness. Finally, the investigation identifies what social identities, practices and relations are constructed and validated in the discourse of wedding magazines.

Wedding magazines

Bridal magazines are a thriving part of the global wedding and media industry (Otnes and Pleck 2003; Wilding 2003; Ingraham 2008; Engstrom 2012; Winch and Webster 2012). As a subgenre of women's magazines, they follow the magazines' basic conventions so that readers "possess the cultural literacy to 'read' their texts" (Boden 2003: 59). For this reason, in the analysis that follows some of the findings and arguments echo ones that have surfaced in research on women's magazines, hence revealing yet another site where the dominant discourse of gender is reproduced.

Along with major similarities to women's magazines, bridal magazines have developed a set of their distinctive features, in particular genres such as real-life weddings and wedding countdowns which were found in all magazines examined in this piece of research. Therefore, in the discussion the magazines are presented as a coherent media genre. Nevertheless, it needs to be pointed out that each title has its individual profile. To illustrate, in comparison to the other magazines in the sample, *Wedding Ideas* puts more emphasis on readers' opinions and ceremonies on a tight budget. Others are more aspirational. *Cosmopolitan Bride*, for instance, relies more extensively on experts' opinions, and features more high-fashion images. Also, each magazine has developed its own variation of the genre of real-life weddings. Importantly, none of these disparities concerned the aspects of discourse that have been of primary relevance in the current study.

Like other print media, bridal magazines need to remain sensitive to the ongoing changes and emergent trends among media audiences and wedding consumers. For example, because the magazine industry has witnessed a considerable loss of consumers after many of them have turned to the online media, the magazines need other ways of keeping pace with the new media audiences. Hence, to offset the decline, they appeal to readers as Internet users by inviting them to their websites (Ingraham 2008; Winch and Webster 2012). Moreover, although wedding magazines remain primarily focused on the white middle-class, they also address multicultural audiences. Finally, in her investigation of American wedding magazines, Ingraham (2008: 130) reports that their current profile reflects people's enhanced sense of the world around them and how it has affected their lifestyles. This can be seen, for instance, in the presentation of wartime weddings (after September 11), environmentally friendly weddings, destination weddings, etc.

At the same time, it needs to be emphasized at this point, despite their responsiveness to the changing landscape of social life and new trends in media consumption, the magazines have been unquestionably subscribed to the traditional wedding culture and conservative ideologies underlying it. To illustrate, they still rely on the same sort of literature as a reservoir of symbolic resources. As Ingraham (2008: 135) observed, "[b]ridal magazines rely heavily on fairy-tale and story-book romance themes in advertising, articles and organization to sell everything one needs to produce their own wedding spectacle". The wedding imagery and discourse are gendered, socially exclusive and reproduce heteronormativity (Boden 2001, 2003, 2007; Otnes and Pleck 2003; Ingraham 2008; White 2011; Nash 2012). Also, they unify beliefs about the commonality of consumption and fetishize it by promulgating its identity-constructive and expressive role. In this sense, the sample of bridal magazines analyzed for the purpose of the inquiry is not unlike many other bridal magazines (and wedding media) examined by researchers in the UK, Australia and the USA.

The extensive market of women's magazines indicates that the practice of reading lifestyle magazines has been particularly popular in this gender group. Bridal magazines, as a subgenre of women's magazines, are an important part of the media market – reading both types of the magazines is an established cultural practice of contemporary times. As discussed in Chapter 1, the erosion of tradition and the individualistic ethos of late modernity have left people wanting an alternative source of authority and inspiration in the pursuit of their identities. Cognizant of this trend, media cater to specific types of readership whom they provide with different information depending on their age, gender, hobbies, professions, lifestyle choices, etc. Brides are one such group of readers to be addressed. In this sense, the growth of the wedding media – bridal magazines, websites, self-help books and movies – can be seen as the result of people's enhanced need for self-reflexive work on one's life and of their reliance on expert systems. At same time, despite the decline of traditional values, the importance of wedding as 'the day' in a woman's life seems unchallenged. Therefore, bridal magazines, which strongly rely on the romantic narratives of weddings and emphasize the 'lifetime' dimension of the event, immediately appeal to many women getting married.

'Wedding-ideological complex'

In her examination of English bridal magazines, Boden (2003: 59) points to "inclusionary strategies by bridal magazines to generate the sense of a shared commonality among those currently planning their wedding". Discourse-wise, this means that the magazines construct collective subjectivity of their readership – a community of readers who are similar and emotionally close to one another solely due to their gender (see Talbot 1995). The "implicit assumption of collective subject" (Weedon 1997: 98) is a vital feature of the discourse. The subject position of the reasonable majority implied in it impresses on the reader the obviousness and 'common-senseness' of what is stated. Therefore, when reading bridal magazines, one is presented not only with information and inspiration, but also with ideology:

It is indeed a peculiarity of ideology that it imposes...obviousness as obviousness, which we cannot fail to recognize and before which we have the inevitable and natural reaction of crying out...'That's obvious! That's right! That's true'. (Althusser 1984: 46)

Wedding magazines interpellate their readers to specific subject positions by encouraging them to recognize "the 'obvious' roles, positions and inter-pretations which the text maps out for them" (Mills 1995: 73). (At this point, however, whether or not women are indeed hailed by any ideology underlying the magazines is beyond the scope of investigation.)

In bridal magazines, the 'obviousness' is implied to the reader by drawing on the established and widely circulating discourses, including the dominant discourse of gender as a central axis of wedding culture. Discussing its place in the wider circuit of the Western popular culture, Ingraham (2008: 119) sees it as *wedding-ideological complex*, namely the numerous sites of popular culture which "work as an ensemble in creating many taken-for-granted beliefs, values, and assumptions within social texts and practices about weddings". Although some studies (Currie 1993; Montemurro 2002; Kalmijn 2004) note their positive role (for example, in terms of how they assist individuals at the stage of life that generates insecurities), the practices regulating contemporary wedding culture have predominantly been found to be socially exclu-sive and oppressive. For instance, it has been noted that established wedding conventions erase homosexuality from the culture and repro-duce entrenched gender binaries (Currie 1993; Lewis 1998; Howard 2003; Schweingruber et al. 2004; Montemurro 2005).

By narrowing the scope of investigation to bridal magazines, this project gives an account of but a small part of the ideological machinery. At the same time, the book posits, the whole wedding culture and ideol-ogies underlying it are textually mediated and thus this level of the wedding-ideological complex needs to be addressed with appropriate attention. Hence, the discussion below examines how bridal magazines perpetuate the established narratives and imagery of the wedding-ide-ological complex, as well as whether/how the magazines generate new socio-semiotic resources related with it.

Constructing the obviousness of the wedding-ideological complex – editor's letter

Investigating bridal magazines in terms of the subject positions into which their readers are hailed basically focuses the current chapter on what is assumed in the magazines about women reading them. As explained in Chapter 1, this book considers that interpellative power is enacted through the establishment of intertextual and interdiscursive connections between texts – the subject of a given discourse finds it as coherent (and obvious) because he or she is literate in the 'intertexts' that constitute the discourse. Based on that, the analysis of bridal magazines presented in this book consists of tracing meaning construction across rather than within texts. This approach is also grounded in the common media practice of reading such magazines, which after all consists in glossing over the texts rather than focusing on specific articles. Yet, the coherence of wide discourses is constituted on both levels – the one of the whole magazine and the one of a single text. Therefore, in the analysis below the latter level will be discussed to provide a full account of the discourse processes discussed.

The text chosen for this analysis is an editor's letter ("Editor's letter") in the issue of *You & Your Wedding* (7–8/2009), which was used as a prompt in the interviews in the second stage of the study. It provides a powerful lead-in by hailing the reader into the subject position of the commodified bride (referred to by the editor as a 'modern bride'). The commonsense ideological assumptions related to this identity category are abundant in the text.

As will be evident from the analysis below, although there are many contexts in the popular discourse where a 'modern bride' is mentioned, in the magazine the 'modern bride' is a local identity category that is not necessarily synonymous with what it means in general. In the construction of it, the discourse of the magazine relies on multiple ideologies. Apart from reproducing them, texts in the magazine (for example, the editor's letter itself) render some ideological contradictions that are, however, suppressed in the local discourse. It is only upon a more detailed analysis that the identity is found to accommodate ambiguous and incongruous values and conflicting subject positions.

To begin with, the title *Celebrate your style!* hails the reader as a style-conscious woman. With part of its headline ("your style") typed in pink, this feature of the magazine exemplifies how the discourse of bridal magazines operates through various modalities. The phrase – marked by the color, which is widely recognized as coded for gender – implies the bride's exalted femininity. Next, the opening assertion ("One of the best things about being a modern bride is creating a wedding that expresses your personality") contains an existential presupposition. Lack of any contextual or explicit explanation implies readers' familiarity with the notion of the 'modern bride' – it is obvious that she exists, as is what makes her unlike other types of brides. By the same token, the formulation that expressing your own personality is "[o]ne of the best things about being a modern bride" implies that there are many others, of which the reader should probably know. That the expression of one's own style is accomplished by means of specific commodities is implied in the following statement: "Hearing your guests say 'That's just so you!' is the ultimate compliment to your dress, flowers, service and all other wonderful things that come together to make your big day so special." Given the editor's assumptive tone, she takes for granted that readers of *You & Your Wedding* consider reliance on the commodities enumerated not only obvious but also desired.

The presumptive mode of the text contains the ideological contradiction that the 'modern bride' accommodates, namely the one that the 'modern' approach to weddings is expressed by means of commodities that belong to the long-established set of bridal artifacts. Tellingly, the "other wonderful things" include:

> Fabulous alternative cakes, seasonal flowers, memorable entertainment, real weddings full of meaningful readings, music and colour themes and fashion and hair accessories ideas.

The ultrafeminine code is reinforced by the typography of the text – the words are typed in the pink boldface. Another visual reinforcement of the code is the exposition of gendered artifacts (which include, for example, mini mascara, lip gloss, stilettos and flowers) accompanying gender marked lexis (*"fabulous* cakes"[2]) – all this hails the reader to the subject position of the 'modern bride'.

On the textual level, it is presumed that the reader (the 'modern bride') has always dreamt of getting married and that the wedding day is the most important time of her life. This presumption recurred explicitly and implicitly in all magazines examined in the study as one of their most common repertoires. In the specific editor's letter discussed here it is reproduced indirectly:

> Hearing your guests say "That's just so you!" is the ultimate compliment to your dress, flowers, service and all other wonderful things that come together to make your big day so special.

The formulation "to make your big day *so* special" presupposes that the 'special' character of the day is generally agreed on. Likewise, the assumption that the wedding day is a particularly important event for women is embedded in the existential presupposition of "your big day". It is later reinforced through the reiteration of the 'big day' repertoire in many places in the magazine.

As will be noted many times in the analysis, wedding magazines often position their readers as members of a gender (bridal) community. In the editor's letter that was chosen for a closer analysis this can be observed, for example, in the closing invitation:

> Finally, don't forget to log on to our buzzing website at youandyour-wedding.co.uk for your daily fix of bridal inspiration and gossip. See you there!

The phrase "*our* buzzing *website*" implies the existence of the community of *You & Your Wedding* readers in more than one way. First, that there is a community that the reader shares with editors and other readers is overtly signaled by the plural possessive 'our'. Second, the word 'website', together with the predetermining pronoun, constructs a group of people involved in online activities, hence *assimilating* (van Leeuwen 2008: 37) them. The adjectival premodification 'buzzing' accommodates the popular images of female friends immersed in chatting and gossiping. In this way the construction triggers conceptual schemata that do not need any further contextual information and, hence, imply the obviousness of a community of 'modern brides', that is, like-minded women and consumers. Finally, the compliment in the final invitation ("for your daily fix of bridal inspiration and gossip") presupposes that using the website is the reader's routine and that she finds it a valuable source of ideas. In this way, the brief invitation naturalizes specific reader and consumer practices.

The editor's letter is a telling example of van Dijk's argument that a swift manipulation of genre and discourse can serve as a resource of power construction. Thanks to the ambiguous relation between the propositional content and the non-propositional (pragmatic) effect of the editor's letter, the text imposes on the readers of the magazine its ideology of commodified bridal femininity without being "bluntly manipulative" (van Dijk [2001] 2009: 302). The content of the text corresponds with its generic identity (Eggins [2004] 2007). Editor's letter is an opinion piece written by the senior editor's letter staff or publisher of a magazine to highlight its most important issues; because it exposes the identity of the magazine, it is its most social part.[3]

Introducing readers to the discourse of *You & Your Wedding* (7–8/2009), the editor's letter promises a relatively light read, an enjoyable esthetic experience typical of women's glossies, as well as a heavy concentration of wedding topics. The text constructs a confiding personal relationship with the individual reader. This is evident in the selection of direct forms of address, such as the interrogative mood ("Got a question for the team?"), imperatives ("be inspired, find that perfect personal touch", etc.) as well as the use of pronouns. The interpersonal relationship with the reader is produced by means of other modalities. For example, the editors' portrait photos make the relation between them and the recipient closer, more intimate. Their frontal gaze and smiles suggest an interactive, friendly positioning. The editors' engaged attitude is textually reinforced by means of captions ("Meet your team...Our in-house experts are here to help!"). The deictic 'here' in "Our in-house experts are here to help!" is a cognitive device establishing a common perspective, as if symbolically leading the reader into the shared world of bridal imagery.

The appearances of a cordial and disinterested relationship that the editors offer to magazine readers are indeed 'bluntly manipulative'. The editor's letter is set on enticing the recipient to let herself be drawn into the world of bridal inspirations. Evidently, the authors of the text took great care to present the bridal world as inviting. This subliminal construction of the reader's affinity with the magazine can be seen in the frequent appeals to her 'positive face' (Brown and Levinson 1987), that is, the need to be liked and admired as well as to see other people care about our wants and feelings. For example, constructions such as "Your team" and "Our in-house experts are here to help" establish the relation of trust between the staff journalists and the reader. She is given by them the promise of being pampered, entertained and guided in preparing a wedding, which, the editor claims, will arouse admiration of significant others.

On the whole, as a media genre, an editor's letter is expected to be a telling opening of a magazine. Its representational value is thus a compelling reason to investigate it. Indeed, by means of numerous linguistic and visual resources the editor's letter analyzed here constructs the obviousness of the bridal identity that is reproduced throughout the whole *You & Your Wedding*. The meanings and subject positions offered may impress on its readers the factuality of the issues that are mentioned in the article and, subsequently, encourage them to live their weddings through the consumption of traditionally gendered products and services. The remaining part of the discussion will show that structures and repertoires constructed in the editor's letter are reproduced not only in other texts in the specific issue of *You & Your Wedding* but in all magazines included in the sample.

Femininity in media discourse

The media constructions of femininity have earned a long, consistently expanding list of critics among social and discourse researchers. The media's production of a false community of women has been criticized for its erroneous assumption of a homogenous, raceless and classless, womanhood (McRobbie 1981; Talbot 1995) as well as for a 'symbolic anni- hilation of women' (Tuchman 1978). The media's dominant discourse of femininity includes the notorious constructions of 'compulsory hetero- sexuality' (Rich 1980) as well as of women's bodies that "always need fixing" (D. Smith 1988: 47). Clearly, the media-produced images trivi- alize and misrepresent women (Ganahl et al. 2003) and reinforce body insecurities in them (Greer 1999). Even postfeminism, with its original aggressive recodification of traditional femininity, has been misappro- priated by the media industry. As Negra (2009: 12) argues, "postfemi- nist popular culture...codifies and essentializes femininity, relentlessly insisting that all women are bound together by a common set of desires, fears, and concerns". Finally, both femininity and feminism have been subject to an enhanced commodification (see 'commodity feminism' Goldman et al. 1991; 'commodified femininity' Benwell and Stokoe 2006; 'consumer femininity' Talbot 2010). Redefined by consumerism and translated into its imagination, the commodified femininity and feminism have been considered as particularly manipulative and destruc- tive ideologies because they promote self-actualization and liberation through consumption.

It seems reasonable not to expect to learn anything new about women and men from bridal magazines because their presence on the media market depends on the continuity and strength of wedding tradition. The producers of the magazines have their grounds for avoiding the counter-hegemonic discourses of gender, which, after all, defy the soci- ocultural templates sustaining the long-established gender order, of which the 'big white wedding' is an essential part. With this in mind, the purpose of the discussion below is not to determine whether or not bridal magazines reproduce traditional concepts of femininity but to examine how they draw on the established discourses of gender when communicating with their readers.

However, it can also be expected that the magazines cannot totally ignore the surrounding reality and the ways in which late modern trans- formations in society are reflected in the wedding culture. Therefore, given the growing popularity of the counter-hegemonic discourses of gender and their increasing visibility in popular culture (Genz and

Brabon 2009), it is worthwhile to explore how the magazines, which are in their essence conservative, orientate to the contemporary culture and society (for example, it is interesting to check whether they accommodate any of its new elements, such as pregnant brides or brides who remarry).

Bridal femininity – lexis

The magazines' preoccupation with hegemonic femininity is evident in the deployment of the adjectives 'feminine' and 'girly' and their derivatives. Even a brief glance over the magazines makes evident that the words are their mantra repeated in various kinds of texts:

> Known for her unashamedly feminine drapery and corsets, Stephanie Allin's new boutique is a haven of girly gorgeousness. (*Cosmopolitan Bride* 12–1/2010)
>
> Glide down the aisle in a dress inspired by femininity. (*Brides* 7–8/2008)
>
> The embroidery on the bodice and at the hem gives this gown a regal, grown-up feel without losing any of its femininity. (*Perfect Wedding* 4/2008)

Used in a defining role, the words reveal the authors' presumption that readers have the same understanding of what 'typical' femininity is. For instance, the last example in the set implies that there is something contradictory between "a regal, grown-up feel" and a feminine look – what the latter means then is supposed to be known. Yet, the actual obscurity of such formulations is not immediately observable because the words are highly conventionalized; they evoke some impressionistic, socioculturally constructed associations. In the examples above, 'femininity' and 'girliness' are also essentialized by the premodifications such as "unashamedly feminine" and "girly gorgeousness". Assigning femininity and girliness various qualities implies that they represent obviously meaningful entities that come in different forms. Because of the intensity with which such expressions are regurgitated in the magazines, the discourse of dominant femininity is normalized and reinforced.

Dominant gender discourse is reproduced in the magazine also through the deployment of gendered lexis, that is language features that belong to what Lakoff (1975) called 'women's language'. Even though Lakoff (1975: 59) presented it as a stereotypical notion of women's speech, the gender coding of the features that she enumerated as marked for white middle-class femininity (increased politeness, refinement etc.), has been found to thrive in many contexts.[4]

In the magazines, the vocabulary of dominant femininity is used extensively, which reinforces the emergent identity of the 'modern bride' and positions the reader as the subject of dominant gender discourse. The examples of gendered vocabulary provided below designate names of flower species (a) and precise color terms (b), they represent expressions for conveying opinion (c) and pertain to details, attention to which has been seen as typical of women (d):

a. Names of flowers species:
    The wedding blooms blossomed out of martini-glass centrepieces that incorporated white *bouvardia*, cream *freesias, lisianthus* and *eucalyptus.* (*Cosmopolitan Bride* 7–8/2009)

    I loved my bouquet, which was a mix of blue *hydrangea*, lime green *roses*, white *peonies lisianthus* and *hypericum*. (*You & Your Wedding* 11–12/2009)

b. Color terms:
    Turquoise accessories. From *teal* to *aquamarine*, we love this selection. (*Wedding Ideas* 56/2008)

    For a sophisticated look, mix calming pale *turquoise* with a deep espresso *brown*. (*You & Your Wedding* 11–12/2009)

c. Expressions for conveying opinion:
    Add the *perfect* finishing touch to your big-day outfit with Dune's *stunning* summer 2009 bridal collection, which includes *gorgeous* retro-inspired peeptoe platforms, diamante-studded sandals and *cute* matching clutches. (*Cosmopolitan Bride* 7–8/2009)

    Hello lover! This month we've been 'carried' away with the hype surrounding *Sex and the City* movie...we have some *fabulous* SATC-inspired goodies to give away. (*Wedding Ideas* 56/2008)

d. Attention to detail:
    Display your chosen colours and themes in your wedding cake and its decorations, taking into account the colours of bridesmaids' dresses, the flowers and so on. (*Wedding Ideas* 55/2008)

    My wedding colours were duck-egg blue and white. We thought the most perfect favour would be something silver presented in a box from Tiffany's. We couldn't have chosen a better idea and the reception room looked spectacular with everything colour-coordinated. (*Perfect Wedding* 4/2008)

Because women obviously do not talk in the way illustrated above, the editors' reliance on such speech patterns may seem puzzling but leaves no doubt what femininity bridal magazines reproduce.

Heteronormative narrative of romance

It has been mentioned that as part of the wedding-ideological complex, bridal magazines draw on the socioculturally recognizable codes that surround the whole wedding media market. One of the organizing concepts of the wedding imagery perpetuated within it is the notion of the 'royal wedding'. In their coverage of royal and celebrity weddings, the media impress on recipients the importance of a sophisticated, informed consumption of the wedding event, and in doing so they reinforce the heteronormative discourse through the appealing power of images used. As Ingraham (2008: 141) notes, the 'royal' narrative of patriarchal and heterosexual gender order is present in people's lives even after they stop believing in fairy tales and playing with toys:

> In bridal magazines and in children's toys, references to fairy tales and princesses dominate, although less so today than in the 1980s. In bridal magazines since the 1950s, advertisements have frequently made reference to the bride as "princess," "royalty," or as having an "empire." Along with the demise of the British Empire, colonial references have also disappeared, but the ideology of romantic love linked to fairy tales and princesses prevails. Children still pretend to be princesses waiting for their handsome prince to arrive, the story of Cinderella continues to be popular, and Cinderella themes continue to echo through the wedding market.

Quite expectedly, the heteronormative romance is a narrative underlying many texts in wedding magazines. The storyline implying that one's ultimate happiness depends on the 'and they lived happily ever after' is connected with the presupposition that the reader would like her wedding to resemble the royal ceremonies which she knows from fairy tales and that in organizing the event she draws direct inspiration from their imagery:

> HALSWELL. Exclusively yours... What could be more romantic than your celebration in a historic 17th century mansion set deep in the

Somerset countryside. ... *Turning once upon a time into happily ever after,* (*Cosmopolitan Bride* 6–7/2009)

Put your best foot forward with these fabulous shoes that are perfect for dancing the night away during *that Cinderella moment*! (*Perfect Wedding* 4/2008)

True bride. *Fairytale dresses* for brides on a budget. (*Wedding Ideas* 54/2008)

The linguistic constructions of a fairy-tale romance are reinforced visually with many models wearing tiaras, ribbons, etc. Another assumption that surfaces texts in the magazines is that women treat the wedding day as a grand finale of a romantic story. Consequently, the bride is presented as a woman undergoing a transformation into a princess:

"*Unleash your inner fairytale princess*, and don't be afraid to think big!" says Peta. (*You & Your Wedding* 7–8/2009)

What could be *more princess-perfect* than a sweetheart necklace teamed with pale pink organza and dainty roses! (*Perfect Wedding* 4/2008)

I'm so excited about wearing a tiara. It's going to *make me feel like a real princess*. (*Wedding Ideas* 56/2008)

Along with the 'fairy-tale' repertoire, the one of the 'dream day' reinforces the presupposition that all women hope to get married and while waiting for the day to come, they plan it thoroughly:

[W]ith *everything you've always dreamed of* – from wedding dresses, accessories and jewellery to favours, photography (*You & Your Wedding* 7–8/2009)

Find *your dream dress.* (*Wedding Ideas* 58/2008)

Dreaming of a fairytale gown? You will find it at Rookery Manor. (*Wedding Ideas* 57/2008)

Such constructions clearly evoke popular fairy tales and their heroines waiting for their dreams to come true in the person of the beloved man. Thus, like the interpretative lines of the seemingly innocuous popular fairy tales, the media constructions perpetuating them carry the ideological load of the dominant, heteronormative gender discourse. The wedding imagery in the magazines, along with that in other media, "works ideologically, conveying to the observer/reader what they should believe about romance, weddings, marriage, and heterosexuality" (Ingraham 2008: 151).

The 'modern bride' as a hybrid identity

Although from the discussion above it may seem that the reader of wedding magazines is addressed in a somewhat infantile way, the subject position of a 'modern bride' is a more complex construction. In her investigation of English wedding magazines, Boden (2001, 2003) observes that the bride which they construct, and which she calls the 'superbride', incorporates two identities – the rational 'project-manager' and the emotional 'childish fantasizer'. Both were identified in the current investigation.

The 'project-manager superbride'

In addition to what was noted by Boden, it is observed in this book that another function of the position of the 'project-manager' may be to offset the infantility and naivety of the 'childish fantasizer', which position could be seen above in the presuppositions that every woman dreams of getting married and having a 'royal' wedding. Correspondingly, while stepping into the role of a princess offers the reader some transformational potential, it inevitably puts her in a submissive position. The constructions of the reader's managerial role in preparing the wedding spectacle, by contrast, help her to regain the position of agency and self-empowerment.

The 'superbride' is referred to in the current discussion as a 'hybrid' because the managerial incarnations of the 'modern bride' accompanying the more conventional constructions of bridal femininity generate a significant amount of ambiguity. They reflect tension underlying women's wedding experiences – the split between the feeling of responsibility for the organization of the 'perfect' day and the idea of living her fairy-tale fantasy of a great romance. Therefore, the vagueness of the emergent subjectivity reflects wider trends in the contemporary wedding culture. The ambivalence of the emergent developments has been deftly summarized by Walter (2010: 130) as the rise of a 'new traditionalism', that is the reconfiguration of the traditional gender repertoires in the way that they are offset and validated by the business-like rhetoric of strategic planning, informed choice and deliberate actions.

Positioned as a skilled consumer of wedding industry, the 'project-manager superbride' is supposed to give the reader an idea that a contemporary bride is not only enchanted with the fairy-tale imagery but that she also feels responsible for creating it. Thus, until the moment when she transforms into the 'princess', she needs to assume the identity of a consumer and worker (Boden 2007: 8). By virtue of the tasks she is assigned, the 'project-manager superbride' possesses features that have not been ascribed to women by traditional gender discourse. Indeed, in the study some texts were found to position the reader as task-oriented, self-assured and agentic. These texts are mainly wedding checklists and countdowns, which instruct readers how to organize a wedding without oversights and missed deadlines. For example, brides are informed what actions to take at what time:

> One month to go. Type up a list of any must-take shots and send it to your photographer. (*You & Your Wedding* 11–12/2009)
>
> One month to go. Run through the ushers' and best man's duties with them. (*Perfect Wedding* 4/2008)
>
> As soon as possible. Organise wedding insurance. (*Cosmopolitan Bride* 7–8/2009)

The no-nonsense style of the instructions starkly contrasts with the style adopted in the examples presented above in the discussion, where the reader is hailed as a 'childish fantasizer'. Clearly, managing wedding organization has little in common with the girlish dreams of becoming a princess getting married in a grand style. The actions that the 'project-manager superbride' is supposed to take defy the stereotypes of women's passivity and submissiveness:

> High-maintenance maids and mums driving you mad? *Turn divas into bride-pleasers* with our guide to getting the good from your girls. (*Cosmopolitan Bride* 12–1/2010)
>
> *Don't be afraid to delegate* – modern weddings are all about teamwork, so involve your parents, best friends and, of course, your fiancé. (*You & Your Wedding* 7–8/2009)
>
> When organising a wedding, you're not just its star player, you're also a manager – a role that makes you the centre of attention and chief decision maker. (*Cosmopolitan Bride* 6–7/2009)

Nevertheless, these constructions of a self-determining and agentic bridal subject are ambiguous. Firstly, it could be argued that all three statements above carry the assumption of the bride's disinclination to take up a managerial role. They are based on the presupposition that it needs to be pointed out to the readers that they can behave assertively in relation to their significant others and wedding suppliers. Additionally, in the last example, the managerial role is constructed as accompanying the traditional, 'esthetic' function of the bride. Reminding the reader of her other role in the wedding event, the sentence puts her back to the traditional position of the object of gaze. Hence, it is a telling illustration of the fact that the position of bridal empowerment and agency does not annul the traditional bridal position of an esthetic object in the wedding spectacle.

For still another example of the hybridity of the 'superbride', among actions that readers are reminded to take, 'checklists' also enumerate body practices that reproduce traditional feminine identity:

Two weeks to go. Practice walking in your gorgeous shoes! (*You & Your Wedding* 11–12/2009)

2 weeks before. Break in your wedding shoes. Sandpaper soles for extra grip when you're walking down the aisle. (*Cosmopolitan Bride* 12–1/2010)

18 months to go. Begin fitness regime. (*Perfect Wedding* 4/2008)

As will be elaborated on below, the practices of walking down the aisle and fitness regime are part of the media discourse of gender in the sense that they contain its central assumption of a woman's bodily imperfections as well as of her discontent with the body and willingness to discipline it. By encouraging brides to be strategic in the 'management' of their own bodies, the discourse confers power on them. Yet, the ideological contradiction this renders is that women's involvement with the bodily regimen recommended in the magazines is contingent on their acceptance of media's power to set beauty standards.

Non-traditional brides

Although the discourse of bridal magazines draws centrally on the imagery of the 'lavish white wedding', the magazines feature also some, but not many, constructions of a relatively less conventional bridal femininity, which are not associated with the managerial incarnation of the 'modern bride'. These constructions, the book suggests, are by no means used as forms of coded criticism of the femininity of the 'lavish white wedding'. Given how marginally and inconsistently this defensive bridal femininity is mobilized in the discourse, it can be argued that it is used to manifest the apparent inclusivity of a discourse community which is, as a matter of fact, committed to the traditional ('emphasized') femininity. To illustrate, in a caption from a fashion file, the reader is addressed as a fashion-conscious customer:

> What's new and on for brides this minute. Not sold on the big white dress idea? Carolina Herrera's Spring 2009 show provided inspiration in the form of a sleek and elegant cream jacket with matching ankle-crazing slim-fit trousers. Think classic Sixties Jackie O retro with a hint of Audrey Hepburn's oh-so-chic style. (*Cosmopolitan Bride* 7–8/2009)

On the one hand, the caption opts out of the symbolism of the white wedding, with the (most probably, strategic) reference to 'the big white dress' as an emblem thereof. This is reinforced by the alternative gown offered (a cream jacket with trousers), which represents an unambiguous antithesis of a classic white puffy dress. On the other hand, the defensive code is subsequently undermined by the "hint of Audrey Hepburn's oh-so-chic style", which repositions the recipient by reinstating the discourse of dominant femininity.

Another ambiguous construction of the non-traditional bride can be found in an article "Wedding file debate" (*You & Your Wedding* 7–8/2009). The text confronts opinions of two brides – one of them decided to keep her dress and 'treasure' it on a special dummy, whereas the other talks about trashing it in a garden bath. Clearly, the text exploits the symbolic potential of a wedding dress. (Hence, as an addition to the main argument developed below, the two stories could compel reflection on the number of powerful and ideologically contentious meanings the wedding dress has accrued.) The subsequent elements of the brides' narratives are indexically linked to the imagery of the 'big white weddings'. Given their global popularity and the wide currency of their imagery, to anybody literate in popular culture the interpretative frame for reading the stories is set on their paradigmatic relation to this tradition, namely, the dissimilar ways of handling the wedding dress index two opposite bridal identities:

Table 3.1 Brides in a "Wedding file debate"

The non-traditional bride (Lucy, married Mike on 9 April 2008 in York.)	The traditional bride (Joanna, married Lee on 11 July 2009 in Dumfries.)
I'd always wanted *a different dress* and ended up finding the perfect design, *second hand, in a red-grape colour,* for £500. *I don't really like traditional photographs.* ... When I bought it, I always had, in the back of my mind, that I'd *do something fun with it* afterwards.	Quite a large group of us, including my mum and best friend, went to choose ... [M]y parents have been very generous and *spent a fortune on my dream dress.* *[T]here's no way that I could ever bear to trash my dress.* ... I've decided to invest in the *dressmaker's mannequin to display it at home.*

Quite expectedly, the 'traditional' bride recapitulates the repertoires that usually feature the spectacle of a 'big white wedding' (for example, the time-established ritual of buying the wedding dress together with female significant others, the assertion of generational ties through the acknowledgment of parents' financial support, the 'treasuring' of the dress). Because of the antithetical configuration of the narratives, the progressive meanings of buying a second-hand wedding dress and of trashing it readily yield themselves to interpretation.

Yet, what is apparent on the surface of the narrative should not be taken for granted. Subverting the traditional repertoires of the 'big white wedding', the non-traditional bride follows its (reversed) logic and hence involuntarily contradicts her stated dislike of conventions. For instance, the subversive identity she is working up in her bridal ritual is challenged by the traditional position of the object of gaze, which she adopts by participating in a photo-shoot. Moreover, the disparities in the brides' relationship to the dress are in fact minor:

Table 3.2 Brides in a "Wedding file debate"

The non-traditional bride (continued from Table 3.1)	The traditional bride (continued from Table 3.1)
[T]here was *no way I wanted to sell it.* The dress itself had got a bit grubby and holey around the bottom on our wedding day, so I *didn't feel as bad* as I would have if it had still been pristine.	I want to be able to *treasure my dress forever.* I use our spare room so *it will take pride of place* in there.

Both women equally ascribe a non-material, symbolic value to the wedding dress. (Indeed, the idea that a bride may not have an emotional attachment to her gown and other wedding artifacts would militate against the magazines' advertising agenda.) Therefore, the narrative of trashing captures the paradox of modern weddings, which, in fact, still take a lot of inspiration from the established paradigm and hence reinstate it. Markedly different from traditional wedding photography, 'trash-the-dress' photo sessions are seen as a way of defying gender clichés, but, as has been demonstrated above, these sessions in their own ways adhere to the templates (see White 2011).

Thus, it needs to be pointed out that generally in the magazines the rejection of tradition is superficial. It is enacted mainly in terms of an esthetic choice. The subversive subject positions that the reader is offered actually reinscribe the old-established elements of wedding culture and the entrenched forms of gender subjectivity. The sample of magazines analyzed in this study did not include 'nonconventional' brides whose presence would mark a more profound resistance to the established notions of bridal femininity – pregnant, older, disabled or lesbian. Non-white women appeared only in a few real-life weddings.

Object of gaze

Wedding magazines are firmly committed to the idea that a woman lives her wedding as an esthetic experience. Presenting the bride as the central part of the 'big white wedding' spectacle, the magazines construct her as an object of gaze:

> Fashion-conscious brides *enjoy the spotlight* in a dress inspired by the latest catwalk trends. (*Brides* 7–8/2008)

> You need to look your best if you're to feel *confident in the spotlight* and being *in the centre of attention* all day long. (*Brides, Wedding Planner* 2008)

> You're guaranteed to *be the star attraction* on your wedding day so make sure you look the part by following these 10 bridal beauty commandments. (*Perfect Wedding* 4/2008)

In the constructions above, the reader is presumed to know and accept her position in the wedding spectacle. The first sentence in the set implies that brides find being gazed on pleasant. The same implicatures underpin the constructions of gaze that draw on the language of popular culture.

For instance, the examples below rely on the culturally recognizable images of celebrities posing for photographers and admiring spectators:

> Hiring a professional will bring out your true star quality. (*Brides, Wedding Planner* 2008)

> There aren't many times quite as exciting as when you walk down the aisle towards your future husband. This is probably the closest you'll get to your own red-carpet moment. (*Perfect Wedding* 4/2008)

> Jenny designs show-stopping dresses for our very red-carpet moment. (*Brides* 7–8/2009)

The premodifications 'you', 'your own' and 'our very' assume readers' familiarity with celebrity culture as well as that they have internalized its cult of stars. After all, the constructions are premised on the presupposition of the reader's anxiety to experience her 'red-carpet moment'. Evidently, the repertoire of celebrating one's 'red-carpet moment' is used in the constructions of wedding preparations in such a way that it gives an impression of the repertoire of a Cinderella being translated into the language of popular culture.

Because the bride is repeatedly constructed as the object of gaze, it could be argued that these constructions reveal male focalization (Mills 1995), that is to say, they reconstruct reality from what has traditionally been considered as a masculine perspective. Indeed, many language structures represent the bride through the eyes of a heterosexual man, apparently reproducing the male gaze (Mulvey 1988):

> *Your groom loves the woman he sees* every day, but it's natural to want to look utterly glamorous on your wedding day. (*Brides, Wedding Planner* 2008)

> [I]t didn't matter what anyone else thought about my day – I could tell from his smile that *he thought I was gorgeous.* (*Cosmopolitan Bride* 7–8/2009)

> *Dazzle your darling* as you walk down the aisle looking radiant with a little help from our experts. (*Perfect Weddings* 4/2008)

The constructions of the gaze represent varying degrees of the sexualization of the female body. Though relatively infrequent in comparison to the constructions of the purely esthetic gaze, the constructions of an overtly eroticized bridal body do appear:

> Get the right underwear for your dress to *show off your best assets, just like Marilyn.* (*Wedding Ideas* 5/2008)

> Be inspired by this retro *pin-up; sexy stockings,* figure-shaping corsets and *sassy knickers* are the way to *sex up your style* and *give him a honeymoon treat!* (*Wedding Ideas* 56/2008)

In the structures, the male gaze is reproduced either through the emphasis on the bodily parts that are usually the objects of heteromasculine attention or through the presuppositions that the bride's primary goal is to arouse her groom's admiration or desire. In the sample of discourse data in this study, the other constructions of explicitly eroticized bridal body were found in one advertisement (discussed below). What needs to be noted at this point, however, is that in the sample there was no text that directly dealt with brides' sex life, in the way it often happens in women's magazines. The explanation this book offers is that the marginal presence of overt sexuality in wedding magazines shows how strongly their discourse relies on the conservative discourse of gender and its inherent figure of the virgin bride.

Moreover, it was observed in the study that many constructions of the bridal body reproduce a type of gaze that does not represent what is commonly understood as the heteromasculine perspective:

> Blossoming romance. Celebrate your marriage in a beautiful dress embellished with pretty floral detail, wear a striking flower corsage and surround yourself with stunning scented blooms. (*You & Your Wedding* 7–8/2009)

> Be an English rose with butterflies and bunting. (*Cosmopolitan Bride* 6–7/2009)

> There's a hint of enchanted garden about this beautiful dress with the trailing floral design – it's sure to sweep your Prince Charming of his feet. (*Perfect Wedding* 4/2008)

Judging by the gendered lexis of the constructions, they seem to express a woman's perspective. Nevertheless, even if that is the case, the female gaze is also a form of objectification. Deliberately aimed at a female readership, the constructions are devised to trigger in them the desire for a certain look that they would like to consume themselves (for example, in the mirror reflection or in the visual wedding recordings). Hence, even if not positioned as the objects of the male gaze, women are positioned as esthetic objects.

The line between the male and female gaze perspective is often vague. An example of the ambiguous focalization can be found in the text below. It is an advertisement of a women-run photo lab where brides are taken sexy pictures that they later give as wedding presents to their grooms:

> Looking for the perfect wedding gift for 'h2b'? Well here's a gift that we guarantee will put a smile on his face – a private portfolio of his dream girl – you! At theboudoirbook we're passionate about pictures. We're an all-female team of skilled professionals, so we really do understand your issues. We'll make you over, style you, light you and then photograph you, bringing out your real beauty in a collection of flattering, seductive pictures. We can even airbrush your photos at no extra cost, eliminating cellulite, stretchmarks, blemishes, wrinkles and much more.
>
> With a range of packages to suit all budgets, and lots of photographic styles to choose from, we know you'll be thrilled with your portraits.
>
> And so will he! (*You & Your Wedding* 11–12/2009)

First of all, the text constructs collective gender subjectivity in the sense that the "all-female team of skilled professionals" addresses the recipient directly and assures her that as women "they understand her issues". The male focalization of the text demonstrates how through the accommodation of the male gaze women have become both the objects and the subjects of esthetic and erotic consumption. The fetishistic, self-consuming gaze on the female body is very much in evidence in the assertion "you'll be thrilled with your portraits". The constructions such as "flattering, seductive pictures" construct the woman's 'thrill' as a form of erotic tension, experienced vicariously with her husband. Finally, the offer of airbrushing is followed by the enumeration of body features that are constructed as imperfections ("cellulite, stretchmarks, blemishes, wrinkles and much more"). With the presupposition that she will wish to have them removed, the offer positions the reader not as the object of male desire but as the object of self-surveillance.

Visual construction of the bride

Wedding magazines, as a subgenre of women's lifestyle magazines, are typically richly illustrated. Their reliance on the visual modality may not be conspicuous due to the increasingly multisemiotic nature of media communication in general. In response to the "period of upheaval in the landscape of communication" (Kress 2001: 72), more and more linguists examine texts together with other semiotic forms (see Graddol and Boyd-Barrett 1994; Fairclough 1995b; Kress and van Leeuwen [1996] 2006, 2001; Bauer and Gaskell 2000; Rose 2001; Scollon and Scollon 2003). Yet, the analysis of images in wedding magazines provided below, apart from recognizing their overbearing presence, seeks to bring to attention their vital role in the magazines' gender discourse.

Modalities of the gaze

Images in wedding magazines reinforce the textual constructions of gaze. Models in the magazines are positioned in the pictures either as if surreptitiously observed or they meet the spectator's eye. These two types of positioning correspond with what Kress and van Leeuwen (2006) distinguish as a 'demand' image and an 'offer' image. The former, when the participant's gaze meets that of the viewer, establishes a specific kind of relationship between the two (Kress and van Leeuwen 2006: 122–3). For instance, in the case of bridal imagery, the model's mouth is usually in a gentle smile, which may suggest affinity or desire. The 'offer' image is created when the participant looks out of the frame, and when his or her gaze does not meet that of the viewer (Kress and van Leeuwen 2006: 124). This means that in such cases brides are presented as subject to contemplation or consumption. Therefore, both types of gaze objectify women. No matter if the models look out of the frame or at the viewer, "[b]oth of these modalities of the gaze help realize traditional discourses about women, showing them either as seductive or as socially intimate and manipulative" (Machin and Thornborrow 2003: 461).

Iconicity

As noted, in the study women of color were found only in real-life wedding texts – they were absent from all advertisements as well as the magazines' regular fashion and style features. The representations of brides in the magazines and in the majority of all wedding media are dominated by the imagery of the Western popular culture, which is evident in the racial homogeneity of the images:

> Women's experience with weddings and the wedding industry is racially structured. Over and over again the icon of the beautiful white bride in the beautiful white bridal gown is replayed and reinforced, sending a clear message to young and old alike that what counts as beautiful and marriageable is white. (Ingraham 2008: 140)

It is not only the American and British media that perpetuate the images of a Caucasian, classically attractive woman as the iconic representation of a bride. For example, adding to Ingraham's critique of the racial exclusiveness of bridal imagery in the US, in her analysis of Australian bridal magazines, Nash (2012) observes that because of their reliance on the Christian and Greco-Roman imagery, the magazines' visual discourse homogenizes the bridal body by exposing the pictures of mostly young, slim, Anglo-Australians.[5]

How the iconic representation of the bride constructs the 'obvious' is notable in the advertisements for bridal gowns which usually only provide images with minimal textual information and contextualization (only store addresses, and sometimes information about discounts). In turn, the presentations invite recipients to make cognitive leaps requiring culture-specific knowledge. On seeing a picture of a model in a wedding dress, which is accompanied only by the address of a store, the recipient needs to overcome the apparent information gap. After all, at no stage do such advertisements exhort the reader to look like the models; their primary function is to direct the consumer to the store. Clearly, in the message hence communicated it is presupposed that the consumer will consider the model's appearance as the appropriate and desirable bridal look. A similar observation is made by Ingraham (2008: 117–8) in reference to an advertisement for perfumes:

> Estée Lauder has long used an advertising campaign for its perfume depicting a white, blond flower girl in a white dress looking up into the eyes of a white, blond bride in a white wedding gown. The only text in the ad says "Beautiful," establishing the white bride and the future bride as standard-bearers of what counts as beauty.

By being exposed to such advertisements, women are positioned as both familiar with the traditional bridal esthetics and aspiring to the looks of its central figure – the iconic bride. Importantly, Ingraham's observation demonstrates that the iconic bride is not just a local figure of the wedding-ideological complex but she pervades the whole culture (for example, the cosmetic industry). This can be regarded as a gauge of the degree to which the icon has been naturalized and keeps reproducing the exclusive idea of the bridal body.

Color

Apart from gaze and iconicity, the symbolic power of bridal imagery draws much of its appeal from its 'grammar of color' (Kress and van

Leeuwen 2002), that is, the consistent ways in which color is used in the imagery as a semiotic resource. The regularities meant here concern the color-coding of pictures featuring in wedding magazines – strong saturation, low modulation and a culturally constructed, gendered palette.

As was indicated in the analysis of the editor's letter, colors in wedding magazines serve their local function of coordination. A cursory look at the typography of the magazines shows how consistently pink is correlated with titles and highlights. This gives an impression of stylization as well as reflects the attention to detail to which wedding consumers are regularly encouraged. Importantly, the stylistic harmony reinforces the code of traditional femininity at other levels of ideological meaning. First of all, the parameters of color, saturation and modulation are configured in a way that the visual truth constructed in the magazines is based on the *sensory modality* (van Leeuwen 2005a). This mode of visual truth is

> based on the effect of pleasure or displeasure created by visuals, and realized by a degree of articulation which is amplified beyond the point of naturalism, so that sharpness, colour, depth, the play of light and shade, etc., become – from the point of view of naturalistic modality – "more than real". (van Leeuwen 2005a: 170)

In sensory modality, colors are "used not to denote general meanings...or to express the essence of something in an artistic image...but for its soothing, stirring, or unsettling effect" (van Leeuwen 2005a: 170). This type of modality is thus used where pleasure matters, for example in perfume advertisements and in the exposition of food. Thus, in the imagery of the magazines, brides are constructed as esthetic objects in the same way this happens on the textual level.

Additionally, visuals in wedding magazines can be regarded as creating *abstract modality* (van Leeuwen 2005a), that is one in which the truth value of an image is judged not on the basis of how faithful a representation it renders but on the degree to which it depicts the underlying essence of a given object. In bridal magazines, sensuality created by rich color saturation is subliminally linked to hegemonic gender discourse in which femininity is hypersensual and esthetic. Another ideological code implicated in the 'grammar of color' is that of the gender coding of the magazines' most extensively exploited colors. The predominant pink, blue and white colors have their specific sociocultural connotations of exalted femininity. The symbolism of white triggers the associations of innocence. Pink connotes softness, delicacy and vanity (see Koller 2008).

Moreover, low color modulation (especially in professional photo sessions) gives the representations the abstract and non-real connotations of fairy-tale fantasies. This strengthens the coherence of the magazines' discourse by indirectly reinforcing the discursive construction of wedding as a long-awaited realization of every girl's dreams. Interestingly, such a configuration of the two modalities is not uncommon. For instance, Chen (2010: 229) observed abstract-sensory coding orientation in an educational context, which she explains in terms of "tension between the educational purpose and pleasure principle". In wedding magazines the bridal body is both conceptual and sensually appealing. This, the book proposes, can be seen as functionally related to the other features of the magazines' visual discourse – iconicity and gaze. Icons are in their essence abstract and conceptual while the object of gaze is supposed to appeal to the spectator.

Clearly, colors are an important, fully fledged mode of meaning construction in the socio-semiotic system of wedding magazines. From the systemic-functional perspective (Halliday 1978), colors in the magazines examined perform all three metafunctions of a sign (see Kress and van Leeuwen 2006: 229–30). They were found to serve the ideational function of denoting a specific group of people (women, brides) and the interpersonal one of compelling women's positive identification with a community of shared knowledge. Their textual role consists in giving the magazines a coherent and distinctive stylistic quality through the selection and coordination of the palette.

Pertinently to the argument made at the beginning of the discussion, the use of color in the construction of the iconic bride is also ideologically meaningful. As Kress and van Leeuwen (2002: 355) observe, "the affordances of modulation are various and...strongly value-laden". As such, the parameters discussed above are 'motivated signs' (see also Kress and van Leeuwen 2006) – the meaning they are given arises from the interests and intentions of the sign-makers. The consensual mode through which the two modalities of bridal imagery operate makes evident their social (and ideological) implications. Apparently, it is also on the level of visual discourse that the reader is positioned as the subject of dominant gender discourse in which the bride embodies innocence and hypersensual femininity.

On the whole, the role of images in wedding magazines shows that their discourse needs to be understood (and investigated) in terms of its multiple modalities. In concluding the analysis it needs to be underscored that the images of brides have a strong affective and meaning-making power because they work subliminally. Similarly to presuppositions and implicatures, the images draw on the recipient's sociocultural knowledge so they are likely to compel meanings that cannot be elicited from their propositional content without background knowledge. This means that, similarly to texts, they imply 'the obvious' and hence need to be considered in terms of their interpellative power. At the same time, images are even stronger than language structures because they are more effective in grabbing the attention of the recipient – even the least interested one.

Men in bridal magazines

Structured by the traditional fault lines of masculinity and femininity, wedding experience accompanies the "creation of shared reality" (Bulcroft et al. 1997: 464) based on the couple's tacit agreement to comply with the established gender roles. As could be seen in the examples above, the rituals of personal transformation accompanying wedding preparations are constructed as the practices of femininity through which a woman attains and validates her bridal identity. The absence of men in those constructions (apart from their role of passive spectators) reproduces the stereotypical view that they do not attach comparable importance to the wedding event.

The same assumption is realized by means of other interesting constructions of masculinity, which perpetuate marked gender binaries:

> Us girls know fabulous shoes complete an outfit but our other halves need a little guidance. (*Cosmopolitan Bride* 7–8/2009)

The dichotomy between 'us girls' and 'our other halves' is reproduced through two main repertoires – of the man's apparent inability to cope with wedding preparations and of the groom being a part of the spectacle organized by the bride. As the latter repertoire hence indicates, grooms are also constructed as the objects of gaze:

> You've got a gorgeous groom, a ring that rocks and shoes that send you head over heels. Complete your superstar-bride moment with Michael Kors' showbiz scent. (*Cosmopolitan Bride* 12–1/2010)
>
> CAN YOU BELIEVE... your groom can get a spray-on ab-defining six-pack from St Tropes which highlights his muscles in the same way you use your Touche Eclat – genius! (*You & Your Wedding* 11–12/2009)
>
> How can I stop my groom from looking stiff in our photos? (*You & Your Wedding* 7–8/2009)

Interestingly, unlike in the case of the bride, who is the sole object of the gaze, most of the corresponding constructions of the groom imply that he shares the position with the bride. Yet, this time she is given a considerable amount of agency because it is the bride's decision how the man should look and she is in charge of his appearance. In this way the groom is considerably de-agentialized (van Leeuwen 2008) by the controlling gaze of the bride:

> Make sure all the groom's party have sorted out their cufflinks – you don't want ushers to wear dress shirts with flapping sleeves. (*You & Your Wedding* 7–8/2009)
>
> Organise the groom's and groomsmen's suits. (*Cosmopolitan Bride* 12–1/2010)
>
> My fiancé and his best man are quite short but they want to wear morning suits. I'm worried the suits will swamp them. (*You & Your Wedding* 7–8/2009)

That the problems tackled here and there are gendered is evident in that often it is not the groom but basically men (best men and the groom's mates) who appear inept at taking care of their looks. Regarding the relations of agency, in the constructions of the groom as the object of gaze, the bride is positioned as the 'project-manager superbride'. Such configurations raise the question of whether the bride's agency necessarily excludes the groom's agentic position, and whether the position of an esthetic object is indeed so damaging to his masculinity. The incongruity of the masculine and feminine positions once they are reversed reveals how limited and inflexible are the forms of experience that hegemonic gender order offers. The apparent conflict could be explained as the consequence of its constitutive binaries being premised on the sets of fixed oppositions.

As for the other repertoire mentioned, wedding magazines reinforce male–female dichotomy by means of the recurrent idea that men do not participate in wedding organization. Sometimes their lack of involvement is produced indirectly; for example, men are not mentioned in the accounts of family disagreements about preparations. Their emotional detachment from the event is also constructed directly:

> I wonder if my groom's actually interested in our wedding. He just says 'whatever you like, darling'. Is he just super-lazy? Jessica, Exeter
>
> "Your groom is suffering from a condition known as napkin malaise", says Matt Rudd, author of 'William Walker's First Year of Marriage: A

Horror Story' (HarperPress, £6.99). "When he proposed, he pictured a beautiful wedding to the woman of his dreams and a lifetime skipping through meadows – not the wedding planning. Men don't care about napkins, favours, horses and carriages or anything confetti-related. This is not super-laziness, it's genetics. Give him some heavy lifting and you worry about the napkins." (*You & Your Wedding* 11–12/2009)

Of course, the text is written in a clearly ironic way. The author uses the appealing 'Mars-and-Venus' rhetoric and artfully plays on the popular themes surrounding weddings (such as horses and carriages). Yet, with or without the touch of irony, the underlying sexism of the text cannot be denied. As noted by Benwell (2003), in media discourse irony is a regular way of handling sexist overtones – it is a strategy of expressing misogynist claims by simultaneously invalidating them and subverting critique they would otherwise evoke (see also Stevenson et al. 2000).

Finally, men were found essentialized along the shared repertoire of the groom's 'embarrassing wedding moment' when he is moved to tears. To illustrate, one of the articles in *You & Your Wedding* (7–8/2009) deals with grooms' public displays of emotions (for instance, while making vows or delivering a speech). Because the issue is discussed on a problem page, it is already constructed as problematic by the genre. Moreover, the topic could possibly be presented without the category of gender, as concerning all people whose extroverted behaviors may embarrass or confuse wedding guests. Yet, the whole discussion revolves around the category of gender; a groom crying in public is presented as not living up to the demands that have traditionally been put on men. This idea is reinforced visually. The couple stand with their backs to the camera as if escaping the public gaze. This implies a moment of crisis that is not supposed to be part of their wedding spectacle. Also, the gravity of the situation is implied by the monochromatic coding of the picture, which is very unlike the majority of photos in the magazines.

Repertoires of the bridal body

Perfection and 'normative discontent'

Many analysts of the popular wedding culture observe that brides are subject to numerous disciplinary bodily regimes that revolve around diet and workouts preceding the 'big day'. In the culture where thinness is the key feature of the normative female body (see Bordo 1993), the critical condition of fitting into the wedding gown is not surprising. For example, in the studies of Australian (Prichard and Tiggemann

2008) and American (Neighbors and Sobal 2008) brides, more than half were found to wish to lose a specific amount of weight (10 kg) before the wedding day. According to Nash (2012: 5), in the mainstream Australian bridal magazines the narrative of weight loss has become the one that marks "the appearance of the bride".

The magazines examined in this book were also found to construct losing weight as part of the established rituals of the bridal body. Additionally, it is observed here that apart from a direct reinscription of the media's repertoires of the female body, wedding magazines hybridize them with the discourses of the wedding-ideological complex. First of all, as Nash (2012: 5) notes, the media's emphasis on the importance of losing weight before the wedding has led to "a new visual and cultural vocabulary for dealing with brides and bridal bodies". In the emergent lexis the ideal bridal body is synonymous with 'sexy' and 'toned', the attainment of which is a time-bound, regimented process. Hence, such constructions are typical of the wider media discourse of the female body. Secondly, it is proposed here, another dominant discourse of bridal magazines, which constitutes the emergent hybrid, is one of the "ethic of perfection" underpinning the popular wedding culture (Otnes and Pleck 2003: 8–9). To illustrate, in what Nash (2012: 5) calls "a new visual and cultural vocabulary for dealing with brides and bridal bodies", the magazines' preoccupation with perfection is evident in the *overwording* (Halliday 1978; Fairclough 1989) of the notion, that is, a substantial amount of lexis denoting it:

> Copy our covergirl's perfectly pretty look with Chanel cosmetics. (*You & Your Wedding* 7–8/2009)
>
> Whatever your look leans towards, a flawless complexion is essential, so take action to repair winter-ravaged skin. (*Wedding Ideas* 55/2008)
>
> Each lucky bride will attend at least seven consultations to achieve that all-important 'like-a-glove' fit. (*Perfect Wedding* 4/2008)

All the sentences above presuppose that the reader is not (or does not consider herself as) 'perfect enough'. The desired appearance is to be 'copied' or 'achieved' by 'taking action' and 'repairing'.

Moreover, sometimes the ideal bridal body is constructed by means of presuppositions and implicatures concerning what is not considered as 'perfect':

> Here's how to survive hours in spotlight without cracking, smudging or smearing. (*You & Your Wedding* 11–12/2009)

Firstly, the main clause in the sentence hails the reader as the object of gaze ("Here's how to survive hours in spotlight"). Secondly, the embedded clause suggests what may, but should not, happen with the bride's appearance ("cracking, smudging or smearing"). In this way, the sentence appeals to the bride by playing on her awareness of the surveilling gaze, her submission to the arbitrary standard of the ideal bridal body and her determination to attain it.

That the reader will take action is another recurrent presupposition that surfaces the discourse. The arbitrary presupposition that women eagerly subject themselves to the regime of body discipline is based on the assumption of women's 'normative discontent' (Tiggemann and Lynch 2001), namely, that they always find their looks not good enough and in need of constant improvement:

> Every bride wants gorgeous undies on her big day as well as lingerie that smoothens out any lumps and bumps. (*Perfect Wedding* 4/2008)
>
> The wedding's approaching and your bottom is still wobbling. (*Cosmopolitan Bride* 7–8/2009)
>
> Tried everything to get that glow, but think your skin's still so-so? A little skin type know-how is all you need. (*Cosmopolitan Bride* 12–1/2010)

The examples above illustrate the magazines' presumption that the target reader has already worked on her looks and, hence, that she is not satisfied with her body. It is also taken for granted that she has failed in her pursuits. This constructs the woman as dependent on specialists and specific commodities that will help her to fight against her imperfections.

Evidently, the constructions of the picture-perfect bridal body, as well as the indications of what 'spoils the picture', render specific information about the appropriate shape, size, skin complexion, etc. For example, the body should not be pale or chubby:

> Unless you're blessed with naturally sun-kissed skin, self-tan is essential but it needs to be flawless. (*You & Your Wedding* 7–8/2009)
>
> If there's one bit of your body that can never be too voluminous it's your eyelashes! (*Perfect Wedding* 4/2008)
>
> "I tried all 'miracles diets'...but this time I had to do something that would work – I was getting married and I could not imagine myself floating down the aisle in w white dress looking like a baby hippopotamus." (*Wedding Ideas* 5/2008)

In the formulation "blessed with naturally sun-kissed skin", the premodifier "naturally sun-kissed" is not only informative, it is ascribed an evaluative function by "blessed". The message communicated in the second example in the set above is a form of interpellation. Given how straightforwardly the reader is informed that she should be concerned about the size of any single part of her body other than eyelashes, the sentence positions her as a member of a community in which this potentially debatable statement needs no justification. Finally, the last example in the set is part of a reader's self-account, but even though self-directed it is offensive to plus-size women who are hereby (indirectly) compared to a baby hippopotamus.

Undeniably, bridal magazines are centrally premised on the wider media discourse of the female body. This is evident in how repeatedly their readers, confronted with the textual and visual constructions of the model-beautiful iconic bride, are put in the position of self-evaluation and self-surveillance. As Boden (2003: 62) posits, "femininity is conceptualized as 'picture-perfect', triggering visual pleasure for the bride as well as her audience for conforming to the cultural requirements of a successful bridal appearance". Another feature which the discourses of the female and the bridal female body share is how much they say through what is omitted in their constructions of the body. After all, the bridal beauty is also embodied by air-brushed and ageless white models, which makes the iconic bride another media-based exclusive construction of femininity.

Body as the object of knowledge and discipline

Like the wider media discourse, wedding magazines construct the female body as the object of knowledge provided by cosmetic technology and science. The reader is provided with numerous instructions concerning dietary recommendations, information about new surgical and cosmetic procedures; established conceptions are contended by media expertise:

> It's a myth that you shouldn't wash your hair on your wedding day. (*Cosmopolitan Bride* 7–8/2009)

> "Knowing your skin type is absolutely essential to creating a routine that addresses your skin's needs and keep it healthy and glowing", revels Beverly England, skincare expert for Darphin. (*Cosmopolitan Bride* 12–1/2010)

> Their professional make-up artist will give you application tips during your consultation and provide you with samples for home trials. (*Brides, Wedding Planner* 2008)

Additionally, the bridal body necessitates constant control. The wedding day is constructed as the time that requires a heightened awareness of one's look and keeping everything in check:

> Be prepared with a kit bag packed with powerful products to deliver an instant beauty boost at the very last minute. (*Wedding Ideas* 56/2008)

> To attain real glamourpuss status, you need to pay attention to every inch of your body, from the tips of your toes to the top of your head. (*Perfect Wedding* 4/2008)

> Never forget that your back is on show! (*You & Your Wedding* 11–12/2009)

At this stage of discussion, some readers of this book may consider that the examples could well serve as illustrations of the other repertoires of the female body that have been mentioned in the discussion above. For instance, "pay[ing] attention to *every inch of your body*" can be regarded as yet another realization of the repertoire of bodily perfection. In the last example in the set, the reminder presupposes the reader's awareness of all other parts of her body that are also 'on show', which hence reinforces the notion of gaze fixed on the bride. The repertoires are indeed strongly connected and this intricacy, this book argues, is their strength. After all, recipients' internalized docility and sense of surveillance allows issuing commands without justifying them. The tight intensity of the repertoires may increase one's vulnerability to commodification. As Boden (2003: 68) states, "anxieties can stimulate consumer desire and ensure potential consumers are receptive to deeper psychological underpinnings of advertisements".

Many of the constructions of the bridal body entail more or less explicit recommendations of specific products and services:

> If you want to wow on your hen night, dazzle your groom on your big day and shine on honeymoon, we've teamed with *cult beauty brand Bourjois* to offer you a free *Bourjois 3D Max Gloss*. (*You & Your Wedding* 7–8/2009)

> Mix *show-stopping gowns* with *cosy accessories* for a wow-factor look. (*Cosmopolitan Bride* 12–1/2010)

> Phillipa Lepley is known for her *miracle-working corsages and bodices* which create a perfect hourglass shape. (*Brides* 7–8/2008)

The examples above repeatedly deliver the same culturally dominant idea that the bride is the object of esthetic pleasure. The premodifiers such as "show-stopping", "wow-factor" and "miracle-working" contain two pieces of information. For one thing, because they are the hyponyms of 'pretty', the sentences apparently provide fashion- and beauty-related recommendations. For another, the premodifiers imply that the ultimate goal of bridal body practices is to grab attention, which implicitly communicates women's desire to be looked at and arouse admiration.

The repertoire of self-surveillance is also realized by reminding the reader that she needs to be alluring but not flamboyant:

> *Don't overdo with the accessories* – having too many can look unsophisticated (*Brides* 7–8/2008)

> [S]ometimes it's easy to get carried away with the whole bridal thing. *Resist the temptation to pile on the make-up.* (*Perfect Wedding* 4/2008)

> [B]rides look beautiful with *minimal but magical accessorising* (*Cosmopolitan Bride* 7–8/2009)

Apparently, the rules of the bridal body regime are more complex than it may seem as both doing not enough and doing too much have their negative consequences. To insinuate that seems a logical step for the magazines as this puts even a relatively knowledgeable reader in the position of wanting clarification, which reinforces the relation of power between her and the editors.

The notion of beauty regime is taken to its extreme in the genre of wedding countdown:

> Just got engaged? Alice du Parcq has your pre-wedding beauty countdown. (*Brides* 7–8/2008)

With the implicature that engagement begins a period of an intensified, carefully planned work on the body, the statement could begin any wedding countdown. In this regular feature of bridal magazines, the practices of body discipline are constructed as scrupulously organized in time:

> For two weeks before and right up until the big day, get eight hour sleep a night, drink two litres of water each day and have a full-body exfoliation treatment three times a week. (*Wedding Ideas* 56/2008)

Start a proper maintenance regime at least four months in advance and have hair regularly trimmed. (*Perfect Wedding* 4/2008)

For the best results, start your fitness and skincare routines at least six months before your big day. (*Wedding Ideas* 56/2008)

As can be seen, the whole genre of wedding countdowns works on the presupposition that all activities mentioned need to be done – the point is not what to do but when and how often. The assumptive tone with which readers are hailed as the 'docile' objects of self-discipline is particularly notable in the imperative mode of the short directives:

Eight months to go. Start your fitness plan. (*Brides* 7–8/2008)

Six to nine months to go. Begin a beauty regime. (*You & Your Wedding* 7–8/2009)

One week to go. Have a spray tan. (*Perfect Wedding* 4/2008)

On one hand, wedding countdowns adopt the managerial rhetoric of a proactive attitude to one's body and position the reader as in charge of her body. On the other hand, the book contends that such pieces of advice position the reader as submissive by taking for granted her compliance with the media-based regime of bridal body.

Exposed to such discourse, one can internalize the idea that the body, due to its unsatisfactory nature, cannot be left on its own, unaided by the workings of diet (a), cosmetics (b), workouts (c) and technological devices (d) (see Jeffries 2007):

(a) *Plan your meals* and plan your shopping around it. And stick to the plan! ... Don't go shopping when you're hungry. ... Better still shop online. (*Wedding Ideas* 5/2008)
Drink chamomile tea by the bucket load and *swap spicy foods* for bland ones. (*Cosmopolitan Bride* 12–1/2010)

(b) Getting wow W-day skin doesn't mean trying every treatment going – *get the cleanser* sorted and all you need is *a skin-type-specific moisturiser,* a once-weekly *exfoliation and a serum* to combat any specific worries, such as ageing or oiliness. (*Cosmopolitan Bride* 12–1/2010)
Do a quick *exfoliation* with Boots Exfoliating Gloves every morning before jumping in the shower and *apply moisturizer* afterwards. (*Brides* 7–8/2008)

(c) Wherever you are, *clench your bum* as tightly as you can, hold for a count of 10 then relax and repeat. (*Cosmopolitan Bride* 7–8/2009) *Shadow boxing* is a great way to tone up. (*Cosmopolitan Bride* 7–8/2009)

(d) To get last-minute svelte, invest in a pair of Revital Lipo Contour shorts, £49.99. As well as shaping, *the cosmetic-surgeon-developed underwear* features double-layer fabric that constantly massages the areas where fat, fluid and toxins build up under the skin. (*Cosmopolitan Bride* 7–8/2009)
The reason for its longevity is the effectiveness of *Guinot's high-frequency electrotherapy wands.* When massaged into the skin, the wands send mild currents into the facial muscles to stimulate collagen production. (*Brides* 7–8/2008)

As can be seen, the commodified bridal body is not only subject to different forms of discipline but is also fragmented. It is separated into 'problem areas' that need separate attention (see Mills 1995; Talbot 1995; Balsamo 1996; Benwell and Stokoe 2006; Jeffries 2007). Specific body parts are linked to particular forms of effort – reducing fat or skin imperfection, coloring, augmentation, toning, etc. The conceptualization of a woman's body as consisting of separate zones is reinforced by the visual representation of women's heads, lips, nails, legs, palms, etc.

Cinderella's transformation

The examples provided so far are the local variations of the repertoires of the female body that are widely exploited in the general media discourse. By concentrating on what one can or should do to change her appearance, they produce a forcible message – a woman's body "always needs fixing" (D. Smith 1988). The persistent encouragements to deal with the 'natural' bodily flaws by means of recommended products, reinforced by the images of air-brushed photographs of models and product recommendations are commodifying strategies. Additionally, it has been demonstrated above that wedding magazines have their own repertoires of bridal body, which are derived from the wedding-ideological complex. The most notable example of that, this book proposes, is the repertoire of bridal transformation.

In their discussion of wedding and pre-wedding rituals, Winch and Webster (2012: 54) observe that the apparently straightforward appeals to strive for physical perfection have their underlying logic of self-transformation that takes place through the process of "self-branding":

> In a society in which women are sold the idea that their body image is in need of improvement, wedding media persuade brides that they can be renewed through a perfect wedding. By investing in the correct brands to produce the correct branded spectacle, the bride can shed her inadequate bodily chrysalis and emerge as the perfect bride.

Simply put, the rhetoric of bodily transformation may lead the reader to consider the consumption practices which are part of body discipline in terms of self-management rather than submission to the media's 'dictatorship'. As has been noted above, in bridal magazines getting married is conceptually linked to a woman's transformation into a princess. The exhortations such as "Unleash your inner fairytale princess" (*You & Your Wedding* 7–8/2009) imply a 'fairytale princess' dormant in the reader who needs to be awoken on 'that special day'. Like the constructions of the normative discontent, the fairy-tale fiction has been weaved into the discourse of commodification:

> Reveal your inner princess with glittering gems and a super-seductive make-up. (*Perfect Wedding* 4/2008)
>
> Look and feel like a princess in a gorgeous designer gown. (*Wedding Ideas* 54/2008)
>
> Perfect your princess look with a terrific tiara or crystal crown, for a royal style that is pure vintage glamour! (*Perfect Wedding* 4/2008)

The commodification of bridal transformation clearly highlights the results of the practices of body discipline. Becoming the 'princess' whom the reader is presupposed to have dreamt of as a child is apparently one of them.

Recontextualized in the discourse of wedding magazines, the practices of body discipline are constructed as part of a transformative process that is not only empowering but pleasant. Consequently, in the constructions of consumer docility, the subject position of a consumer hybridizes with the one of a 'childish fantasizer' living her dream of a royal wedding:

> Fancy indulging in some pre-wedding pampering with your groom or your hens? (*You & Your Wedding* 7–8/2009)

Mirror Mirror's two stores have a way of treating every bride like a celebrity. (*Cosmopolitan Bride* 12–1/2010)

WIN! A pre-wedding pampering package. (*You & Your Wedding* 11–12/2009)

The notions of pleasure and indulgence are deployed to expose the advantages of more or less luxurious commodities and services, the consumption of which means also subjecting oneself to body discipline. The presence of the notion of pleasure next to that of discipline has been observed by Ingraham (2008: 7–8) in her examination of the American wedding culture:

[A]s well as selling the bridal identity to us as a "pleasure", bridal magazines in fact promote the disciplined female body – disciplined not only through diet, beauty, regimes, costume, gesture and posture..., but also through conforming to the more traditional properties of wedding etiquette and formality.

Importantly, however, in the magazines examined in the current study, the repertoires of pleasure and discipline are handled so ambiguously that they often seem difficult to tell apart:

And the pampering doesn't stop there – you'll have your teeth whitened by cosmetic dentists Swiss Smile (swiss-smile.co.uk) before celebrity make-up artists create your perfect bridal look. (*You & Your Wedding* 7–8/2009)

As well as being wonderfully hydrating, this effective skin treatment uses mild, pain-free electrical currents to tone up your facial muscles and tighten dull skin, so it's good for those with slightly older complexions. But it's not all beams and lasers. There's a pampering cleansing and massage ritual. (*Brides* 7–8/2008)

Need a tougher approach? The New You Boot Camp's Luxury Fitness Break combines a hardcore week-long exercise marathon with treats such as four-poster beds. (*Cosmopolitan Bride* 6–7/2009)

Clearly, in the discourse of the commodified bridal body, pleasure, realized through the repertoire of 'being pampered', is intertwined with the sorts of experiences that are not primarily associated with pleasure (teeth whitening, electrical currents, hardcore exercise, etc.). To regard this as an illustration of the media's production of docility is one way of seeing such an organization of the repertoires. Another one proposed here is to understand such constructions of bridal transformation in terms of how they reflect late modern mentality. The magazines apparently imply that practices leading to the attainment of the 'perfect' bridal body are not less enjoyable than the moment of attainment itself. This reflects the late modern approach to identity as a 'reflexive project of the self', as constantly 'under construction', in which the idea of 'becoming' is "more desirable than being" (M. Jones 2008: 12).

Commodified bridal femininity

The constructions of consumption often feature the repertoire of fun – similar to that of pleasure, this repertoire even more openly interpellates the reader as a 'childish-fantasizer superbride' by alluding to the idea of women's irrational and compulsive consumer behaviors:

> SHOPPING HEAVEN. Wearing your gown is only half of the fun – choosing your dream dress at a luxurious bridal boutique and being treated like a princess is an essential part of wedding planning for any bride (and her mum!). (*You & Your Wedding* 11–12/2009)

> Once the dossier is done, the real fun starts – wallow in dream dresses from designers such as Sassi Holford and Benjamin Roberts. Best mates are welcome but don't be surprised to lose them – AP has the biggest collection of bridesmaid dresses in the country. By appointment only. (*Cosmopolitan Bride* 12–1/2010)

> Prepare to lose yourself in this Aladdin's cave of a store. (*Cosmopolitan Bride* 12–1/2010)

The constructions of bridal indulgence recontextualize the culturally recognizable practices of (commodified) femininity – shopping sprees during which women find mutual understanding and strengthen emotional bonds between one another. The underlying assumption that the reader and her companions share the fondness of shopping produces the collective subjectivity of female consumers. Such constructions illustrate how by adding the social and affective dimensions to consumption, popular wedding culture turns consumption into the "pleasure of ultimate femininity" (Boden 2003: 61ff.).

Apart from taste and preferences, members of the bridal consumer community share the knowledge of the market. This is noticeable when the reader is positioned as well versed in, for example, available brands:

The original Crouch End shop stocks fairytale dresses from the likes of Ian Stuart and Pronovias to their one Mirror Mirror. (*Cosmopolitan Bride* 12–1/2010)

The advertisement works on the presupposition that the names should be telling enough for the reader. Basically, the subject position of an informed consumer reflects how brides are addressed by the wedding market. As Boden (2003: 60) observes, "[b]rides must make themselves knowledgeable enough to discern their wedding style and to make informed purchases to achieve coherence in style throughout the whole wedding occasion". Another way in which the subject position identified here corresponds with the wider wedding-ideological complex is that it reinforces the notion of bridal self-transformation through 'self-branding' (Winch and Webster 2012). The manifest conviction about the reader's consumer knowledge adds authenticity to the idea that she is capable of managing the process of transforming herself into the 'perfect' bride through an informed selection of goods and services.

Another form of consumer interpellation which essentializes women can be found in the constructions of a community of readers:

You can find much more than just great advice from other brides-to-be forum – how about some friends for life, too? (*Wedding Ideas* 53/2008)

As has been noted at the beginning of this chapter, the target reader of bridal magazines is assumed to "possess the cultural literacy to 'read' their texts" (Boden 2003: 59). Thus, because the implications of intimacy and like-mindedness surface the whole media genre of women's lifestyle magazines, the established ethos of a reader community (Talbot 1995) should be transparent to the readers of bridal magazines. In turn, the magazines become the site of the gender practices of exchanging opinions and offering mutual support:

My shoes were from Gina (gina.com) – I wanted something sexy, feminine and elegant, says Gina. (*You & Your Wedding* 11–12/2009)

Charlotte Gardner, 33, married Chris Leventis, 34, at Bickleigh Castle last November. "I would highly recommend a weekend wedding, even if it means asking slightly fewer people." (*Brides* 7–8/2008)

Let yourself be pampered. I hired a make-up artist and she was worth every penny! Charlene. (*Wedding Ideas* 54/2008)

Readers' personal recommendations of specific services, products, venues, etc. are substantiated by their first-hand knowledge. The intimacy is constructed through, among other way, the personal tone of the advice. The shared subject position of well-informed brides and magazine readers is bolstered by the use of neologisms that are used by both readers and journalists:

Stress-free ways to manage your mumzilla. (*Brides* 7–8/2008)

Getting wow W-day skin doesn't mean trying every treatment going. (*Cosmopolitan Bride* 12–1/2010)

Dita's glamourpuss style is dramatic and inspiring – perfect for sassy brides! (*Wedding Ideas* 56/2008)

Indeed, it could be argued that the exchange of knowledge by means of media serves the media's pragmatic function and that seeing an ideological agenda behind it is tendentious. Yet, what this analysis seeks to call into question is not that wedding magazines provide consumer information but that they often address readers as consumers covertly. For example, in the magazines the reader's membership in the bridal community is conditioned by her acceptance of consumer subjectivity. (As noted in the discussion preceding the current analysis, harnessing gender solidarity in generating consumer loyalty has deservedly earned a long list of critics among media and feminist writers.) Another implication of the commodifying interpellations that this book seeks to problematize is that consumption is constructed as one of the 'technologies of self', hence part of the 'reflexive project of the self'. To illustrate, the following example comes from an article about choosing the right wedding dress. It includes advice from a life coach:

Once you've chosen your look, trust your instinct. "If you lose the courage of conviction about a decision, such as which dress to buy, take a 10-minute timeout to clear your mind, then go back to the shop", says life coach and hypnotherapist Caroline Carr (caroline-carr.com). (*Cosmopolitan Bride* 7–8/2009)

Of course, there is nothing controversial about encouraging women to make careful consumer choices. Yet, the fact of by whom the advice is given constructs the purchase of a bridal gown as a practice of self, rather than a mere consumer choice. This logic was manifest also in the "Wedding file debate" (see pp. 68–70), where the trashing and treasuring of a wedding dress were found constructed as the acts of bridal identity.

But, a counterargument could be advanced here that societies have always developed some material forms of cultural activity, which assisted them in their experience of the surrounding reality. Seen from this perspective, nothing alarming should be found in the assurance that a new collection by Victoria Jane

> offers to the brides-to-be the emotion of their gown; a gown that translates their dreams and emotions, bringing to life their personality. (*Perfect Wedding* 4/2008)

Yet, it is not the intention of this study to unconditionally debase all wedding rituals linked with the commodity market. Instead, it hopes to encourage consideration of the degree to which media seek to integrate commodity consumption with the contemporary wedding culture. In light of what has been asserted in this volume about the threats of 'liquid modernity' (Bauman 2004), this is a timely reflection. Because the power of tradition has loosened its grip on once rigid social and cultural conventions, it seems worthwhile to consider whether (and if yes, how) the original meanings and functions of wedding rituals and artifacts have changed. For example, the data presented above show how the choice of the appropriate gown is handled in media discourse to regulate consumer behaviors, as well as verify the media's informative function and prove the media's socially facilitating role (after all, the magazines apparently assist brides in establishing a mutually supportive community). By the same token, in reference to the two examples above, there is no point in denying the symbolical value of the wedding gown, but perhaps it should be reconsidered whether relating to one's wedding gown from the ambiguous, media-constructed subject position presented above is an act of the bridal or the consumer identity.

Finally, as the examples above illustrate, the practices of bridal transformation revolve around the body. Apart from the implications that this may have for the body (if the magazines' instructions are followed), the commodification of this transformative experience may affect one's self-reflexive relationship to the body. Following Baudrillard (1988: 129), the contemporary forms of consumption have effected a 'split' in the body as a result of which it is now treated as 'capital' and 'fetish'. While the former requires economic investment, the investment in the latter is non-physical. In fact, the fetishized bodies are the "the objects of salvation", which have "taken over that moral and ideological function from the soul" (Baudrillard 1998: 129). It, then, follows from Baudrillard that the constructions of the bridal body in wedding magazines both commodify and 'fetishize' it. The process of fetishization is evident in the constructions that blur the boundary between the bodily and non-bodily practices:

> Ritva Westenius is a *city-based sanctuary*. The service is subtle and catering. (*Cosmopolitan Bride* 12–1/2010)
>
> [W]ith this facial you're immediately soothed by a *hot-towel foot ritual that lulls you into a state of bliss*. (*Brides* 7–8/2008)
>
> This therapist's continuous hands-on contact *puts you in a head-to-toe state of ease*, which is perfect for brides who need to *clear their racing minds* of planning dilemmas. (*Brides* 7–8/2008)

Obviously, the textual-discursive focus of the current study is narrow in comparison to the vast area of the sociocultural sites encompassing the wedding-ideological complex. Yet, the book proposes, media texts are apparently limited – only if they are seen conventionally, as separate units that are once written or said. However, following the notion of text delineated in Chapter 1, due to their intertextual and interdiscursive relations with other texts, discourses and practices, the salience of media texts in the production and reproduction of social meanings cannot be overvalued. Media texts serve their meaning-constructive role thanks to their recontextualizing properties. Because recontextualization is an ongoing media practice, it has been mentioned more than once in the discussion so far; many of the examples which have so far been provided could be regarded as its vivid illustrations although they have been used to explain other issues. The purpose of the remaining part of the chapter is to address recontextualization specifically.

Recontextualization: hidden ideologies

In Chapter 1 it has been proposed that thanks to its meaning-productive capacities, intertextuality is one of the key mechanisms of power production and mediation. It is through 'intertexts' that subjects of dominant discourses are hailed. Accordingly, this book takes a 'decentralized' approach to media texts by assuming that their meanings "depend on intertextual relations with many other genres, diachronically or synchronically. Texts relate to other texts, represented by the media…thus already adding particular meanings or decontextualizing and recontextualizing meanings" (Wodak and Busch 2004: 106).

Wedding magazines constitute an integrated, internally cohesive discourse that is intertextually and interdiscursively related to other discourses pervading the wedding-ideological complex. It may seem confusing to the reader to learn from the discussion at this point about the cohesion of the discourse after several contradictions have been enumerated. Their presence in the magazines is not denied here; yet it is at the same time noted that the incongruity of specific practices and relations may not be recognized by average readers because those practices and relations are recontextualized in the discourse of wedding magazines.

As explained in Chapter 1, recontextualization effects social changes and it is usually accompanied by at least one ideology. To specify, this book relies on Critical Discourse Analysis (CDA) to understand ideology as discursive "constructions of practices from particular perspectives (and in that sense 'one-sided') which 'iron out' the contradictions, dilemmas and antagonisms of practices in ways which accord with the interests and projects of domination" (Chouliaraki and Fairclough 1999: 26). This corresponds with the Gramscian concept of hegemony according to which the contemporary forms of power are based on the contestable, continually negotiated notions of common sense. Also, following Foucault, it has been proposed in this book that the emergent systems of knowledge (the 'truth') are fundamentally language-based.

The role of language in the production of knowledge is also emphasized in Haraway's (1988) theory of 'situated knowledges', from which it follows that all knowing subjects possess meaning-making tools, that is, 'semiotic technologies' (Haraway 1991: 187). Information, Haraway contends, "is just that kind of quantifiable element that allows universal translation, and so unhindered instrumental power (called effective communication)" (Haraway [1993] 1999: 284). Accordingly, knowledge is 'coded', that is to say, translated into "a common language in which all resistance to instrumental control disappears" (Haraway 1999: 284). In view of that, bridal culture constructed in wedding magazines can be regarded as a form of 'situated knowledge', and recontextualization that is at work in the magazines – as a 'code' which renders coherent their account of wedding culture.

The ideological coherence of discourse is attained by rearranging social practices, hence through recontextualization. In this process, the meaning of the recontextualized social practices can be covertly changed, for example by establishing new relations between the practices or between social actors involved in them. The appealing power of the mechanisms consists in that they create the appearances of the naturalness and legitimacy of the re-reconstructed order:

Recontextualization not only makes the recontextualized social practices explicit to a greater or lesser degree, it also makes them pass through the filter of the practices in which they are inserted. The way this happens is rarely transparent to the participants of the recontextualizing practice, and is usually embedded in their common sense, ... and in what they take the purposes of the recontextualizing practice to be. (van Leeuwen 2008: 13–14)

The social practices of getting married and consumption are recontextualized in the magazines ('filtered' through their perspective) and assigned to the locally established identity of the 'superbride' (Boden 2001, 2003). This impresses on the reader the 'obviousness' of the compatibility of traditional femininity and commodification. Simply put, it works to convince magazine readers that a modern woman getting married expresses herself through her transformation into a princess, in a process that necessitates a series of informed consumer choices. These mechanisms, thus, have ideological implications because they 'mystify' relations between social practices (see Barrett 1991: 167).

Therefore, below I will investigate how the genre of real-life weddings reconstructs social practices related to getting married. The texts are given closer attention at this point because they are interesting examples of both generic and discursive hybridity and they illustrate social implications of hybridization. (For another example, before the discussion proceeds to the main illustration, readers may wish return to the "Wedding file debate" (see pp. 68–70), to consider how the recontextualization of 'treasuring' and 'trashing' a wedding dress in the magazine constructs the practices anew, as acts of bridal identity and established elements of the contemporary British wedding culture.)

Real-life weddings

Real-life weddings narratives are long-running (usually 3 to 4 pages long), richly illustrated stories of wedding days which newlywed couples share with magazine readers. Due to the professional coverage that they get from the magazines, real-life weddings follow the convention of professional fashion shoots. Additionally, they have some features of media reportage, social column, reader letter, diary and advertisement. The hybridity of the genre, however, concerns not only the formal features of the texts but also social practices recontextualized in them as real-life weddings arrange side by side practices which until recently were not obviously related. An underlying contradiction this renders is one between the personal and spiritual dimension which wedding ceremonies are expected to retain and the new idea of wedding spectacles based on informed and calculated consumption.

Narratives of late modernity

The most notable feature of the genre of real-life weddings is their reliance on the traditional wedding discourse. Yet, in their marked conservatism they are truly late modern media texts. The mere fact that people tell their wedding stories reflects the late modern pursuit of the human need to narrate their lives. Following McKee (1999: 12), people's "appetite for story is a reflection of the profound human need to grasp the patterns of living, not merely as an intellectual exercise, but within a very personal, emotional experience". As discussed in Chapter 1, the late modern dissipation of the traditional systems of knowledge and moral codes has been followed by the emergence of the 'tribulations of the self'. The genre of real-life weddings illustrates implications of one of them – the sense of an internal dissonance and conflict between 'unification and fragmentation'.

On one hand, to develop coherent stories of their lives, individuals need "a sense of continuity and order in events, including those not directly within the perceptual environment of the individual" (Giddens 1991: 243). On the other hand, the coherence is threatened by the destabilizing nature of the post-traditional society and its mediatized culture. As Benwell and Stokoe (2006: 22) observe, "[p]erpetually immersed in myriad signifiers and images, the self is subsumed and substituted by this bricolage of imagery". The "collage effect" (Giddens 1991: 26, 84), which the media images and texts produce, provides their readers with a plurality of identity choices.

Yet, real-life weddings seem to be unlike many other media narratives in that they represent coherent narratives that give "a reassuring balance to difficulties in sustaining the narrative of the self in actual social situations" (Giddens 1991: 199). Contrary to the media's focus on the crisis of post-traditional relationships (their exploitation of the topics such as increasing divorce rates, loss of trust, the 'epidemic' of single men and women, etc.), real-life wedding texts bring placating stories of happy relationships, in which couples tie the knot in a truly late modern way. Importantly, as the following discussion demonstrates, apart from perpetuating the established narrative patterns and familiar wedding imagery, the texts assimilate into the wedding experience the consumer discourse, hence a discourse that could be considered as destabilizing the traditional notion of wedding, and thus needs to be naturalized in the new discourse order.

Rhetoric of romance

Proposing the notion of the 'superbride', Boden (2003: 75) finds it a consumer identity "constructed in order to incorporate the relevance of the manipulative view of consumption in the Romantic theme". This rhetoric of romance is also vividly present in the genre of real-life weddings, which overtly exploit it in the constructions of wedding events and in the couples' retrospective accounts of proposals:

> On the way to the castle our car stopped. There was a horse and carriage waiting to take us on. (*Wedding Ideas* 53/2008)
>
> I could not have imagined a more romantic moment when Ben proposed as we sat under the stars. (*Wedding Ideas* 56/2008)
>
> After Lisa sealed their partnership with a (slightly early) kiss in the church...the couple entertained 150 guests at Chiddingstone Castle in Kent. "I grew up nearby and always dreamed of having a wedding reception at the castle," says Lisa. (*Cosmopolitan Bride* 6–7/2009)

The discussion has so far provided numerous indications that the wedding has been turned into "a fantasy-laden, cultural event that is dependent upon consumption" (Boden 2003: 153). As can be seen, real-life weddings are the feature of bridal magazines which bring the most telling illustrations of how the commodification of wedding experience is legitimated by means of the romantic themes.

The deployment of romance narratives is an established practice of the whole wedding market. In their investigation of wedding media, Winch and Webster (2012: 52) observe that "[t]hese narratives are usually aspirational, and tap into popular consciousness in order to encourage the consumer to engage with, buy into and invest in the brand. Consequently, branding strategies converge easily with powerful romance narratives." Likewise, in her study of American wedding reality TV, Sgroi (2006: 117) finds the narratives as the "glue binding the wedding to commerce", and notes that "reality TV narratives enable a fusion of story and advertising" (Sgroi 2006: 125).

The examination of bridal magazines brings many examples of the relations mentioned above. Substantiating Sgroi's observation, in the advertising discourse of the magazines the relation between commodities and modern romance is explicitly enunciated:

Traditional dresses with a twist spell *pure romance* (*Brides* 7–8/2008)

> *Inspired by Romeo and Juliet*, the Summer 2008 range retails at £1,000 or under, and features innovative fabrics and unique embellishments. (*Wedding Ideas* 55/2008)

> *Romantic fiction.* Tell your own story with an amazing, detailed gown from the new Ronald Joyce collection. (*Perfect Wedding* 4/2008)

The accessories such as tiaras, veils and jewelry that give the bride's look the regal gracefulness are enumerated in both advice articles and overt advertisements. The deployment of the same theme in advertising texts and in readers' narrative contributions to the magazines is a telling example of hybridization and the ensuing commodification of wedding culture. By providing readers with real-life wedding stories that are premised on the popular romantic theme, the editors of bridal magazines manifest their awareness of the market. Illouz (1997: 26) observed that nowadays people use commodities and services in creating their "romantic utopias" – "the romanticization of commodities and the commodification of romance" reinforce each other. Hence, by yoking people's old sentiments with their fondness of consumption and managerial attitude to life, the genre resonates with the late modern sociocultural trends.

To entice readers to consume, the stories of real-life couples include the exposition of specific artifacts, which is often immediately followed by the name of the store where they can be purchased:

> Jenny wore a beautiful strapless dress – Emerald by Amanda Whatt (amandawhatt.com), with a beaded corset bodice and full skirt. "It was from Pronuptial in Romford (pronuptialromford.co.uk) and I tried on hundreds – my poor mum!" (*You & Your Wedding* 7–8/2009)

As can be seen, in the discourse of wedding magazines the positions of reader and consumer overlap. Therefore, this book suggests, such a construction of weddings as both an emotional and a financial investment conceals the unlikeness of romance and consumption because the immediacy with which the positions are intertwined generates the sense of the naturalness of consuming one's wedding.

Community of readers/consumers

Another way in which the contradiction is 'ironed out' and the consumerist approach to wedding is impressed on the reader consists in constructing reader solidarity. As could be seen in the constructions of commodified femininity, the apparent community of readers is in fact a community of consumers exchanging advice. In real-life weddings the sense of membership (and hence of the commonality of wedding consumption) is evoked, for example, when the narrating couples address readers directly with their tips and personally recommend specific services, commodities and venues:

> Bride's top tip. "Having a wedding planner was the best thing I ever did. Toni did everything, and she also saved us money by shopping around and negotiating discounts. Everything was prepared before the wedding, so the day was totally stress-free." Find out more at isisevents.co.uk (*Wedding Ideas* 58/2008)

The merging of these positions, the book contends, is a covert practice of power in the sense that it takes place in the instructional content of the real-life narratives.

Another observation made in this piece of research is that because of this way of positioning the readers the genre of real-life weddings reveals two ways in which contemporary weddings accommodate the seemingly contradictory qualities of a public and private event. Namely, apart from bringing the weddings to wide media audiences, they also make the preparations a form of a community practice – it is not only the family and the couple who participate in the process, the readers also have their (symbolic or actual) share in it.

Importantly, rather than contributing to the development of a new tradition, this book finds the media genre as reflecting (and reinforcing) the established trends of the popular wedding culture. Other media also offer couples gallery space where they post pictures and brief descriptions of their weddings (for example, the back pages of popular magazines and websites). As Winch and Webster (2012: 57) argue, the possibility of having one's wedding photographs published next to celebrity weddings encourages people to "emulate the self-branding promotional spectacle" that celebrities usually present. Interestingly, despite their growing visibility in popular media, no references to celebrity weddings in the real-life wedding texts were identified in this study. This can be considered as an indication that despite their fundamentally hybrid constitution, real-life weddings are an independent and consistent chapter.

Individualism

Despite their distinctive reliance on the traditional gender configurations, real-life weddings encourage readers to undermine the time-established wedding conventions, which reflects the ambiguous relation of late modern culture to tradition.[6] Beyond the confines of the conventionalized wedding ceremonies, real-life couples are free either to demonstrate that they still feel connected to them or to individualize their wedding. At the same time, in real-life weddings, even the couples who choose conventional ceremonies personalize them in varying degrees, as a result of which all the texts reflect the late modern culture of individualism (Baumeister 1986; Giddens 1991).

Moreover, real-life couples are positioned as both aware and in control of the elements that make their wedding spectacles meaningful:

Thalia and Tom's creativity turned their wedding into a true *reflection of their personalities. (Cosmopolitan Bride* 12–1/2010)

Choose a wedding cake that *lets your personality shine through* (*Brides, Wedding Planner* 2008)

Personalized decorations. Make your *wedding day a true reflection of yourselves* by including little *personal touches* like these that won't break the bank. (*Wedding Ideas* 53/2008)

With couples assuming responsibility for organizing the wedding spectacle and its attendant meanings, real-life weddings are regarded in this study as the materializations of the late modern 'reflexive project of the self'. That this project is premised on consumption is evident in how the couples are positioned as potential consumers – the texts feature appeals to readers' consumer tastes and choices ("personal touches like these that won't break the bank", "choose a wedding cake"). Consequently, real-life weddings accommodate the paradox of the commodified self, which consists in pursuing individuality among mass-produced commodities and widely available services:

Let real-life brides inspire you with weddings that are truly individual. (*Brides* 7–8/2008)

Beverly and Mal's chic wedding had lots of memorable details – steal their style to personalise your big day. (*You & Your Wedding* 11–12/2009)

20 pages of inspiring real wedding pages (*Cosmopolitan Bride* 6–7/2009)

As can be noted, the instructions how to express one's individual self can be found in the mass-produced magazines – evidently, individualism does not emanate from the inside, it is a result of externally provided inspiration.

Esthetization

The emphasis on the 'spectacular' attained through a careful selection of fine details reflects the enhanced esthetization of late modern culture. In this way, the genre of real-life magazines shows another form of managing the 'reflexive project of the self' – constructing one's identity through the choice of lifestyle. As a range of beliefs, attitudes and choices made in life, it has replaced the traditional social indicators such as class and race: "People use lifestyles in everyday life to identify and explain wider complexes of identity and affiliation" (Chaney 1996: 12). Nowadays lifestyle choices, Chaney notes, are expressed through shared consumer behaviors which express one's individual taste: "Strongly held beliefs and commitment to family values are likely to be symbolised by particular types of esthetic choice, just as militant feminism is likely to be associated with particular ways of dressing, talking and leisure" (Chaney 1996: 96).

The esthetization of culture has been taken up by producers, marketers and advertisers. The commodification of identity has been reinforced by the media and advertising discourses in which commodities have been infused with a new kind of meaning: "producers have begun to elaborate symbolic systems to transform them into lifestyle signifiers" (van Leeuwen 2005a: 145). Media offer their recipients membership in groups affiliated on the basis of esthetic likes and dislikes. As members of the emergent 'interpretative communities' (Fish 1980), individuals articulate their interpretations of the world through their affiliation with a specific way of consumption. In the analysis, real-life wedding texts were found to distinctly articulate the relationships between the couples' consumption of specific products and services and their lifestyles, tastes, sociocultural affiliations and fascinations:

> As yoga aficionados, they gave their day a natural, green feel. "We tried to leave as light a footprint as possible by having the ceremony and reception in the same place, *eating local, organic food and donating the flowers to a home* for the elderly." (*Cosmopolitan Bride* 6–7/2009)

> We wanted our wedding to really represent who we are. We held the ceremony outdoors under beautiful trees with *colourful garlands, and*

instead of a string quartet…we hired a mariachi band. (Cosmopolitan Bride 6–7/2009)

It was important to us that our wedding reflected our Caribbean culture. So we chose a fresh ivory and green colour theme and took a lot of time planning *a Caribbean-themed menu* from caterers Burrell Catering (burrellcatering.com). (*You & Your Wedding 7–8/2009*)

As can be observed, specific details are explicitly constructed as revealing something important or intimate about the couple. This book proposes that such constructions of the personalized and esthetisized wedding spectacle exemplify "myself-that-could-be" through consumption (Belk et al. 1996). This shows in what sense media, as an expert system providing lifestyle information, reinforce the distinctly late modern reliance on commodities in the pursuit and expression of one's sense of self.

'Pure relationship'

The de-traditionalization of life has also affected the shape of contemporary relationships in Western societies. It has undermined the value of religion, which has consequently been replaced with romantic love as a new site of seeking meaning in life (Beck and Beck-Gernsheim 1990; Illouz 1997). This prompted a major shift in the idea of marriage from 'institution' to 'relationship' (Finch and Summerfield 1991). Referring to the emergent type of intimate relationship as 'pure relationship', Giddens (1992) underscores its emotional and economic equality between partners. Substantiating that (but rendering a marked inconsistency with the rest of the magazines' discourse), real-life narratives redress the traditional gender imbalance of wedding culture. They are the odd occasions in the magazines when the groom is constructed as participating in the wedding preparations and experiencing the wedding event as intensely as the bride. Contrary to what is usually either directly stated or implied in the bridal magazines about men's 'natural indifference to napkins', in these narratives the decisions about all wedding details are presented as shared:

We arranged tables in a U-shape and had an Indian-style buffet so everyone could mingle from the start. (*Brides 7–8/2008*)

The venue was key for us – we love architecture and once we found Templeton, everything fell into place. (*Wedding Ideas 57/2008*)

Because they were such a strong pink colour, we wanted softer tones for the wedding party. (*You & Your Wedding* 7–8/2009)

Real-life wedding texts manifest the least gender imbalance in the discourse of bridal magazines due to their deployment of inclusive forms of narration – the personal pronouns 'we/us/our', or the bride and groom interchangeably narrating their wedding experience. When the narrating voice belongs to the journalist, the use of 'they' also implies the couple's equal involvement in the wedding preparations and ceremony. Also, the visual representation of the bride and groom is proportionate.

Thus, due to the inclusive forms of narration, if regarded as a form of romantic fiction (or at least texts that are centrally premised on it), real-life weddings are not as obvious as the traditional stories exploring the theme of romance. The constructions of men's emotional investment in wedding organization upset the established configurations of agency by assigning them roles that have commonly been associated with women. However, it would be ungrounded to state that the texts totally subvert the power allocation that is typical of traditional romantic narratives (see Wetherell 1995). Other repertoires deployed in the narratives rewrite traditional themes (for instance, in the accounts of the bride's arrival in the church, she is positioned as the object of gaze; the accounts of proposals made by the man mobilize the traditional forms of men's heroic agency).

Last but not least, the repertoire of 'pure relationship' needs to be contextualized both in the magazines' gender and commodifying discourses. As regards the latter, the constructions of grooms' involvement in wedding preparations may be the magazines' strategy of naturalizing men's consumer behaviors. The inclusive forms of representation attest that men approve of lavish weddings and live their weddings through consumption similarly to women. In the discourse, which is supposed to encourage consumption, it seems reasonable to try to preempt the potential contradiction that grooms may see between traditional masculinity and the consumption of wedding artifacts that are elsewhere in the magazines presented as women's object of concern.

On the whole, the commodification, esthetization and individualization of the life course, as well as transformations in the intimate life, have rendered a new form of wedding experience that 'real-life weddings' aptly illustrate. These three patterns can be identified in the dominant repertoires and meaning structures of the discourse of commodified weddings. The construction of weddings in the texts suggests that weddings have ceased to function as solely social and religious rites of passage and have taken on the role of cultural performances wherein couples enact their romance through wedding commodities. In this sense, the texts show how the discourse of commodification forges a link between self and consumption, hence how "[i]ndividual needs of personal autonomy, self-definition, authentic life or personal perfection are all translated into the need to possess, and consume, market-offered goods" (Bauman 1989: 198). As demonstrated, the texts interlace the private and the public, the traditional and the modern, the real and non-real (lived and staged, or 'magical'), the individual ('personalized') with the mass-produced. Still, as a result of recontextualization and hybridization the otherwise mutually exclusive qualities are incorporated into the single, seemingly coherent texts, which in the long run may confuse the reader. The question this leads to is whether the antagonisms dissolved in the genre of real-life weddings can be suppressed in the weddings in real-life.

Hybridity of advertising discourse

Real-life wedding stories are a prominent example of hybrids because they accommodate features of many media genres, mobilize several established repertoires of late modernity as well as marshal its established discourses (media, consumer, expert, etc.). As indicated in the examples above, through these complex discursive and generic configurations, the magazines follow their distinct agenda of encouraging consumer behaviors in their readers. Another form of hybridity on which the magazines rely extensively in stirring consumption was found in texts that were presented as advisory. These were 'macro-genres' (Martin 1994) – features written by staff journalists and incorporating other genres. To illustrate, in the wedding magazines analyzed, many articles were accompanied by boxed-off sections where readers share advice and experience, and provide personal assessments. Some of the boxed-off sections contained readers' tips contributed by brides on the magazines' websites, to which readers were regularly invited. Others included statistics and advice from experts quoted. All this makes evident editors' general policy of validating their informative role and of including readers' voices in discourse. Most importantly, however, such generic hybrids are used in the mystification of the magazines' advertising agenda.

Consequently, the advertising agenda of wedding magazines is manifested not only in the strong presence of advertisements side by side with articles.[7] In the current investigation, the discourse of advertising was identified in other features of the magazine not readily associated with advertisements. For instance, a "Gossip file" in *You & Your Wedding* (7–8/2009) features the following article:

> Psst, guess WHAT?
>
> ♥ Worried about tottering down the aisle in heels? "Madonna and Gwyneth never put a foot wrong," says Alexander Technique teacher Chyna Whyne. "Madonna has a great sense of balance from her dancing background and Gwyneth (right) oozes confidence. To make your entrance in high heels, avoid leaning forwards or bending your knees as this shortens your silhouette – not a good look on your wedding day! Log on ... walkinstilettos.com

Both the direct address in the headline and the presupposition in the opening question position the addresser and the addressee of the message in a relation of intimacy. The underlying incongruity in the relation stems from the non-obvious purpose of the text. As mentioned, the article was found in a "Gossip file". Indeed, referring to celebrities by their names only and the secretive "Psst" give an air of an informal interaction. The allusions to women's chitchat reinforce the bogus community of readers, who are provided at this point with some comforting acknowledgment that their anxieties are shared and can be effectively handled.

Yet, in the text the reader is also provided with an expert's instructions on how to deal with her (presumed) anxieties about walking down the aisle in high heels. The advice is followed by a recommendation of a website where other forms of help can be found. What the text does not state is that at walkinstilettos.com women are invited to enroll for courses on walking in high heels. Clearly, the hybridization of expert discourse, advertising discourse and everyday discourse accommodates the contradictions that would otherwise be untenable – the underlying antagonism between the practices of instructing, stirring consumption and sharing secrets with others.

Colonization: synthetic personalization

As explained in Chapter 1, drawing on Bakhtin's theory of polyglossia, Fairclough (2009) posits that the co-existence of more than one voice within a text leads to the emergence of 'intertexts'. In his view of the polyglossic relations between texts, Bakhtin differentiated between the primary and secondary genres. The latter (mainly written, more complex ones) internalize the former (the social genres of mundane communication). Cross-examining mutual relations between them may yield some insight into "the complex problem of the interrelations among language, ideology, and world view" (Emerson and Holquist 1986: 62). Likewise, as explained in Chapter 1, following the CDA theory of language, hybrids both generate and respond to changes in social practices when discourses and genres move to different discourse orders and affect their local social practices (see Chouliaraki and Fairclough 1999; Sunderland 2004: 10–3, 29–31).

The major social relation constituted through hybridization in the wedding magazines investigated here is that of interpersonal, close relations among people involved in the magazines' discourse. Both readers and editors are positioned as members of a close community when media genres hybridize with those of personal communication in the process of *synthetic personalization*, that is, "a compensatory tendency to give the impression of treating each of the people handled 'en masse' as an individual" (Fairclough 1989: 52). The linguistic features constitutive of what Baudrillard (1998) referred to as *simulated intimacy* are, among other things, second person singular pronoun, deixis, direct ways of addressing the reader (questions and commands) and informal register.

The strong presence of the features in the magazines' discourse indicates that it has been *colonized* by the discourses and genres that normally mediate interpersonal, intimate communication. Colonization takes place when a discourse or genre that is 'new' in a discourse order prevails over the local one (Chouliaraki and Fairclough 1999: 93).[8] Because discourses mediate social practices, colonization usually entails major social changes within the discourse order. To illustrate, the *conversationalization* (Fairclough 1995a; see also Fairclough and Mauranen 1997) of media discourse, that is, a form of colonization caused by synthetic personalization, has led to the *informalization* of public life (Featherstone 1991), the social effects of which are still debated. For instance, Macdonald (2003: 78) sees the discursive shifts as facilitating "dialogic interaction and multivocality". However, the changes effected by the emergent 'public colloquial' language (Leech 1966; Fairclough 1994) can be seen as part of the tabloidization of information media, which is the manifestation of the global shift to consumer culture (Fairclough 1995b). The culture, following Habermas (1989), has led to the 're-feudalization of the public sphere', as a result of which media audiences are nowadays invariably positioned as media consumers rather than participants of a public debate.

In line with the bleaker understanding of conversationalization, in this book synthetic personalization in wedding magazines is considered as symptomatic of covert power relations between editors and readers. As postulated in Chapter 1, hybridization changes relations between social practices. Because it has been examined here in terms of the subject positions that correspond with specific practices, in this book synthetic personalization is understood as the process of

> constructing fictitious individual persons, for instance as the addresser and addressee in an advertisement, or [as] manipulating the subject position of, or the relationship between, actual individual persons (in direction of equality, solidarity, intimacy or whatever), as in interviews. (Fairclough 1989: 179)

Accordingly, the discussion below presents the examples of synthetic personalization and their implications for the construction of not necessarily transparent subject positions. The examples illustrate how the colonization of the discourse of bridal magazines by the everyday spoken discourse has contributed to the construction of the appearances of communality which hide the magazines' actual advertising agenda.

A relation of closeness between the editors and readers of bridal magazines is simulated in the constructions, suggesting that the latter seek help or advice from the former:

> I've lost weight but my bum and thighs are now really wobbly. *Help!* Carly, Dorset (*You & Your Wedding* 7–8/2009)
>
> I haven't chosen my engagement ring yet – *any suggestions?*
>
> – Have you seen the new Tiffany engagement rings? (*You & Your Wedding* 7–8/2009)
>
> *I'm just dropping a quick note to thank you* for the reception ideas feature on Orange-themed receptions. My wedding colour is bright orange and I had so much trouble finding anything in this colour. Anna Lola (*Wedding Ideas* 58/2008)

Although they are turned to as experts, the magazine editors are addressed informally – the bold imperative and elliptical forms evoke the straightforward tone of an interaction between individuals of at least equal status, if not acquaintances. The informal, unceremonious questions shorten the social distance that is typical of communication between experts and people seeking information. As the second example demonstrates, the proximity is maintained by the editors when they respond in the form of equally casual questions. The sense of reciprocity and informality that this generates is reinforced when the editor's advice is acknowledged by readers who write back, as in the last example.

As for another way of maintaining the appearances of the communal relations between readers and editors, the latter themselves use many features of informal register:

> High heels are *fab* if you can carry them off. (*Wedding Ideas* 54/2008)
>
> For a healthy-looking complexion, don't skimp on *zzzzs*. (*Brides, Wedding Planner* 2008)
>
> *Bring on the bling* in attention-grabbing gold and silver! It's time to shine! (*Brides* 7–8/2008)

Apart from using the informal tone, sometimes editors construct themselves as experts who know what the reader feels and needs. Therefore, they often withdraw from the conventional journalistic way of disclosing information by means of affirmative sentences to address readers with assumptive questions:

> What girl doesn't love exquisite footwear? (*You & Your Wedding* 7–8/2009)
>
> Considering doing your own make-up on your wedding day? Cosmetics queen Bobbi Brown share her tips. (*Brides* 7–8/2009)
>
> Are you a bride on a budget? You can still achieve a unique and stylish look for less. (*Cosmopolitan Bride* 12–1/2010)

Also, the editors manage their own membership in the bridal community when they position themselves to the readers as members of the same popular culture who share enough background knowledge to understand allusions to it:

> Diamonds really are a glamorous girl's best friend. (*Perfect Wedding* 4/2008)
>
> If you want a bit of extra support under your dress without the Bridget Jones moment, check out Slinkies. (*You & Your Wedding* 7–8/2009)
>
> We've been inspired by Carrie and friends this month. (*Wedding Ideas* 56/2008)

> Forget limp locks and tired tresses, a wedding calls for jaw-dropping, camera-loving L'Oréal advert hair. (*Cosmopolitan Bride* 7–8/2009)

The allusive references are particularly frequent in titles and headlines. Reasonably, these are the first textual features to grab readers' attention and, if engaging enough, they may help the author in appealing to the reader. Recognizing the title of a song or a movie scene that is meaningful in a given context but cannot be deduced from it without reliance on the background knowledge may evoke in the reader some affinity with the authors of the text.

Briefly, the consistent use of synthetic personalization puts readers in the agentic subject positions of advisors and information-seekers as well as of the members of a democratic, mutually supportive community. Nevertheless, the conversational style adopted in the magazines does not necessarily reflect the actual forms of participation that are available to readers in the discourse of wedding magazines. This ambiguity results from the fact that the social practices of, for example, sharing information and experience are recontextualized in the magazines' discourse, which, as has been demonstrated in this analysis, has its agenda of encouraging the consumption of goods.

Conclusion

In this chapter, wedding magazines were investigated in terms of their constructions of gender and the relationships that the magazines establish with target readers to make them identify with the constructions. Overall, the social semiotic of wedding magazines was found to draw on the easily recognizable textual and visual representations of bridal femininity and femininity in general. The magazines' reliance on the familiar sociocultural gender codes is particularly notable in the constructions of the bridal body, which are the magazines' local reinstatements of the broader media discourse of the female body. The persistent encouragements to combat bodily imperfections, coupled with the images of the "white beautiful bride" (Ingraham 2008: 140) and product recommendations were considered as commodifying strategies, which pervade contemporary popular media.

The argument developed in this chapter was that bridal magazines take advantage of the familiarity of dominant gender discourse to present readers with new, potentially debatable and incongruous notions and subject positions. Commodifying bridal experience, the editors of the magazines use the commonality of bridal tradition to make their readers accept the commonality of wedding consumption. The inherent contradictions of this practice were brought into focus in this chapter when the possibility of self-actualization through the consumption of mass-produced commodities was doubted. Therefore, taking into consideration the potential confusion or skepticism which commodifying discourse may arouse in readers, it seems reasonable for the magazines to impress on the readers the obviousness of commodified wedding by appealing to them with the imagery of the traditional wedding. After all, the essentialist, heteronormative notions of masculinity and femininity accompany readers throughout their lives and hence must be internalized by the readers to varying degrees. That there are people to whom the heteronormative order is not self-evident was noted in Chapter 2, but the readership of this particular media genre, this book proposes, can be safely assumed to accept it as natural.

Consequently, this chapter sought to identify the role of the local discourses and genres in the formation of the consensus about the obviousness and common-senseness of the magazines' local ideologies. As demonstrated, the magazines' chief mechanisms of meaning construction consist in recontextualization and hybridization. The recontextualization of consumption practices in the discourse of wedding magazines gives commodities a reifying power. This is attained by integrating consumption with the patriarchal, heteronormative model of femininity and reinforcing this in the constructions of the hybrid identity of the 'modern bride'. Accordingly, going to a spa retreat or choosing the wedding dress with one's mother and friends are constructed as a practice of becoming a 'modern bride'. Likewise, whether the bride will buy a tiara or a modern accessory, or whether she will 'treasure' or 'trash' her wedding gown are the acts of bridal self-actualization. The hybridized constructions of commodified bridal femininity were found to generate the expected contradictions of commodification. Additionally, the interdiscursive relations that were identified in the chapter between the discourses of gender and consumerism were found to reproduce the covert relations of power.

Of course, to argue that it is through bridal magazines that the commodified rituals are introduced into popular wedding culture would be ungrounded. What is claimed here is the magazines' undeniable role in the reinforcement of the wedding-ideological complex. The tight cooperation of its elements, the examples of which are provided in this book, illustrates the dispersed foci of power legitimating the hegemonic ideologies of gender, which in turn substantiates this book's concern with the notion of symbolic power. Evidently, the discursive and generic hybrids allow managing subject positions in ways that give the impression of readers' empowerment and participation. Yet, in doing so, they first and foremost give magazine editors more space for manipulating readers into consumption and the acceptance of the repressive forms of gender subjectivity.

Far from claiming that the average reader is definitely unable to recognize the ideological codes and contradictions, this chapter presented what discursive mechanisms may make these antagonisms difficult to identify and confront. In the subsequent part of the analysis the findings will be complemented by examining readers' reception of the texts to see, among other things, how they related to the media constructions of wedding experience. Apart from addressing the specific issue, the interview data will also serve to investigate what discursive mechanisms underlie women's own constructions of their lived experience of getting married (for example, whether these are the same as those that were found in media discourse in this chapter).

4
Reading a Magazine: Methodological Considerations

'Fallacies' in research of media reception

As has been stated, the central intention of this piece of research was to conduct a critical analysis of wedding magazines in such a way that their inherent discourses are not simply 'proven' but interrogated in terms of their implications for readers' subjectivities. This has been underpinned by the book's concern with the feminine subjectivity being extrinsically organized by dominant discourses. The idea here is that this volume, which by itself represents a dominant (academic) discourse, will not contribute to this by allowing women to speak for themselves in the study.

Another reason behind devising the reader-inclusive framework of research was related to the controversies around readers' 'actual' attitude to popular media. As Machin and Thornborrow (2003) observed, women's magazines such as *Cosmopolitan* take a trivial and tongue-in-the-cheek approach to matters discussed. Consequently, "[o]n the one hand, the reader learns, perhaps subconsciously, how the discourse hangs together, yet, on the other hand, can dismiss it as not serious, just fun, and thus disarm critics and picture them as dour and humourless" (Machin and Thornborrow 2003: 456). On a similar note, in what she calls the 'fallacy of meaningfulness', Hermes (1995: 16) claims that researchers make the "unwarranted assumption that all use of popular media is significant". In agreement with that, the analysis of wedding magazines presented in this book has been conducted with the awareness of the possible differences between the results of the current exploration and the ways in which the magazines are read in the mundane contexts of media consumption. Yet, the study has never claimed to account for women's routine media consumption. As explained in Chapter 4, the main interest behind this research was to see how women negotiate their subjectivities in relation to dominant gender discourses, which are reinforced in the popular media. This aim, the book posits, does not require from the analyst to approach participants in their daily contexts of media use. Media research should include studies that approach media reception from different angles. Ethnographic studies of media practices render fascinating data but this should not be the premise on which the methodological value of research interviews should be denied or under-played. For example, well designed interview questions enable eliciting from participants media-related talk that presents different levels of reflexivity. (Other advantages of research interviews will be addressed in the discussion below.)

In Chapter 2, it was proposed that some approaches to the textual production of meaning are inapplicable to research on the reception of popular media texts. Based on the abstract notion of a reader (recon-structed from the formal features of texts), they do not tell much more than how the author wanted his or her text to be interpreted (see 'intended reader' Wolff 1971). A mode of analysis that this book finds more applicable involves the 'dominant' reading (Brunsdon and Morley 1978), which implies an overtly critical approach to text. This way of examination does not concern "the writer's intention ..., but a position (or positions) which the text offers or proffers to the reader within a particular historical moment, because of the range of ideological posi-tions available which make that text understandable" (Mills 1995: 72). However, although closer to the primary concern of the current volume, it needs to be noted that the 'dominant' reading is a top-down approach to text reception, based the contestable figure of a subject "read off the text" (D. Smith 1990: 4). As such, it suffers from the 'fallacy of inter-nalism' (Thompson 1990), which is the assumption of individuals' internalization of the surrounding ideologies (see the discussion of the Frankfurt School in Chapter 2).

Therefore, following the critical, academically informed analysis of wedding magazines in Chapter 3, in Chapter 5 the study proceeds to interviews with women who approached the same media discourse from the perspective of their lived experience. Consequently, insights from Chapter 3 will be enriched with information provided by 'embodied' readers, that is, individuals who actually (physically, emotionally, cognitively) dealt with the texts investigated in previous chapter in the volume and to whom getting married was part of recent experience. The construction of this research project stems from its interest in D. Smith's (1990) distinction between the 'subject-in-discourse' and the 'subject of one's actions'. The former allows the exploration to maintain its focus on how individuals' textual encounters are implicated in the hegemonic gender ideologies; the latter complements this analysis by compelling reflexivity of how the encounters are embedded in the individuals' social practices. This stage of the investigation, however, had a few contextual limitations that are briefly discussed below.

Gendered texts and contexts

Firstly, the chief aim of confronting women with bridal magazines could be considered as limiting the aim in that it made the interviews notably gendered contexts. The purpose of this study was to see if women find themselves interpellated by media as gender subjects and if they regard the subject positions offered as oppressive or inferiorizing. However, the interviewer's intention was to avoid hailing the interviewees in ways that would increase their reflexivity of gender positioning and subsequently provoke their self-reports. Simply, rather than generate the interviewees' talk about media's depictions of femininity, the examination was intended to occasion textual encounters in which the salience of media gender discourse would not be made immediately apparent to the readers.

Consequently, to lessen the appearances of the direct relevance of gender, the participants were informed that the purpose of the interviews was to collect information about the British wedding culture. The prompt magazine, it was explained to them, was included in the interviews as part of the culture. One of the priorities during the interviews was to make sure that texts in the prompt were referred to in this way and that the conversations flowed smoothly to gender issues, with no apparent intentions of the interviewer. Thus, although the current discussion focuses on the reader and gender subjectivities that the participants negotiated, the interviews did not concern gender issues only. They included questions about the local wedding traditions (proposals, preparations, ceremonies, honeymoons, etc.) and various issues concerning contemporary marital relationships.

Generic identity of a research interview

What could be regarded as another major methodological limitation of this study is the well-established generic identity of a research interview (the conventionality of this type of interaction). The unequal division of power that is typical of the genre, and the participants' expectations concerning their role in the interaction must have affected the interactive dynamics of the conversations. (The power differential was particularly evident in the guiding role of the interviewer at the beginning of the meetings, before the women took more initiative.) Thus, to reduce the differences between private reading and reading in a research-based context, the interviews took the form of lengthy conversations in the home of each participant. Also, each woman was given her own magazine and took at least one evening to read it. To make the context less cued by the power relations typical of research interviews, in some of the questions the interviewees were able to choose the topic and subject position. (For example, the last question asked was "Is there anything more I should have asked you?" and the participants usually proposed additional issues to talk about.)

Still, research interviews, as pointed out by Miller and Glassner (1997: 101), do not yield any straightforward information about the social world of the interviewee. Language used in the specific research context is significantly shaped by the interviewer. In this study, my questions must have had some influence on readers' text-related talk and the stories they told. Moreover, the participants' expectations about my research goals, knowledge, etc. may have influenced what they said. Finally, what is at work in the mundane use of discourse is made more profound in research interviews because of the 'essential visibility' of the interactions (Edwards 1995). The participants must have thus been oriented to talk rhetorically (see Bamberg 2006). (Because they felt that their outlooks were made apparent ('visible') in the talk with the researcher, they took into account whether their claims were appropriate in the specific context.)

This, however, is not regarded in this book as a research limitation. Instead, it is argued here that even if the heightened self-presentation concerns affected the interviewees' positioning, their constructions of intended self provide valuable data. Firstly, speakers' *rehearsed identity work* (Taylor 2005c) is not absent from mundane social interactions. People enter them with some agendas, put on specific faces (Goffman 1959), and perform what Butler (1990: 34) refers to as "the foundational illusions of identity". Secondly, as Atkinson and Delamont (2006: 169) argue in relation to narrative work, its rhetorical properties should not "be treated as an issue in the quality-control of information". The rhetorical work is an interesting piece of data by itself because the way in which speakers make their stances accountable illuminates their moral and ideological dispositions (see Drew 1998). As will be seen from the analysis, in this study the informational value of the rehearsed selves in data interpretation was particularly evident when the identities were found to cast some light on the self-accounts from the less monitored moments of the conversation. Therefore, the interviewees' subjectivities, even though negotiated in a research context, will be seen to afford some insight into the women's relation to the dominant discourses of gender.

Finally, although research interviews have been criticized for their inability to lend insight into mundane discourses, many discourse analysts defend this way of data collection. Because interviews are a well-established, popular part of the contemporary Western culture, both for the interviewer and the interviewee, they are as natural and as familiar types of interaction as ordinary conversations (Atkinson and Silverman 1997; Shakespeare 1998) and, like mundane interactions, they are commonly recognized as occasions for the discussion and negotiation of certain meanings (Westcott and Littleton 2004). Thus, more and more linguists treat unstructured interviews as a rich source of normative cultural meanings and narratives (Scollon 1995; Benwell 2007). Interviews foreground specific topics and many people partake in them willingly because they consider their life experience as relevant to research aims (Taylor 2001). For instance, in the current study the participants considered their experiences interesting and valuable enough to present them in the interviews. They seemed to treat the conversations as an opportunity to tell their stories, which was particularly evident when the women added new plots and topics, and offered to show me their wedding photos and film recordings.

Identity of the reader and speaker – synthetic approach

In line with theories discussed in the previous chapters, the study presented in this volume takes a *synthetic approach* to the speaker (see Wetherell 1998; Taylor and Littleton 2006). Accordingly, speakers' self-accounts and their positioning to the discourse of the magazine are regarded here as both situated and social. The examination of these two aspects of speaker identity entails two disparate research frameworks.

Following conversation analysis (CA) and ethnomethodology, identity is considered here as *performative*, that is to say, multiple, occasioned and contingent on how one is positioned in talk (see Antaki and Widdicombe 1998; Abell et al. 2004). Because the notion of performativity implies that speakers are *action-oriented* (Heritage 1984), discourse produced in the interviews (media-related talk and participants' self-accounts) is considered here as social actions which participants performed, dependent on the tasks and goals that their utterances were designed to achieve. Moreover, CA recognizes that meaning-making processes take place intersubjectively, as individuals negotiate and display shared understanding of what is going on in their interactions. The intersubjective construction of meaning pertains to the current research context in two major ways. Firstly, as mentioned above, speakers' identities must have been to some extent co-constructed by the interviewer – by my researcher's status and my questions. Secondly, in the analysis of the participants' accounting work,[1] attention is paid to the relationships that they established intertextually with other subjects (say, significant others absent from the immediate interaction).

The other methodological framework included in the current examination of media reception has been compelled by the study's 'decentralized' view of text. As has been explained, in its critical engagement with discourse this study approaches individuals as "social historical subjects" (Wodak 2001b: 3). Yet, observing links between the local enactments of identity and socioculturally available discourses is part of CA methodology (see Sacks et al. 1978; Schegloff 1996; West 1998; Speer and Potter 2000; Stokoe 2000). Dedicated to the contextually immediate minutiae of the "technology of conversation" (Sacks 1984: 413) and to the principle of "ethnomethodological indifference" (Garfinkel and Sacks 1970: 345), CA disregards both hidden power relations and social categories which preexist the context of interaction. Thus, the conversational analytical approach is inconsistent with the critical perspective from which this book interrogates the questions of feminine subjectivity (for more discussion see Weatherall 2002).

While this book agrees with the conversational analytic view that identities are performative and contextually contingent, it additionally considers that identities are *constructed* (Gergen 1994a; Mishler 1999). Namely, in line with the poststructuralist view of subjectivity discussed in Chapter 2, in the subsequent part of the analysis it is assumed that identity cannot be limited to the contextually immediate actions of speaking. Every local context of interaction is part of a wider sociocultural frame. The broader (discourse, social, cultural, etc.) processes underlying it need to be addressed, even if they cannot be directly validated in language data. In advance of the controversies that this inclusive methodology of exploring gender may arouse, it is contended in this book, after Sunderland (2004: 22), that "gender can be *constructed, performed, represented* and *indexed*... Associated with social constructionism and post-structuralism, *construction* and *performance* are members of the same field."

Analytical tools – Critical Discursive Psychology in media reception

In relation with what has been stated above, in this investigation identity is understood as *positional*: "Identities encompass (a) macro-level demographic categories; (b) local, ethnographically specific cultural positions; and (c) temporary and interactionally specific stances and participant roles" (Bucholtz and Hall 2005: 592). Based on that, following the methodology of Critical Discursive Psychology (CDP),[2] interviewees' accounts are considered as local (contingent on the pragmatic rules of an interview) and intertextual (related with other texts, discourses and contexts) (see Wetherell 1998, 2003; Wetherell and Edley 1999; Parker 2002; Korobov and Bamberg 2004; Reynolds et al. 2007).

In the immediate context of the interviews, the study assumes that individuals were 'positioned by who they already had been' (see Taylor 2005a). The occasioned performances and actions of identity were to a significant extent the reproductions and reconstructions of the previous ones. From the perspective of the critical discursive tradition, the routinely repeated accounts of self are a regular means of self-construction. As "the cumulative fragments of a lived autobiography" (Davies and Harré 2009: 265), they constitute one's discursive habitus (Bourdieu 1977). Corresponding with the notion of habitus, but at the same time more illuminating language-wise, is Wetherell's (2007: 668) idea of *personal order*:

> Personal order is derived from social order but is not isomorphic with it. A person…is a site, like institutions or social interaction, where flows of meaning-making practices or semiosis (Hodge and Kress 1988) become organised. Over time, particular routines, repetitions, procedures and modes of practice build up to form personal style, psycho-biography and life history and become guide for how to go on in the present.

Defining 'personal order', Wetherell accentuates its stability. The iterated performances develop into dispositional interactive behaviors. The situated "psychodiscursive practices" (Wetherell 2007: 668) become our acquired identities, but not in the cognitive understanding of self (see also Wetherell and Edley 1998). The practices, Wetherell (2007: 676) explains, are "not necessarily expressive outpourings of a deep inner psyche…[but] procedures or routines that people know how to do in talk, making meaning as they go".

At the same time, the book emphasizes that although the lived experience of self is to a significant degree non-reflexive, individuals' agency and capabilities of reflexive insight should not be disregarded. As mentioned above, rather than 'emanate' from one's inside, identities are locally 'done', 'performed', interactionally 'accomplished' and socio-culturally 'constructed'. In their discursive practices, individuals "*actively* produce social and psychological realities" (Davies and Harré 2009: 262, emphasis added). Moreover, this book posits, accentuating individuals' active involvement in the construction of the realities is particularly important in the critical approaches to self because it precludes analyses based on the reductive understanding of subjectivity. The concept of self proposed here implies that individuals are constantly interpellated by ideologies – but rather than put in specific positions, they are offered temporary attachments to the positions, which they can reject.

Clearly, so far, 'subject position' has been one of the central concepts in this volume; it will also be used in the subsequent analysis of the spoken data because it closely corresponds with the book's idea of identity as experienced in discourse:

> Once we take up a Subject position in discourse, we have available to us a particular, limited set of concepts, images, metaphors, ways of speaking, self-narratives and so on that we take on as our own. This entails both emotional commitment on our part to the categories of person to which we are allocated and see ourselves as belonging... and the development of an appropriate system of morals (rules of right and wrong). Our sense of who we are and what it is therefore possible and not possible for us to do, what it is right and appropriate for us to do, and what it is wrong and inappropriate for us to do thus all derive from our occupation of Subject position within discourse. (Burr 1995: 145–6)

Based on this understanding, rather than as merely a rhetorical figure of critical discourse studies, this book considers 'subject position' as a versatile conceptual tool applicable to the investigations of the discursive mediation of identity. The previous chapter demonstrated the applicability of the notion in the analysis of media discourse by exploring how the construction of available subject positions in wedding magazines leads to the production of bridal identities. In the further part of the exploration, the notion will be used to conduct an analysis that does not downplay the role of the reader's identity in media reception.

Technically, this means examining the socioculturally available subject positions that individual readers drew upon in their situated encounters with media texts.

Another quality of identity that needs to be addressed is its *indexicality* (Silverstein 1985; Ochs 1992; Bucholtz and Hall 2005). Discourse structures which constitute a given subject position acquire meaning in relation to the context of use. The indexical processes of identity construction entail:

> (a) overt mention of identity categories and labels; (b) implicatures and presuppositions regarding one's own or others' identity position; (c) displayed evaluative and epistemic orientations to ongoing talk, as well as interactional footings and participant roles; and (d) the use of linguistic structures and systems that are ideologically associated with specific personas and groups. (Bucholtz and Hall 2005: 594)

The temporarily occupied positions are linked not only to the immediate interactional context, but also to macro-scale categories. In their positioning practices, discourse users draw on socially shared meaning resources: "When interviewees report on experience, they do so from different social positions and in greater or lesser agreement with recognizable cultural scripts" (Järvinen 2000: 386). Accordingly, in the study, individuals' positioning in relation to texts and their personal narratives are seen as intertextual and polyglossic – "shaped by previously presented versions and also by understandings which prevail in the wider discursive environment" (Taylor and Littleton 2006: 23). The prevailing understandings which help speakers establish culturally shared, contextually functional frames of interpretation are referred to as *interpretative repertoires* (Gilbert and Mulkay 1984). These are meant as "systematically related sets of terms (Potter 1996) that can be recognized in the familiar and well-worn images that are known and understood through shared cultural membership" (Reynolds et al. 2007: 335).

Used to maintain coherence and transparency of self-accounting work, interpretative repertoires are resources in the construction of self-narratives (see Taylor and Littleton 2006) and in interactions. Nevertheless, both narrative construction and interpersonal communication entail contradictions and ambiguities, that is, *ideological dilemmas* (Billig et al. 1988). More specifically, "[t]he competing arguments and values which people draw on in making sense of their lives pose many dilemmas. Ideological dilemmas are linked with interpretative repertoires, since speakers work with the inconsistency in the repertoires they draw on and try to reconcile contradictory argumentative threads" (Reynolds et al. 2007: 336).

The accounts accompanied by repair work are referred to in this volume as troubled subject positions. More specifically, intertextuality of self, in the form of pre-established discursive and sociocultural constructions of identity, both facilitates and constrains identification practices. The constructions cause *identity trouble* (Wetherell 1998) when one's provisionally enacted identity contradicts "other identity claims or positionings given by her or his life circumstances" (Taylor and Littleton 2006: 25; see also Taylor 2005a, 2005b). In such cases, troubled subject positions disrupt the internal cohesion and cohesiveness of one's self-account. Alternatively, it can also be considered that "[a] speaker may encounter trouble (Wetherell, 1998) in identity work by taking on, through the flow of discourse and its accompanying subject positions, an identity which in other contexts and in other discourses is negatively valued" (Reynolds et al. 2007: 336).

Briefly, the analytical tools adopted in the current stage of the analysis correspond with what has been claimed in this volume about subjectivity established in discourse. Indeed, because the critical premises and conceptual units of discourse theory informing this study determine methodology developed in the project, they inadvertently shape its findings. Yet, it is stressed, they do so neither less nor more than any other frameworks, including those that claim their 'sociological neutrality'.

Interviews

The data come from interviews that were conducted in August 2010 in Manchester and Newcastle (UK).[3] The selection of participants was based on their availability for the interview during the period of data collection. In that way, time limit was a significant obstacle in reaching the individuals who met all criteria.[4] Each interview lasted approximately an hour and a half. The participants were assured anonymity and confidentiality and asked to sign a consent form for the use of data from the interviews in academic work.

Eleven women volunteered to take part in the study.[5] To address the diversity of feminine experience manifested in text reception practices, the women invited differed in terms of age, ethnicity, education, sexual orientation and professional background. However, within this volume it is found impossible to accommodate the analyses of all of them because of the complexity of the picture that the conversations altogether rendered. Consequently, selecting the interviews for the purpose of the current publication, I decided to investigate conversations with the women to whom wedding experience was the most immediate. This immediacy of the experience affected the quality of data by rendering autobiographic information that was related to the media texts (even though, as will be seen, mostly indirectly). This allowed me to explore the subjectivities that the women established in their wedding narratives side by side with the subjectivities that they established in their embodied experience of reading bridal magazines. The interviews with Mary, Cara, Debby and Suki were selected for the purpose of the current publication because they were either about to get married or had not long done so, while the other participants related to the topic from less immediate perspectives.[6]

Another criterion by which the interviewees were selected, namely, their reading preferences, was also considered in the conceptualization of the present volume. The aim of both data collection and of the current discussion was to gather a proportionate number of responses from two types of readers – women who claimed to read wedding (and women's) magazines regularly and avidly, and those who did not claim reader involvement with such magazines. Including the latter was not particularly informative in terms of reader practices but it was considered indispensable to provide an analysis that spans a wide range of feminine subjectivities.

Still, identification of the preferences appeared less obvious than was expected. Although before the interviews some participants professed to regularly read wedding and women's magazines, in the interviews the majority presented themselves as reluctant readers. Consequently, so as not to rely on the participants' self-reported data, the credibility of which was undermined in that respect, in the discussion the degree of affiliation with the discourse of wedding magazines will be identified on the basis of data derived from the immediate context of the interviews. Depending on the degree, the women will be referred to as the 'invested' and the 'uninvested' readers (Benwell 2005). As will be seen, this rough classification is based on the observation of relevant discourse practices (for example, careful reading versus cursory reading, acknowledging versus dismissing the instructive value of media texts).

The mode of examination presented here is referred to as 'symptomatic reading', that is, the investigation of interview transcripts which "directs the attention to processes beyond the text" (Currie et al. 2007: 381). In the analysis of the interviewees' media-related talk and of the accompanying identity work, attention is paid to the wider discourses that were more or less explicitly present in the immediate context and shaped the locally established subjectivities. The discourses made themselves present in the interviewees' talk because the women talked about their experience while referring to the prompt texts, as well as because they were asked about the experience. Consequently, the participants constructed two major (interrelated and often overlapping) forms of subjectivity – one connected with their relationship to the media discourse and one emergent from their self-accounts that did not directly concern the prompt texts.[7]

As has been explained in this chapter, the interviews concerned the British wedding culture and the interviewees' own experience of getting married; the magazines were referred to as an accompanying part of the culture. The point of reference for media-related talk was a specific issue of *You & Your Wedding* (7–8/2009). Because it served to encourage the women to relate to media discourse, in the discussion it will be referred to as a prompt text. It will be seen from the discussion of the data that I sought to ask each participant questions concerning the same articles in the magazine so that a comparative analysis of text reception would be possible.

Each of the texts chosen for the purpose of the interviews was related to a specific finding from the critical analysis of the magazines. For example, in the magazine discussed with the interviewees, there were two advertisements strongly premised on the hegemonic discourse of gender. One of them was an advertisement for a wedding venue and it extensively drew on the symbolic imagery of fairy tales. It was referred to in the interviews based on the finding that the repertoire of a fairy tale is extensively drawn upon in the media discourse. The other advertising text was a "Gossip file". As explained in Chapter 3, it was a hybrid of an advertisement and a gossip column encouraging women to log on to a website where they can learn how to walk in high heels. The other articles which were critically analyzed in Chapter 3 and will be referred to in the subsequent chapter are "Editor's letter" and "Wedding file debate".

5
Reading a Magazine: The Interviews

Mary

Mary,[1] a 34-year-old office worker, temporarily on a maternity leave, got married a year before the interview. Mary's parents came to the UK from Germany. Her husband is a Mexican and works in the local hospital as a GP. In the conversation before my interview with Mary, both claimed to be practising Christians and said that they planned to have a second child. Among all participants in the study, Mary was the most invested reader. Mary claimed she had read wedding magazines regularly before her wedding and found some of the articles instructive and inspiring. In comparison to the rest of the interviewees, she read texts in the prompt magazine in much more detail.

Despite Mary's involvement with the discourse of the magazine, it would be an oversimplification to consider her as thoroughly vulnerable to its interpellating practices. To begin with, while singling out the articles that appealed to her, Mary made a series of regular positionings that revealed her awareness of the discourse. In the extract below, Mary talks about the editor's letter in the prompt magazine (see pp. 56–59):

Extract 1.1

R:[2] Did you pay any attention to it?

Mary: Yeah, it's sort of that ((your)) wedding reflects the person you <u>are</u> basically. And I <u>do</u> think if you stick <u>too</u> much to just magazines, you don't actually take your own style, you take somebody else's. Cause like…Lots of things we did at our wedding, I didn't really get from magazines, you know like the paper decorations on the ceiling. And the Mexican band we didn't get from the magazine. You know, we sort of tried…We sort of looked back and said, you know, what is important to us and that how we can represent our culture cause that's what we wanted to do. […]

R: Is that how modern brides express their personality?

Mary: To some extent, yeah ... I think so because, um ... Like for the flowers for my bouquet I chose my favorite flowers, and all my friends knew they were my favorite flowers, and I had green, as a sort of my favorite color, for the bridesmaids' dresses and little accents on the table.

The sequence exemplifies how Mary juggled the subject positions of an invested and uninvested reader. In the extract, she accepts the magazine's repertoire of 'wedding personalization', which repertoire was found in Chapter 3 to be a part of the magazines' commodifying discourse. Mary talks about color and flower themes as expressive of the bride. Although elsewhere in the interview, when narrating her wedding experience, she also relied on the discourse of a commodified wedding, it is noticeable that for Mary the identity of a commodified bride was troubled. For instance, in the extract above she first constructs her awareness of the threat that the media pose to their consumer's identity ("I do think if you stick too much to just magazines, you don't actually take your own style, you take somebody else's"). Subsequently, Mary denies being influenced by the magazine, which might be indicative of her identity concerns ("Lots of things we did at our wedding, I didn't really get from magazines", "the Mexican band we didn't get from the magazine", "we sort of looked back and said, you know, what is important to us"). Generally, the extract suggests that Mary sought to position herself as a knowledgeable and rational subject of her actions, and as a reflexive media consumer.

Another example of how ambivalently Mary established her reader subjectivity can be found in the extract below:

Extract 1.2

Mary: [...] when they sort of give different tips ... I always like sort of real-life weddings. =

R: = Mm

Mary: I quite enjoy that. Because ... it seems ... I don't know, it's just nice to see what other people planned and did and stuff.

R: Would you consider presenting your wedding in such a way?

Mary: No! I'd just pick what I like and ignore the rest 'cause I think I would never copy someone's wedding. =

R: = But would you like your own wedding to get a coverage in a magazine like this one?

Mary: Probably ... M: ... not, it depends what would be involved. If somebody from the magazine would have to be present at the wedding, I wouldn't like that. Cause I was actually against having a professional photographer.

On the one hand, Mary takes the position of an invested reader, for example when she constructs her 'voyeuristic' pleasure of seeing what other people did ("It's just nice to see what other people planned"). On the other hand, she objects to the idea of hiring a professional photographer which is linked to the magazine's repertoire of wedding as a professionally organized 'spectacle'. Her reader detachment is reinforced also by means of hedging ("sort of real-life weddings", "quite enjoy that") and when she constructs herself as a selective and judicious media consumer ("I'd just pick what I like and ignore the rest 'cause I think I would never copy someone's wedding"). At another point, Mary produced a more explicit detachment from the discourse of the magazine:

Extract 1.3

Mary: Looking at the bride here, people may think, "Oh, I have to be this skinny, I have to be this made-up". I think the whole magazine is a little like that, including real-life weddings to some extent I reckon, 'cause they pick all the nicest aspects of it. I guess lots of people get more out of the beauty tips than I, but...those who usually wear make-up get some inspiration from those.

Mary qualifies her endorsement of the magazine's discourse by pointing out the artificiality of the wedding spectacle presented in the texts. By no means is she hailed to the subject position of a member of a 'community of readers'. Mary indexes her lack of involvement in it by separating her reader identity from the one of more engaged readers, which position is propped up by means of the distancing, generalizing construction "lots of people".

The ideological dilemma that accompanied Mary's reader positioning was particularly visible in the disjunctions between her 'official' (for the record) reader positionings and the accounts she constructed when flipping through the magazine, in think-aloud comments on what she saw on the subsequent pages. For instance, elaborating on her view of real-life wedding articles, she presented the magazines as geared at stimulating consumerism:

Extract 1.4

Mary: Gives you an overview of what you can achieve, but it would cost you so much money, it basically encourages people to spends lots of money on weddings.

Conversely, in the think-aloud comments, which she produced at a lower speech volume, while looking for another article, she said:

Extract 1.5

Mary: ° I think the first one was a bit over the top... Probably the one I could copy... oh, I like the flowers, they're quite nice... Italian touch ....°.

The 'media pleasure' implied in Extract 1.5 is unlike the opinions in the other passages presented above. The idea of 'copying' somebody's wedding poses an ideological contradiction to Mary's emphasis on the need to retain one's own style in Extract 1.1. Apparently, it is possible to retain some degree of criticism in relation to the magazines' discourse of commodification but at the same time be appealed by the commodities which are presented in them. A similar note is made by Grimshaw (1999: 99) in reference to the discourses of gender when she argues: "It is perfectly possible to agree in one's head that certain images of women might be reactionary or damaging or oppressive, while remaining committed to them in emotion and desire." Therefore, it is not impossible to be aware of the influence of bridal magazines and to allow oneself to be affected by them.

As explained in Chapter 4, in the prompt magazine there were texts where the reliance on the hegemonic discourse of gender was remarkable, for which reason each of the interviewees was asked about it at some point of the conversation. One of them was a "Gossip file", hence a text encouraging women to log on to a website with instructions as to how to walk in high heels (see p. 106); each of the participants was asked about it so as to see their reactions to the interpellations the text contained. Mary resisted the interpellation, but she did not take up the discursive space that this opened for a deconstructive reading:

Extract 1.6

R: = Did you see it? =

Mary: = Oh yeah! That made me... sort of... laugh a bit =

R: = So, you did pay any attention to it? =

M: = I just skipped it through basically... I mean, I more read the headline and then a little bit, and if I'm interested I read the whole paragraph... Let me have a look, um... ((flipping pages, in the end makes no further comment))

Mary's reaction to the text indicates that she did not take its advice seriously – her laughter indexes the uninvested reader self. Yet, although she indirectly rejects the self-disciplining practice to which women are invited in the article, she does not elaborate on it. Mary also reacted with laughter to an advertisement that extensively drew on the imagery of fairy tales:

Extract 1.7

R: What did you think of it?

Mary: It sounds sort of expensive. ((laugh)) That's, that's sort of my initial... Yeah, that's probably right, I mean, I thought it was a dress advert but it was a place. It's a place, isn't it?

R: Yeah. And did you feel like in a fairy tale?

Mary: No, I just... I don't know, I just...

R: So why do you think they refer to fairy tales here?

Mary: I don't know; they're playing on women dreaming of the wedding before, isn't it. Sort of fairy-tale wedding. Because I think the first weddings anybody becomes attached with, are in fairy tales, when you read fairy tales as a child. You read *Cinderella*, that's the first wedding you come across I reckon, in a way... I can see the way people say it, or what they mean by it, but for me it doesn't really... You know, somebody said to me "What's your fairy-tale wedding?". And I was, like, "I don't know".

In the sequence, Mary initially makes no involved positioning; she recognizes the popular interpretative repertoire of fairy-tale weddings only after it has been referred to by the researcher. At that moment, she takes the subject position of an informed media critic and constructs her awareness of media discourse by means of a few discursive resources – the distancing "they", the evaluative "play on" and a falling intonation in the question tag. Nonetheless, she does not overtly object to the dominant gender discourse underlying fairy tales.

Mary drew on wedding magazines intertextually. For instance, talking about how she worked on her looks before her wedding day, she constructed her body along the dominant repertoires of the media discourse of the bridal body:

Extract 1.8

Mary: Didn't pay really that much attention because first of all, when I got married, I invested in some really good make-up. I thought a fake tan would be nice, sort of the faintest fake tan 'cause obviously if it's too dark, it doesn't look right, so I invested in that. I had never one before so I went there a month before the wedding, tried it out and said "Oh yes! It actually looks nice". So that was the only thing.

As indicated in Chapter 3, wedding magazines construct a suntanned body as a standard feature of bridal looks. In her self-accounting work in Extract 1.8, Mary internalizes the repertoire by constructing getting a suntan as her own decision based on her own taste ("*I thought* a fake tan would be nice"). What lends itself to at least two interpretations is Mary's statement that she wanted "*the faintest* fake tan 'cause obviously if it's *too dark* it doesn't *look right*". For one thing, this echoes the magazines' repertoire of keeping one's look in control and avoiding flamboyance. For another, Mary's emphasis on keeping her tan in check may be a form of repair work, in the sense that she could have seen some identity trouble in admitting to being influenced by the magazines' advice (an underlying repent can be found in how she caps the disclosure with the emphatic "So that was the only thing").

Mary produced her detachment from the media discourse of the female body on many occasions:

Extract 1.9

Mary: Because...I just think it's very difficult to say, to see a dress in a magazine and say, "Ok, that's the dress I want". I think it's much better to go to the shop and try on some dresses, so you know what actually suits you. They're obviously...all these models here, are skinny people and you know, a dress that suits <u>them</u> would not necessarily suit <u>me</u>. So yeah, I just skipped those right away...Make-up was another thing that I skipped I have to say...

In the sequence, Mary positions herself as a critical, selective reader unaffected by the model beauty propagated in women's and bridal magazines. She does so in the accounts of her practices of media consumption ("I just skipped those right away", "Make-up was another thing that I skipped") and when she constructs an explicit distinction between the model body and her own body claiming that "a dress that suits *them* would not necessarily suit *me*".

Mary's constructions of her lived bodily self paralleled her qualified engagement with the media discourse of female beauty. For example, in Extract 1.10, Mary explains her personal motivation behind improving her appearance:

Extract 1.10

R: Why did you find it so important to look better at your wedding?

Mary: I just wanted to feel confident. I just wanted to feel as good-looking as I can. For example, for the wedding on Saturday I'm not going to make any big effort or [any]thing but I will still make more effort than I did this morning because, you know, you just want to feel good about yourself. And for me it's...I don't know...I just feel more confident when I know I look good. For me it was very important to look like myself at the wedding. That was one reason why I didn't want a professional hair, appointment, a make-up and stuff; I didn't want to look <u>completely</u> different.

On the one hand, the repeated link between looking good and feeling good about herself suggests that Mary has reconciled herself to the media imperative of an attractive look. On the other hand, similarly to the distinction made in Extract 1.9, Mary draws a separating line between her body and a model-skinny body. In the sequence above she articulates a distinct sense of her own bodily self ("For me it was very important to *look like myself* at the wedding", "I didn't want to look *completely different*"). Also importantly, Mary's disclosure that she did not want to look "<u>completely</u> different" makes evident her sense of the temporality of the bridal experience and her limited emotional investment in the transformation that it involves. The distance which surfaced in Mary's constructions of her wedding preparations makes them unlike the constructions of bridal transformation that were found in the analysis of wedding magazines. Nevertheless, although this is only implicit in the extract, while talking about what she did not do to 'look like herself', Mary must have constructed her bridal body in reference to the 'iconic bride' (see pp. 74–75). This illustrates the interpretative relation between the female body and the "ideological circle" of socio-culturally available texts and imagery (Smith 1990: 179). Overall, Mary's constructions of the bridal body show in what sense the body is a construct – negotiated and performative.

Another discursive strategy which Mary seems to have worked up for herself in the construction of her bodily experience was the subject position of a woman who cares about her looks but is not obsessed with it:

Extract 1.11

Mary: I did go swimming a little bit more than before. Just to lose a <u>little</u> bit of weight. I didn't really go on a diet or anything like that. I was basically, I was size 12 at that time and I thought, "Oh, it would be better to be size 10 more". All I did was eat a little less of sweets and go swimming once a week rather than you know…So that was the only thing…

The repeated qualifying formulations such as "a *little* bit more than before", "a *little* bit of weight", "*little* less of sweets" and "So that was the *only thing*" seem to work pre-emptively – perhaps to defuse any appearances of alignment with the media discourse of the body. Mary constructs her beautifying practices as based on her own discretion and unlike the thorough body disciplining practices to which women are encouraged in wedding magazines.

Elsewhere in the interview Mary constructed a more explicit critique of the media discourse by taking issue with the imperative of the flawless body that it promulgates:

Extract 1.12

Mary: It's like, I knew that I don't look perfect but ... he:y Ana ... they ... ((baby crying)) 'cause 'perfect' is a very dangerous word. Perfect body for example doesn't exist 'cause the people in the magazines, I mean, he:y Ana ... Sorry, <you don't want that on the recording, do you > ((laugh)) They ... 'Perfect' is a very dangerous word 'cause 'perfect' doesn't really exist in some ways. You can say "I had a perfect day", okay, I mean could be, but ... I don't know, if you look at these people there, a lot of them, I don't know, you can air-brush pictures in the magazines don't you, and people are after cosmetic surgeries and they've gone through diets ... It's just not normal ... No, 'normal' is the wrong word, but you know, when you look at these supermodels who are meant to be perfect, I reckon that lots of them are just too skinny! You know, you look at them and can't stop thinking "That's not nice!" ... I remember once I read an article about people with low self-esteem. And there were all these girls who hate their bodies, you know, especially teenage girls, they hate their bodies 'cause they look at the models who are size 2 or 4, ridiculously small size, but they think that's normal. So I think 'perfect' is a dangerous word, but they do like it in those magazines, so it's 'perfect wedding', 'perfect couple' and I think that's where people sort of start to get themselves into trouble.

In the extract, Mary constructs a position of a highly reflexive media consumer. She is critically aware of the language in the magazine ("So I think 'perfect' is a dangerous word but they do like it in those magazines") and of the one she uses ("No, 'normal' is the wrong word"). Also, she talks from the subject position of a 'cultural expert' capable of a deconstructive reading of media texts ("you can air-brush pictures", "people are after cosmetic surgeries", "that's where people sort of start to get themselves into trouble"). It needs to be observed, however, that this reflexive and polemical positioning could have been related to her rhetorical orientation at the point of the conversation, which can be observed in the injection about the noise of a crying baby.

In many reminiscences of her wedding and when talking about her favorite features of bridal magazines, Mary constructed her role in the wedding preparations in line with Boden's concept of the 'superbride' (see p. 65):

Extract 1.13

Mary: The other thing I like, most of the magazines have the planning part, 'Checklist', because I found it really useful, probably the most useful of the things, the magazines and the books I bought =

R: = Really?

Mary: Yeah, I mean, not everything on the list is necessarily something I would need but it's nice to sort of... There was, you know, at some stage in that year when we were working out the wedding I was thinking "I hope I remember everything, I hope I don't sort of turn around on the day of our wedding thinking 'Y:! I haven't done this!'", you know, like panic, so... That sort of checklist helps to calm your nerves a bit. Make sure that, yes, you've done it so these are kind of obvious things but it must be really stress- stressful to realize "Oh! I didn't organize this bit!" and it's last minute and stuff. And checklists are quite good for that event. Um, and also a timescale. I was also, I was quite experienced in organizing events, 'cause I've done that in my job, 'cause I know sort of roughly what sort of timescale.

As could be seen in the examples of 'checklists' and 'countdowns' in Chapter 3, bridal magazines often present wedding organization as a process that is the bride's responsibility and requires her managerial skills, especially if potential failures are to be avoided. Because editors at the same time construct themselves as helpful at every stage of the preparations, the wedding consequently "becomes a carefully negotiated performance organized by the bride, aided by the industry, given meaning by the culture" (Boden 2003: 70). In the extract, Mary produces her bridal experience along the repertoires identified by Boden. For one thing, she talks about her anxieties, which, as Boden observes, are "purposely mobilized as a method of need stimulation" (Boden 2003: 68). For another, Mary constructs the magazine as helpful in combating her distress ("I was thinking 'I hope I remember everything... you know, like panic, so... That sort of checklist helps to calm your nerves a bit"). Also, she takes the subject position of the 'project-manager superbride' by claiming she was "quite experienced in organizing events" because of her professional background.

Mary positioned herself as an invested reader when she described another of her favorite features, the readers' letters:

Extract 1.14

R: Did you read any of these?

Mary: I skipped through it cause it's the end of the magazine and I ran out of time basically, but I still would have read it 'cause I, I actually quite like that they give different options, because I do think that weddings can be a very stressful time and they can be a very difficult time for family, um, and there can be potential arguments, particularly between the couple and their parents and…I know of…um…a person who, not because of the wedding, but because sort of, because of talking a lot with her dad before the wedding they fell out, and he refused to come to the wedding, and then the whole side of his family refused to come as well in sort of solidarity, and yeah, that's sad isn't it. I mean, so I mean I didn't read the article properly, but from what I gather, the dilemma is that the mother thinks the bride is wasting money and I like it that they give three different options – the softer, the harder and halfway through sort of compro[mise].

R: [When] you read articles like this one, do you pay attention to who's giving the advice?

Mary: No, not really. I think if I read it, I would probably, what I probably would do is I would read the question at first, is it interesting at all, if it was rubbish, I mean something…I don't know if the 'Emotional rescue' question was, I don't know um…'I'm not sure if I should wear a long or short dress', I wouldn't be interested in that, whereas this one is more interesting, so I probably would read it if I had more time and…if it's…Usually in the magazines, it's something inbetween, isn't it, it's not very radical, you know, if it was really strange advice, I would probably check who's writing this. And you know, <u>then</u> I would probably check, or if she's giving really good advice, she's giving really good tips, then I'd probably check who gives that advice.

Apparently, talking about her relation to the texts, Mary reveals her vulnerability to the discourse of the magazine. Her minimal interest in who actually provides advice is one such indication. As for another, the claim that she appreciates being provided with more than one solution ("like that they give different options") implies that she considers the solutions as viable guidance. In this sense, Mary is interpellated to the reader subject position of a woman who seeks advice from 'media experts'. This is an important point to make because these kinds of interpellations can be regarded as the media's form of symbolic power. However, although hailed to this subject position, Mary organizes it as a space for enacting her agency and reflexivity – she emphasizes her control of the situation ("I would read the question at first, is it interesting at all, if it was rubbish", "if it was really strange advice, I would probably check who's writing this"). This, hence, serves as a reminder that the appearances of hailing should not lead analysts to hasty conclusions about people's vulnerability to the media's hidden agenda.

As can be seen, throughout the interview Mary presented an ambivalent relationship to the discourse of the magazine – by juggling the invested and uninvested reader positions as well as by manifesting identity trouble in the constructions of her reader investment. In the sequence below, Mary talks about the "Wedding file debate" (see pp. 68–70):

Extract 1.15

R: So, do English women trash their dresses like the one in the article here?

Mary: Oh, I've read that! Yeah! I just, I just thought, "Oh, am I understanding that right?", 'cause I was a bit like, "Ok?" But then I remembered that I had actually heard that people literally roll in the sea and the sand or something, you know to take photographs, and I've always thought it was a bit strange, 'cause sometimes these photos look fair enough, but I could never trash my dress, I'm sort of on this...um, is this the woman who says 'no'...I mean she's gone a bit extreme, she's putting the dress on a dummy you know, into a spare room and will display the dress, and I think in some ways it's extreme, in some ways it's a good idea because I actually remember, you know these make-over programs where they do up houses, I remember one of them had, um, they displayed a wedding dress in between sheets of plastic, really thick plastic, on an organza wall, sort of, like a print, it was a wedding dress, not a picture of it, so that was the actual wedding dress displayed and I thought it was quite a nice touch, I probably wouldn't do it I reckon... 'cause I don't know where I would put it, but I thought it was quite a nice idea, but yeah, displaying your dress on a mannequin is a bit much I think =

R: = But =

Mary: = But I'm definitely more for the 'keep your dress'. ((sarcastically and dreamy))

At the beginning, Mary displays an affective orientation to the text, which indexes the invested reader identity ("Oh I've read that! Yeah!"). Her reader investment is also evident when she takes one of the sides in the debate ("I'm sort of on this...um, is this the woman who says 'no'...", "But I'm definitely more for the 'keep your dress'"), as well as when she refers to another media account of the same issue. Taking side with one of the readers and supporting them by talking about her personal experience reveal a reading pattern which Currie (2001) terms as 'comparison reading'. In the investigation of media consumption by adolescent girls, Currie found the participants interested mainly in texts written by their peers (such as confessional stories or reader advice) rather than articles about fashion or celebrities. This, she considers, is an indication of the indistinct fault line between the "textual and experiential realities of adolescence" (Currie 2001: 265).[3] The border between the textual and the experiential was also blurred in Mary's relation to the "Wedding file debate":

Extract 1.16

[continued from the previous extract]

Mary: = But I'm definitely more for the 'keep your dress'. ((sarcastically and dreamy)) You know, didn't she say something with her daughter as well, um... "I'd be delighted and I love the idea if I ever have a little girl, she'll be able to wear it one day, too". And I mean, I would never say to Ana in years' time "Oh, I want to you to wear this dress" but... If she gets married, let's say in 25 years and she's like "Oh Mom, what was your dress like", and I would show it to her and if it fit her and she'd like it, I would be <u>delighted</u> if she wanted to wear it. But I definitely wouldn't sort of force her. Ana, yes ((baby crying))... But, I mean, I had my dress cleaned and put into the box, so, and yes... it's definitely something I treasure... And it's silly... really, in a way... so... keeping ((it)) in a box and stuff, but my mom had kept her wedding dress and, yeah, I know, I think it's really special to keep it, °so I have a box upstairs with my dress in it.° And I actually followed their advice on acid-free tissue paper as well... 'cause I had it cleaned by somebody who cleans wedding dresses professionally, and they supply the box with this particular tissue paper.

Extracts 1.15 and 1.16 reveal parallel patterns. In both, Mary does 'comparison reading'. In the former passage, she compares herself to the 'traditional' bride; in the latter, she talks about women who have actually trashed their wedding dresses. Both instances of 'comparison reading' are followed by repair work. In Extract 1.15, Mary makes use of prosody in the construction of her affinity with the 'traditional' bride by marking the disclosure with a sarcastic tone. In Extract 1.16, she constructs the invested reader self as a troubled identity through the deployment of the evaluating adjective 'silly'.

Overall, Mary established her reader subjectivity by negotiating the fine line between revealing her involvement with the discourse of the magazine and maintaining the subject position of an independent and critical media consumer. Interestingly, similarly to how she worked to show her awareness of the magazines' discourse, elsewhere in the interview Mary gave indications of her reflexivity of the established discourses of gender. This was particularly visible in the self-accounts that Mary produced in the less structured parts of the interview, when talking about her general attitude to life, work, marriage and family:

Extract 1.17

R: So is there anything else I should have asked you about?

Mary: ...I don't know...

R: Like, is there anything I should know as, you know, a single person?

Mary: ((laugh))

R: Anything I could possibly get to know from you as a married woman?

Mary: I can't give advice myself 'cause for me it happens the way it is meant to be really, 'cause I remember when I was single, I was thinking like "Oh, I just want to be with somebody", I mean I didn't think that I wanted to be married =

R: = Mm =

Mary: = but it was, definitely, I wanted to be in a relationship.

R: Mm, so what is so wrong about being alone?

Mary: Nothing, I just knew I didn't want it by choice.

R: Mm =

Mary: = And you know, when I bought my own house seven years ago, there was never an option for me to live there by myself.

R: Mm

Mary: Not for financial reasons, but because I don't like living by myself.

R: Mm

Mary: I would feel very isolated. I don't go out a lot so I would feel very lonely I think.

Mary constructs her happiness as dependent on finding a partner ("when I was single, I was thinking like 'Oh I just want to be with somebody'", "definitely, I wanted to be in a relationship"). In this sense, she produces her feminine self by means of the "dominant coupledom narrative" (Reynolds and Taylor 2005: 209).[4] Arguably, reliance on the traditional, heteronormative storyline in accounting for her choices absolves Mary of agency in decision-making. Still, in the narrative Mary constructs herself as an agent of her actions and decisions ("But it was, *definitely, I wanted* to be in a relationship" as well as "I just *knew I didn't want* it by choice"). In so doing, she unfolds a narrative of choice, not destiny, despite her initial reliance on the latter repertoire ("for me it happens *the way it is meant to be*").

Likewise, elsewhere in the interview Mary deployed the 'dominant coupledom narrative' but worked to qualify her commitment to it:

Extract 1.18

Mary: [...] I believe there are people who are single and happy, but I think if I hadn't met Daniel...I mean I would be happy, I mean I wouldn't be desperate, but there would be little tiny...there would be something inside me, like something missing.

R: Mm

Mary: The same with when Daniel and I got married, we both knew we wanted children, and if I never had children I would feel like, yes, there's something missing.

R: Mm

Mary: 'Cause I don't know, obviously there is nothing wrong about not having children, and not being married, and everybody is different, but for me, it would be like "Oh, there is something missing".

Two parallel constructions can be identified in the sequence. Mary first contends the heteronormative narrative by admitting the possibility of resisting it ("I believe there are people who are single and happy", "obviously there is nothing wrong about not having children"). However, Mary next subscribes to this repertoire ("but I think if I hadn't met Daniel", "but for me, it would be like 'Oh, there is something missing'"). She also reinforces the position through the repeated formulation "something missing" finalizing three subsequent statements. Still in the same extract, it can be seen that the way Mary positioned herself to the dominant discourse of gender bears an important similarity to her reader positioning. As demonstrated, Mary established a polemical relation to the discourse of the magazine without disavowing her reader investment. In the sequence above she hybridizes two competing discourses of gender. In turn, although she basically positions herself as the subject of dominant gender, she is able to problematize it by means of the counter-hegemonic discourse, which belies the essentialist assumptions of traditional gender order.

This line of gender positioning recurred throughout the interview:

Extract 1.19

R: Are men as much into the wedding day?

Mary: No, I don't think so, I don't know, I reckon women are you know.

R: [Mm]

Mary: [the] whole fairy-tale wedding.

R: Why?

Mary: I don't know it's just ... Maybe women are more, I don't know if women are more romantic, but they are definitely more into, for example, they are more into romantic comed[ies].

R: [Mm]

Mary: Or romantic films.

R: Mm

Mary: So I think they get fed this idea of perfect wedding much more than men do.

R: Mm

Mary: And I've heard people a couple of times saying, or the husband-to-be, he said, he called the wedding a 'party' =

R: – Mm

Mary: And the bride-to-be was like "Don't call that party". ((mocking)) I mean, that was more like a joke really, but I think for men, I mean obviously, it's still special but the actual wedding, yes, it's more like a big party, I reckon.

R: So are you saying that they experience the wedding in different ways?

Mary: At least the planning or the <u>dreaming</u>, especially the dreaming about it before, I reckon.

Talking about gender-dependent approaches to wedding, Mary essentializes women and men – the former are more romantic and dream of weddings, whereas for the latter the wedding is "more like a big party". At the same time, she is apparently aware of the limits of the discourse. She seems wary of passing sweeping generalizations. Firstly, instead of talking about what men and women are like, Mary gives examples of their preferences and behaviors in specific situations, for example when she says "I don't know if women are more romantic, but they are definitely more into (...) romantic comed[ies]". Secondly, when she talks about men, she shuns all-encompassing, generic formulations and refers to what she has "heard people a couple of times saying". Finally, she mitigates her arguments about men's non-romantic disposition by calling the situations "a joke".

Still, despite all these qualifications, Extract 1.19 reveals Mary's endorsement of dichotomous gender discourse. In some of her constructions she reproduces widely circulating gender stereotypes (women like romantic comedies, men are party animals). She essentializes women as romantic and enchanted with fairy-tale weddings by means of double-voiced formulations – women's fixation on weddings is constructed intertextually, through the voices of their fiancés as well as through

women's own voices, which she parodied. Mary's polyglossic constructions demonstrate that speakers can participate in the reproduction of
ideas to which they do not overtly subscribe in their statements, or they
strategically employ double-voicing to subvert the criticism of what
they claim.

The same discursive resources featured in Mary's constructions of motherhood and child-rearing which have not been included in this volume for
lack of space. It needs to be pointed out that the ambiguities and contradictions in Mary's accounts of media consumption, marriage and motherhood were distinctive. Compared to the underlying inconsistency and
variability observed in all interviews, moving along the axis of resistance
and submission, she revealed most clearly in what sense media reception
cannot be considered in terms of the crude dichotomy of submission and
resistance. Despite her investment in the discourse of wedding magazines,
she was able to establish a polemical relation to its specific aspects.

Cara

Cara, a 29-year-old pediatrician, got married one week after the interview. Her parents came to the UK from South Africa. In the interview she
mentioned that together with her fiancé, Bob, she worked among poor
communities in Africa. During our meeting before the interview with
Cara, both emphasized they are committed Christians. Her fiancé, also a
medical doctor, at the time of the interview studied to become a pastor
in the local church. Even though before the meeting Cara claimed she
had read wedding magazines, what she said during the conversation did
not indicate a significant reader investment.

Referring to texts in the magazine, Cara projected her bridal identity.
In doing so, she emphasized how profoundly her lived experience of
getting married was determined by her Catholic faith. Consequently,
Cara's positioning to the magazine was first and foremost mediated by
religious discourse:

Extract 2.1

R: What do you make of all the wedding magazines you have read?

Cara: I have to admit I mainly flipped through them. I haven't read them in
any great detail and some of the things that I did read, I didn't like 'cause I
felt they are very much emphasizing...that it was all about kind of arranging
a perfect day, um, and about being kind of stylish and modern, and it was
quite self-centered and that's not...The Biblical view of marriage is that, you
know, it's all about being married man and woman in the sight of God and in

the presence of people at church, so the day is just a start of your married life together and so in that way it's not about a big performance or ... It's not just about all that day ...

Asked about her personal opinion, Cara initially employs the first person pronoun 'I' and then shifts to a subject position mediated by the discourse of the Catholic Church ("the Biblical view of marriage is that ... "). Throughout the interview she seemed to use this transition to conclude her stances in a forcible way, to provide them with some rhetorical force.

Like most participants, Cara constructed her relationship with her fiancé as unlike other couples' relationships. Compared with the other women interviewed, however, she employed the repertoire particularly often. For example, in the sequence below she first talks about the editor's letter (see pp. 56–59):

Extract 2.2

R: So what do you make of the letter?

Cara: ... All the things about personal touch, I guess, all the things that reflect what you're like, yeah, making things kind of perfect ... as far as you see it. But for us, I guess that's not I mean partly the wedding that we wanted to be ... we don't want it to be driven by other people's expectations because, you know, our marriage is not going to be about creating a perfect day.

Similarly to Extract 2.1, Cara readily abandons the position of a reader. She first indicates her awareness of the sociocultural code of the text and immediately juxtaposes it with her own point of view. The resistance is established from a joint subject position which she shares with her fiancé ("us", "we"). This shift recurred in the interview whenever Cara dropped the reader subject position (or declined to take it) and she later maintained it when she marked her detachment from the popular tradition of lavish weddings:

Extract 2.3

R: Did you read about any of the weddings here?

Cara: I looked into a few of them and I can't help thinking, you know, they say it's real-life weddings, yet clearly the weddings featured here, um ... People just spend loads and loads of money and for both of us, we didn't wanna waste ... You know, weddings are so expensive and that's not a good use of resources. We both worked overseas you know, in countries where people have, you know, not enough money to eat and children are malnourished and it just... For us, it just, for us it didn't seem right to spend 15 or 16 thousand pounds on average per wedding, these [days]

R: [So] you wouldn't present your wedding in the magazine like this one here?

Cara: Um, I couldn't imagine presenting it in a magazine. I think, it's, you know, I would be very happy to talk to people about our day and how we made the decision and what we did, but I couldn't imagine that sort of putting it in a magazine or as... like an advert 'cause in the end it's all about the vows made, being together with people in the sight of God in the church.

As in Extract 2.2, Cara switches from the uninvested reader position to that of a woman in a relationship, which is unlike the others interviewed. Next, the subject position of a person committed to a relationship is changed into that of a member of the Catholic Church. Cara positioned herself in the same way when she was asked about an advertisement which consisted of a narrative and an image that exploited the repertoire of a fairy-tale wedding, the examples of which were presented in the analysis in Chapter 3:

Extract 2.4

R: What do you make of the ad as you read it?

Cara: Um, kind of unrealistic. Um, and it sounds like if you choose the right place to get married then your happiness after that depends on it and... um, you know, Bob and I know marriage is not going to be easy, so, you know, the perfect wedding day is not going to determine what our married life is going to be like, so... in that way we're gonna look to ((the)) church and God to help us in it.

It can be noted that in Cara's positioning patterns, the joint subject position of "we" and "Bob and I" acquired indexical properties because Cara used it repeatedly. She deployed it either to express her denial of popular culture or as a transitional subject position leading to the construction of the Catholic identity. As a consequence, many of Cara's epistemic and evaluative stances were produced even when she made no identity or ideological claims.

The subject position Cara shared with her fiancé was the second major form of polyglossia in her accounting work. The predominant voice in her talk was one of the Catholic Church and it surfaced in Cara's talk in different forms. In the extracts above, the way in which polyglossia surfaced in her accounting work is quite explicit because she announces or gradually concedes to voice of the Catholic tradition. In other cases, the multi-voicedness was quite indistinct as no overt structures separated the speaking subject from the other voice. On the one hand, this form (and degree) of multi-voicedness undermines Cara's agency – it makes evident to what extent Cara's sense of self has been colonized by the Catholic discourse. On the other hand, the choice of a subject position and discourse can be regarded in terms of a 'subversive tactic' (de Certeau 1984), in the sense that she organized for herself a discursive site of resistance. For instance, asked about readers' letters, Cara, unlike Mary, did not construct them as a valuable source of information – she undermined media's authority in that respect by pointing to the support that she obtains from her church community:

Extract 2.5

Cara: I did scan that one actually and I kind of thought I wouldn't get any advice on these things from magazines, um ... I'd get that advice from people at church, from kind of what I know of the Bible, so far as I remember. One of my friends actually was having big issues with her mother-in-law and we talked about it a lot and kind of what the Bible says about it and prayed through it and so in that way I wouldn't get my advice.

How Cara orients herself to the media texts in the extract above is an illustrative example of the highly relational and oppositional identity that she worked up in the interview. As can be observed above, the self was accomplished through strong positive identification with Bob and the Catholic community as well as distinct negative identification with popular culture.

At some points of the conversation, Cara took gendered subject positions. Because they were mediated by contending discourses of femininity, the gender subjectivity she established revealed some notable contradictions. To begin with, Cara referred to the images of femininity circulating in popular culture:

Extract 2.6

R: Did you choose the dress on your own?

Cara: No, with one of my bridesmaids, one of my friends.

R: Did you enjoy looking for the dress?

Cara: To be honest, I kind of saw it as a bit "Oh, I just want it get sort of sorted in that or another way" ... um ... and, um ... I felt sort of funny as well, but it wasn't ... you know, I didn't <u>dis</u>like it, but, you know, some people spend days and days and put a lot of effort into it.

In the extract, Cara talks about a practice that has been socioculturally constructed as one of the ultimate pleasures of bridal femininity. Looking for a wedding dress with bridesmaids was a regular repertoire identified in the discourse of wedding magazines in the previous part of the study. Qualifying her satisfaction from the practice, Cara constructs a subject position of a woman who is not fully affiliated with the media discourse of femininity.

The disclosure in Extract 2.6 was occasioned when, while flipping through the prompt magazine, Cara saw a photo session in which a caption under the title of the shoot presupposes that women love window-shopping. In the sequence below, it can be seen how she went on distancing herself from the media discourse of bridal femininity:

Extract 2.7

R: So what was it ((choosing the wedding dress)) like?

Cara: I felt a bit funny as I was trying on the dresses and a bit sort of artificial and I didn't... you know, I would try them on, have a look at them, but I didn't particularly.

R: Do you think women in general enjoy it?

Cara: I guess, yeah, partly as a novelty 'cause it's a bit different so that's quite funny you know, you can laugh off, you're with a good friend, we can laugh about it a bit. But I think probably some people would enjoy [it].

Throughout the interview, as Cara was taking subsequent subject positions, commodified bridal femininity appeared indexical of the identity she evidently did not seek to work up. Both in Extracts 2.6 and 2.7, the juxtaposition of the media-reproduced femininity and Cara's lived femininity is produced by means of parallel constructions. Her relationship to dominant femininity is indexed with semantically equivalent structures such as "funny", "artificial", "partly as a novelty", "laugh about it a bit". Cara's dis-identification with what she finds as common among women is reinforced through the generalizing references to "some people" terminating both extracts. At the same time, the rejection of hegemonic femininity must have put Cara in a troubled subject position because she qualified her disavowal of traditional femininity with the assertion "I didn't dislike it" and by means of hedging constructions ("a bit", "sort of" and "particularly").

A similar form of indexical work can be identified in the subject position that Cara took in relation to her mother, who regularly appeared in Cara's accounts:

Extract 2.8

R: Did you have like your idea of your wedding dress?

Cara: Um, not really. Originally by mom was going to make it so I went to some shops for ideas and then ended up in one shop. Because our wedding is quite, there's not much time between deciding to get married and the wedding day, so the lady in the shop said "You're not going to have enough time to get anything made for you so just try those from the sale rail, you can get them and just adjust it.' So we just found one on the sale rail and it seemed to be good. And you know, then I said to my mom "Would you be offended if I bought one" and she said "No, no, of course not". Instead, she's making the bridesmaids' dresses.

In the extract, the mother is presented as eager to partake in the wedding organization and someone whose opinion and feelings Cara finds important. The intersubjective relations with the mother were another index of Cara's resistant femininity. For example, in the extract below, Cara was indirectly asked about the "Wedding file debate" (see pp. 68–70):

Extract 2.9

R: = By the way, there is an article, here, about some people trashing their dress, other people treasuring it…

Cara: I don't know 'cause it feels in some ways a little bit of waste just to wear it for one day, but, um…oh I wouldn't trash it just because it…something feels wrong about that. I wouldn't trash it. I can't imagine putting it on a dummy to look on it kind of everyday or anything, and if anyone wanted to use it, and it fitted them, that would be fine to do, um…I don't know, my mom still has her wedding dress which she showed to me the other day, °but I don't know°.

In terms of reader positioning, Cara ignores the researcher's reference to the prompt magazine, hence making clear her weak engagement with its discourse. Because of the apparent unfamiliarity with the article's content, she elaborates on the issue of the researcher's interest by talking about her lived experience. In the sequence, Cara constructs her mother as affiliated with the dominant discourse of bridal community, which is evident in that her mother also treasures her wedding gown. Yet, unlike her mother, Cara is uncertain of her relationship with the discourse, which she implies with the hesitant constructions of her own opinion about the value of a wedding dress (the repeated confession "I don't know"). A similar relationship is established in the sequence in which Cara talks about beauty tips in the magazine:

Extract 2.10

R: Did you find them helpful?

Cara: I've never really been interested in the kind of beauty tips things to a great extent. Um, you know, my mom keeps saying I need to make sure I get some fake tan or something to make my arms looks less white and I just keep thinking "Well, yeah...if I have time I'll think about that", but to me that's not the most important bit about the day. And having said that, like, I <u>am</u> going to pay someone to do my hair and have a friend from my home group who has offered to do a make-up, and I'm normally someone who doesn't wear a lot of make-up, so I'm hoping she's gonna do something really subtle but, um =

Even though the mother is not mentioned in the interviewer's question, Cara, again, refers to her while talking about the practices of femininity that she apparently finds extraneous to her sense of self. (This, hence, is another indication of the notably relational identity that Cara worked up in the conversation.)

Furthermore, as mentioned above, Cara gave misleading information about her reader practices. She claimed she was reading wedding magazines at that time, but this was only weakly substantiated by what she said during the interview. This discrepancy may have resulted from the fact that, as Cara explained later in the interview, she got the magazines from her mother – she did read them, but found them unappealing. In Extract 2.11, Cara mentions her mother while explaining her attitude to women's magazines:

Extract 2.11

R: And do you read women's magazines?

Cara: Um, I do sometimes, not very often...°I do sometimes°

R: Which of them?

Cara: Um, well, in the past my mom...Like, my mom and I would share things and my mom had a subscription to the *Women 'n Home* so I read some of those, but...you know...it's um...not, um, normally...

R: So what do you think about the magazines?

Cara: Um, some of the things that I used to like, some of the recipes...like cooking recipes...and with my mom some of the patterns like dressmaking patterns...um...

The past simple formulations such as "in the past my mom" and "my mom and I would share things" construct distance between Cara and her mother. By talking about what they used to share (Extract 2.11) and her mother's expectations (Extract 2.10), Cara disavows affinity with dominant femininity (to which the mother seems subscribed to). Importantly, none of the questions asked by the interviewer concerned the mother. The fact that it was Cara who created the intersubjective relationship when talking about her practices of femininity may imply the influence of the mother on Cara's lived experience of gender.

At some points in the interview, Cara's affinity with the dominant discourse of gender was less ambiguous than in the extracts above. Namely, constructing her relation with her fiancé, she used repertoires that were identified in Chapter 3 as constituting the magazines' discourse of bridal femininity:

Extract 2.12

R: = There are like beauty countdowns in many of the wedding magazines. Do you also feel like you need get your body to a certain [condition]?

Cara: [It's a balance] of, you know, like, I...want to look as lovely as I can for Bob and so that determines...you know, that determined which of my dresses...that determined the choice of my dress. You know, I asked my friend "Do you think Bob would like it". I tried to find out what things he may or may not like, you know, I wanted to look nice for him on the day, um, and...like I said to him yesterday that, um...now that my dress has been fitted, I can't put any extra weight on 'cause otherwise ((laugh)) I won't be able to fit into it. But I think in the end, you know, we've talked about the fact that as the years go by, you know...age makes your body look less attractive and...that in a way...Bob will have to live with me whatever I look like in the years to come ((laugh)) so [in that way].

R: [So are] you afraid of aging?

Cara: Um, I have been so I've kind of asked him about it but he's very reassuring and, you know.

The extract brings yet another example of the relational links which Cara established with her fiancé in the interview. Talking about her bridal beautification practices, Cara relies on the dominant discourse of gender. By constructing her attractive looks (such as the wedding dress and the right weight) as subject to her fiancé's evaluation, she positions herself as the object of the male gaze, thus within the traditional discourse of femininity. Another interpretative repertoire representing the discourse is one of the aging female body as essentially faulty. Cara subscribes to it when mentioning her concern about the loss of attractive looks and explaining how Bob's assurance of his unconditional approval helped her to overcome the concern.

Cara's identification practices reveal an ideological dilemma implicated in constituting one's self amidst dominant discourses of gender. A comparison of different points in Cara's identity work shows that overt defiance of the media discourse of the female body does not necessarily mean that one is able to construct a relationship with the body which is not constrained by external, socioculturally established standards and regulations. For example, in Extract 2.10 it was demonstrated how Cara rejected the standards of bridal appearance that are arbitrarily set in the wedding magazines (for example, a tanned body and a professionally made-up face). Nonetheless, as can be seen from Extract 2.12, when constructing her confidence about her appearance as conditioned by Bob's approval, Cara positioned herself as the object of the fiancé's gaze (hence, in the same way the magazines interpellate their target reader). A similar inconsistency occurred when Cara talked about the "Gossip file", encouraging brides to practice walking in stilettos (see p. 106):

Extract 2.13

R: Have you read the "Gossip file"?

Cara: It's funny 'cause we were having a conversation about shoes and somebody suggested that high heels were nice, and I said to Bob "I want to wear comfortable shoes 'cause, you know, I want to be able to run around and to walk up to people and chat, and I don't want to be thinking that I have to sit down in the corner 'cause I have sore feet". So he said, "So just wear flat shoes", so I'm going to wear flat shoes. For the sake of style I wouldn't I wouldn't be prepared to kind of compromise my ability to mingle with guests because =

Cara resists the interpellating power of the text by rejecting the reader subject position of a commodified bride. The repeated verb of volition ("I want", "I don't want") additionally indexes her powerful and agentic self. Nevertheless, the empowerment and self-determination are contradicted when she takes the subject position of a bride consulting with her fiancé about her choice, which means yielding some discretionary power to him.

Cara revealed her commitment to the traditional gender discourse also while talking about Bob's proposal:

Extract 2.14

R: How did you feel when Bob proposed to you?

Cara: I wasn't expecting, you know, we talked about it but I wasn't expecting it then, so I was quite surprised but obviously kind of, really happy as well, but also partly I felt that, you know, a sense of disbelief and, for many years I thought that I wouldn't get married and no one would ever ask me to marry them, so partly I thought "Hm, I don't quite believe that it is happening to me".

The confession "for many years I thought that I wouldn't get married" is premised on the traditional cultural storyline of a woman waiting and dreaming of being asked 'the' question. When narrating her life before she was proposed to, Cara gave many indications of her subscription to the conservative view of gender. It was also manifest when she explained her view of marriage:

Extract 2.15

R: So do you think that those differences concern also a couple's married life?

Cara: Um, <u>definitely</u> yeah, 'cause that's the way God's designed it, isn't it. You know men and...He says that the typical role once you're married is that the male is the headship role and the woman is the helpish role...um...So definitely that's the way it is. Yes! There's mutual companion, there's mutual help and joint decision-making and everything, but I think...

R: But how do <u>you</u> feel about this kind of design?

Cara: um, I think, you know, it's not always straightforward 'cause everybody, naturally we are all stubborn and, you know, naturally we are all...Self is the thing we want to take care of first, but I think when men and women live out marriage in the way God's created it, that's the way because God created it and he knows what's he doing 'cause that's the way that works...<u>Perfectly</u>, that's the way it works and knowing that you're committed to each other and marriage is for life, even in the hard times we continue to look to God for help of the church.

The extract reveals a strong intertextual interference from the Catholic discourse. The expressions "helpish role" and "headship role" as well as the apologetic constructions of human condition ("naturally we are all stubborn", "self is the thing we want to take care of first") seem linked to the ideological positions of the Catholic Church. Cara's extensive reliance on the Catholic discourse is particularly conspicuous when she is asked how she feels about the 'God's design'. Despite the interviewer's emphatic distinction between Cara's opinion and the 'God's design', Cara does not change her subject position. In contrast to the earlier positioning in the extract, where she used reported speech ("He says that"), the constructions following the question are not double-voiced.

Moreover, toward the end of the sequence, Cara internalizes the voice of the Catholic tradition as her own by means the mental verb "I think".

Importantly, however, what Cara meant by saying "I think" is difficult to determine and could vary throughout the interview. One explanation may be that Cara has internalized the Catholic discourse to the extent that she considers its values and ideas as ones that she developed herself. On the other hand, the epistemic stance "I think" may suggest that for Cara reliance on the Catholic discourse is a result of her self-reflexive choice to consent to it and live accordingly. This was claimed by Cara in one of her self-accounts:

Extract 2.16

R: So where does your idea of marriage come from?

Cara: Whole mixture I think. I only became Christian kind of late in life, at university and so I started ... You know, most of my ideas would be just assumptions from home, what family life was at home, um, and maybe just a few families that kind of later I saw children whose parents got separated or divorced or, but then later on when I became a Christian was when, you know, that's when I realized that the truths about life including those concerning marriage are, you know, to be found in the Bible, what God's plans are for marriage and that's ... since then, seeing <u>Christian</u> marriages at church, um, and hearing what people have said about marriage has kind of contributed.

In the extract, apart from constructing her commitment to the Catholic religion as a reflexive practice of self, Cara produces two dichotomies. She draws a line between happy, Catholic families and non-Catholic broken homes as well as differentiates between her life before and after becoming a committed Christian. The dichotomization is a crucial moment in Cara's identity work. Constructing the non-Catholic notion of marriage as "assumptions" and the Biblical one as "the truths", Cara displays her epistemic orientation to the traditions. This illuminates her earlier identity work and reader positioning. For example, the construction of lay tradition as "just assumptions" explains Cara's hasty rejections of reader subject position. By the same token, the construction of the Catholic religion as the source of "truths" sheds additional light on how Cara negotiated her gender subjectivity (for instance in the categorical accounts of marriage). In terms of the methodological considerations proposed in the current study, this shows the analytical value of contextualizing media reception in the extended self-accounts that are not directly related to the media. The narrative data, an example of which is provided in the extract above, enable a better understanding of her reader positioning as well as render insight into the idiosyncratic relations between media reception and the recipient's lived experience.

Overall, media discourse, which I expected to be the discursive frame of reference in the interviews, was marginalized by Cara. Because of her evident lack of investment in the discourse of bridal magazines, the point of presenting the interview with Cara might be questioned. Nevertheless, she was included in the discussion because she considered herself as a reader and provided interesting examples of the ways in which the non-invested relationship with the media can be negotiated. What she thus added to the study's findings is the subjectivity of a woman who is familiar with the media texts of (bridal) femininity even though she denies engagement with them; moreover, the woman repudiates the media-based femininity as one-dimensional (consumption-oriented) but establishes her subjectivity by relying mainly on one discourse and two subject positions related to it.

This made the analysis of the interview worthwhile for two main reasons. Firstly, how Cara negotiated her non-invested reader subjectivity richly illustrates the role of lifeworld discourses in media reception. Secondly, because of the consistency with which she rejected the subject position that she was expected to take in the interview, the subjectivity established by Cara in the interaction with the researcher was definitely subversive and powerful. On the one hand, it was proposed that the discourse mediating her resistance essentializes femininity similarly to the media discourse of gender. On the other, in line with what has been emphasized in this book about imposing one's own, critical analyst's ideological view on data, Cara's 'subversive tactic' in relation to media discourse is not discounted here.

Debby

Debby, a 31-year-old mother of three, moved to Manchester to study at a local university, but in the interview she did not elaborate on her education. She decided to stay in Manchester after meeting her husband (originally from New Zealand) and becoming pregnant. At the time of the interview, she worked part-time in a department store. She got married a year before the interview. In the interview, she mentioned her parents were divorced and talked a lot about her relations with her mother. Although Debby was recruited through a Christian network (as a mother bringing her children to the local church-run community center), she recognized herself as an atheist. She was invited to the interview because she claimed to read women's magazines eagerly but only occasionally (as a mother of three, she had less time for it).

To begin with, asked about her general attitude to women's magazines, Debby admitted to reading some of them but questioned their genuineness:

Extract 3.1

R: So what do you think of women's magazines?

Debby: Um, I think, I mean, they are all the same so I sometimes read them and then I'm, like, it's all made up, that's just a made-up story.

Although such a statement could lead to the construction of a highly subversive reader subjectivity, Debby did not involve herself with the deconstructive interpretation of the prompt texts. Throughout the interview, she generally put up an impassive relationship to the texts, as in the extract above. At some points of the interview, however, she was drawn into the discourse of the magazine, for instance when referring to the "Wedding file debate" (see pp. 68–70):

Extract 3.2

R: By the way, did you read that?

Debby: Oh I did read that! Yeah! I didn't really understand that because it's almost like a well-established ritual which I have never heard of, but you know, in my personal opinion it is like, keep it °for sentimental reasons° or sell it, or get away with it, you know.

R: Mm.

Debby: But that's just didn't make any sense to me...

R: Would you do that?

Debby: Trash the dress?! No! Certainly not! ((mocking))

R: Why?

Debby: Because it's a beautiful dress! ((laugh)) Um I couldn't just, um =

R: = Mm

Debby: I couldn't just ruin it... That would be a waste you know, why should I do it?

R: As a kind of rite of passage?

Debby: The wedding day is a rite of passage, you know, and trashing the dress is just pointless =

R: = Yeah...

Debby: But I suppose that will just end up being a tradition that will become popular but, you know, I was shocked when I read that 'cause I have never heard of that...

Debby positions herself as an invested reader by taking both affective and epistemic stances to the text. The latter can be found in the implicature "it's almost like a well-established ritual", where the existential 'be' suggests the factuality of the new bridal custom. The premodifier "almost like" qualifies her statement, but at the same time implies consent that trashing a wedding dress becomes or resembles a form of 'ritual'. The affective orientation to the text is established in the exclamations (e.g., "Yeah!", "No! Certainly not!") and in the acknowledgment of the emotional reaction to the text ("I was shocked when I read that"). Finally, another invested reader positioning is evident in Debby's expression of her own opinion on trashing a wedding dress.

At one point, after Debby expressed her dislike of the infantility of popular wedding culture, she was asked about an advertisement premised on the repertoire of a 'fairy-tale' wedding. This gave her the opportunity to confirm the dislike – this time by referring to a text and an image drawing on the ultratraditional feminine code, which Debby earlier emphatically rejected. Nevertheless, Debby did not take up a reader subject position:

Extract 3.3

R: Did you pay attention to this ad?

Debby: Um... I don't like the dress...

It was mentioned above in the discussion that due to the generic conventions of a research interview, the interviewer had the privilege of asking questions. However, as can be seen in the extract above, the interviewees could (and often did) ignore that arrangement. Reasons for that are, of course, difficult to determine. In the extract above, for example, Debby might have disliked the direction set by the researcher and might have avoided dwelling on the text for sheer lack of fancy. Alternatively, the apparent lack of interest could be an index of Debby's distance to the specific gender discourse.

The latter explanation seems most plausible given how often in the interview Debby marked her subversive gender subjectivity by means of her references to the prompt texts, for instance, the "Gossip file" (see p. 106):

Extract 3.4

R: Would you go to this website?

Debby: ((laugh)) No, I don't wear high heels anymore, but the fact there is a website like that, it's something ridiculous, I mean, some people wear high heels, for example my friend but when she does, it's like y:... ((laugh))

Clearly, Debby takes the position of a woman who is unlike other, 'typical' women. The position appeared one of her central identity resources. For example, in Extract 3.5 Debby manifests her awareness of the discourse of dominant femininity when she positions herself in the relationship of difference from her friend:

Extract 3.5

Debby: You know, this is so expensive =

R: = Window-shopping... have you ever tried it?

Debby: I don't like shopping...

R: But they say 'enjoy the fun [of]'.

Debby: [But] that's exactly why most women really like shopping, you know, my friends, they really like to go and window-shop, maybe try this thing on, maybe that small thing =

R: = What do you think is so enjoyable about it?

Debby: Well, I suppose it's like a female bonding thing, I don't know, they get the day, just spend the day chatting and stuff, but I know, Vicky, one of my friends, she just loves clothes and buying stuff, you know =

R: = Mm

Debby: I think it gives them that sort of ten minutes' thrill, afterwards, you know. I have it when I go shopping ((for)) booze =

R: = Mm

Debby: That's the only time I can slightly understand them if I buy a little bit of ( ) or just little things like ( ) I just go, like, "oooh". I'm like "oooh, look at the little things I've got", I suppose that, as well, is the booze.

The exchange above was occasioned by a photo session presupposing women's fondness of window-shopping. In the extract, Debby draws on the dominant discourse of femininity to construct a highly individualistic gender position. Some of her claims ("that's exactly why most women really like shopping", "it's like a female bonding thing", "chatting and stuff") essentialize women in accordance with entrenched gender stereotypes and help Debby to assert her non-stereotypical feminine self. The self is indexed by the accounts of her shopping habits, that is, buying booze, in which apparently none of the friends joins Debby. Importantly enough, the withdrawal from the traditional practices of femininity is presented as a difference of outlooks and preferences rather than sheer disapproval. In the playful self-parody "oooh I'm like 'oooh, look at the little things I've got'" Debby presents herself as thrilled by shopping and hence manifests some degree of like-mindedness with the friends. By projecting her sense of affinity rather than membership, Debby withholds the ownership of stereotypical feminine identity without completely denying her feminine self.

Unlike other interviewees who routinely positioned themselves as critics of consumerism underlying popular wedding culture, Debby did not problematize the role of commodities in wedding celebration, as can be seen in her relation to the editor's letter (see pp. 56–59):

Extract 3.6

R: What did you make of the letter here?

Debby: It's all about putting your individual mark. If you think about your wedding, you know … white dress, tables, chauffer, that's why the little details are so important to people because that all stand out, you know =

R: = Mm =

Debby: = The dress is white, all the confetti on the table, putting your stamp on it, isn't it, this is how stylish I am, this is … Oh, I suppose I did it with my dress, you know … not alternative, but, you know, wacky or quirky =

R: = Aha

Debby: I didn't want a white dress I wanted an unusual dress, a different dress and that was me, to put my style on it and the same with us going to Vegas =

R: = Mm

Debby: I didn't want a traditional wedding, I didn't want a traditional dress …

Debby recognizes the sociocultural code of the text – she knowingly enumerates the details that are commonly used to personalize weddings. She also acknowledges people's general need to distinguish themselves. The somewhat ironic "this is how stylish I am" is followed by Debby's confession that she did that herself, choosing an unconventional wedding dress and venue (although the interjection "Oh" may imply her genuine surprise upon realizing how her wedding resembled other commodified wedding spectacles). This way of positioning recurred in the conversation as Debby worked up the subject position of a person who is not a media consumer but participates in the popular culture which the media (and hence bridal magazines) are part of.

An analytic challenge that Debby's accounts render is to determine how accurately she estimated her distance from the media discourse. For instance, in the passage below she talks about being unaffected by the magazine's emphasis on consumption, which she constructs as implicated in its discourse of the female body:

Extract 3.7

R: And did you pay attention to the beauty tips in the magazine?

Debby: Yeah, it's all like different types of looks, that's general thing about the magazines.

R: Do you find it useful?

Debby: No, of course not! 'Cause I could, you know, put that make-up ((on)) but I'm not gonna look like them, you know.

R: Yeah.

Debby: Um, in terms of the make-up, the best thing you can do is to go to the make-up artist and ask her what suits your face.

R: Mm =

Debby: = And get her to do a few different looks on you, and see what you like, you know, you may try many things out and say maybe something like that maybe something vampy.

R: Mm =

Debby: = Or maybe something more natural, but in terms of what they are saying, mostly they just want to sell stuff...

In the extract, Debby consistently works up the position of an uninvested reader. Firstly, she presents herself as conversant with the general conventions of women's magazines ("Yeah, it's all like different types of looks, that's general thing about the magazines"). Next, she deconstructs the hidden agenda of the beauty file by means of two interpretative repertoires that featured most interviews in the study. She states that the magazines are geared to stimulate consumerism ("mostly they just want to sell stuff") and that they promote an unattainable model of beauty ("I could, you know, put that make-up ((on)), but I'm not gonna look like them, you know"). The repertoires serve to account for Debby's personal detachment from the media discourse, which she produced by means of an affective stance ("No, of course not!"). However, the practices of femininity that Debby rejects when positioning as a reader are reclaimed in her bridal self-accounts. Although she denies the endorsement of the magazine's discourse of femininity, she constructs her grooming practices in the way they have habitually been presented in women's magazines. As in the media constructions discussed, in Debby's accounts, the female body is malleable, the face takes on disparate appearances depending on the cosmetics applied ("get her to do a few different looks on you and see what you like", "maybe something like that, maybe something vampy, or maybe something like that, maybe something vampy, [...] [o]r maybe something more natural").

Similarly, in her self-accounts Debby consistently reproduced the interpretative repertoire of the 'normative discontent', hence another repertoire of the female body reproduced in the discourse of bridal magazines:

Extract 3.8

R: And did you feel confident about your looks?

Debby: Yeah...for the most part, I suppose, yeah...((laugh)) I mean there are the small things that generally people have, I mean generally =

R: = Mm

Debby: I was, I was happy, the dress was beautiful.

R: Yes, but there is like a regular feature in the magazines 'Beauty count-down', like.

Debby: Oh yeah! I saw that! It's, like, two months, one month before =

R: = <Yeah, yeah>, so what do you think of it?

Debby: Yeah, I did, I was going on a diet 'cause I still had a lot of baby weight to lose, you know.

R: Aha =

Debby: = So I went on, like, a major diet 'cause you know lots of people put on baby weight and then I had this dream of being size te:n ((mocking)) and being really small =

R: = Mm

Debby: And I was doing a lot of fending somewhere around my regular diet 'cause I love food so I was really happy when I did find my dress, and I fit into it so I was, like, "Great, now, so I don't need to lose anymore 'cause I fit into it" =

R: = Mm

Debby:...so just don't put much more on but, you know =

R: = Mm

Debby: I don't need to lose a lot, it fits.

R: So even though you didn't read the articles you still got that feeling that you [should].

Debby: [Yeah!] Well, that's the whole thing your body is meant to be, that's the whole thing about the wedding, you're supposed to look the best you [can].

R: [Mm]

Debby: Ever in your life, your wedding day, that is the best you can look, that's what's meant to be and that's what it means to me.

Debby constructs people's dissatisfaction with their body as obvious and natural by means of definite articles and the generic constructions ("*the* small things", "*generally* people", "*the whole* thing", "*your* body"). Likewise, the interjective usage of "you know" can be considered as indicating Debby's presumption of the interviewer's knowledge of the usual body insecurities that women have after pregnancy. Moreover, similarly to how the wedding dress is constructed in the media, Debby constructs it as the major motivation to lose weight before the wedding and fitting its size as the ultimate verification of attaining the 'right' bridal appearance, although she does so with a hint of irony. The mocking tone in one of her disclosures ("this dream of being size te:n and being really small") indexes Debby's ambiguous relation to the dominant discourse of the female body. Following Benwell (2007: 540), irony is "a versatile device which allows a speaker to articulate certain views whilst disclaiming responsibility for, or ownership of, them". In Debby's positioning, mockery might have worked to minimize the effects of her compliance with the imperative of a skinny figure, which is centrally present in the media discourse of (not only bridal) femininity.

Debby evidently sought to retreat from the subject position of a woman who feels obliged to live up to certain beauty standards also at other points in the interview:

Extract 3.9

R: Mm, and after the wedding?

Debby: Well no, you know, to me that is not a comfortable thing ((that)) I wanna wear everyday, you know.

R: Mm.

Debby: I wouldn't want to be that, to have to do that everyday.

R: Mm.

Debby: I mean, I work in a department store where you have to, like, you have to wear a full make-up and do your hair and, you know.

R: Mm.

Debby: And if I go out, I will do my hair. I mean, today my hair is a mess, but if we go out at the weekend, I'll do it. But I can't do it everyday! It would drive me mad! ((mocking))

R: So why do you do it when you go out?

Debby: 'Cause you want to look your best! You know I, like now I feel a bit fat, scruffy and my hair is messed up and I feel a bit dowdy and so, you know =

R: = Mm =

Debby: = it will make me feel better, you know. I feel more confident in that look, you know =

R: = Mm

Debby: I know that I look nice...you know, rather than hiding and slumping...

Debby's ambiguous relationship to general norms concerning women's looks is signaled in her construction of the source of volition and causality. She uses the verbs of volition in two claims – saying that it is normal for women to want to look as good as possible ("'Cause you want to look your best") and that she would not like to keep a perfect look all the time ("I wouldn't want to be that, to have to that everyday", "that is not a comfortable thing [that] I wanna wear everyday, you know"). In the latter statements Debby constructs herself as the subject of volition. In the first one, volition is to some extent externalized because 'wanting' is constructed as a generic feature. Similarly, the constructions such as "it will make me feel better", "I feel more confident in that look", "that is not a comfortable thing [that] I wanna wear everyday" exteriorize the 'perfected', made-up woman from Debby's lived self. Moreover, similarly to Mary, Debby constructs her bridal self as an identity attained just for one day and in fact unlike her 'actual' self ("But I can't do it everyday! It would drive me mad!"). Having asserted that, however, Debby constructs her submission to the dominant, media-reinforced discourse of the female body, which is revealed in the apologetic tone accompanying the constructions of her everyday shabby looks, as well as at the end of the extract, when Debby constructs this kind of appearance as shameful (a reason for hiding).

Evidently, throughout the interview Debby negotiated the line between the hegemonic and subversive femininities. The distinction between the two was also apparent when she was asked if she would like to have a photo session like the one at which we were looking at one point in the interview:

Extract 3.10

R: Mm. Would you like to have a session like this one?

Debby: What? Just on my own?

R: Yeah.

Debby: I suppose half of me, I'd be lying if I said I wouldn't like ((it)), half of me would and half of me wouldn't.

R: So which half of you would like to to =

Debby: = Half of me would like 'cause, just the practical reason is that, you know, I would really like to have pictures of myself in the house and, you know, I don't even have any room and other pictures, um...you know =

R: = Mm =

Debby: = I have got, you know, the ones of my children and stuff but, yeah...it would be lovely, you know, to spend the day in the ga:rden ((dreamy)) and, um, you know, looking beautiful with people taking pictures of me. °yeah, of course that would be nice°.

Debby's careful wording in the extract indicates identity trouble around the traditional bride. Stating "it would be lovely...to spend the day in the ga:rden...looking beautiful", Debby positions herself as the object of gaze. Yet, this subject position and the images of brides in the magazines reproduce a highly effeminate bridal identity that Debby basically disavowed. Therefore, Debby does some repair work. For one thing, she signals her awareness of the emergent contradiction by referring to the 'halves' of her self. For another, she positions herself as both the object of the gaze and the 'beholder'. Finally, Debby mentions a "practical reason" behind participating in the photo session.

Despite the ideological contradictions, most of which were found in her constructions of the female body, Debby systematically developed a subversive bridal femininity. The resistance she worked up to the prompt magazine was supported with the narrative accounts of lived experience accompanying Debby's media-related talk. As mentioned above, Debby's identity work was based on the interpretative repertoire of being unlike other women; it was hence established intersubjectively – in the relationship of difference from the bridal identity constructed in the wedding magazines. Another form of intersubjective construction of bridal identity was accomplished by the relationship that Debby established with her husband. Although not directly related to her reception of wedding magazines, it illustrates how the binary oppositions between the bride and the groom perpetuated in the magazines' discourse can be used by individuals in constructing their gender and bridal identities. The first constructions of the relation appeared in the interview when Debby was elaborating on the interpretative repertoire of being 'unlike most women':

Extract 3.11

R: Oh! And proposal?

Debby: I think it is generally considered, I mean again, it was the other way round, I was the one to propose to Martin and I think it's horrible, absolutely outrageous 'cause most women they, you know, want to coerce men into... you know. ((laugh)) That sounds terrible but lots of people, they discuss it, they really want to get married but then it's up to men... to actually do the proposal and... many people are interested in how to do the proposal' I've just said "it" ((mocking)) and people want a meal and rent a castle, and the limo, and, you know, people want a big stuff, a big stuff. °I suppose it's a chance for men to be romantic for once in their life and stuff°.

The narrative of proposal that Debby subsequently produced reinforced her defiance of the popular wedding culture, especially of its gender-relevant conventions. In Extract 3.12, talking about how she proposed to Martin, Debby constructs her subversive bridal self by ascribing herself the forms of agency that women have traditionally been denied in wedding tradition:

Extract 3.12

R: How did you do the proposal?

Debby: I did it...I did it properly at meal. Everybody with my mom was going to Centre Parks, and we were going out for the meal, with my mom, my sister and her partner, so we went there. Well, I got there beforehand, I bought champagne and arranged who's gonna come to the table. After we sat ourselves down and then I was gonna, I get on my knee and I propose and then, if he says 'yes' ((laugh)) we can have the champagne and if not I will just run out with the champagne ((laugh)) =

R: = Amazing.

Debby: I was really embarrassed and really nervous and the whole restaurant must have heard it, but I wasn't saying that really loudly and everybody was clapping =

R: = Yeah.

Debby: And got emotional.

R: And what was Martin's reaction like?

Debby: He was shocked. Absolutely...

Of all instances of identity work presented in this volume, the extract above presents probably one of the most illuminating explanations why some consider identity as performative (Goffman 1959; Butler 1990). In their understanding, self is 'a signifying practice' (Butler 1990) which consists in one's selection of the pre-established, culturally available "imaginable and realizable gender configurations" (Butler 1990: 9). In the passage above, Debby constructs her non-traditional bridal identity relying on the highly conventional image of the groom, which the analysis in Chapter 3 found both explicitly and implicitly present in the discourse of wedding magazines. Despite the overall rejection of the major wedding convention concerning who should propose to whom, Debby puts a surprisingly strong emphasis on 'doing it properly'. Narrating her proposal, she employs widely available wedding repertoires, such as inviting family to the restaurant, proposing on the knee, fear of rejection and public humiliation.

As demonstrated in the critical analysis of bridal magazines, the dominant repertoires of wedding clearly demarcate the gendered fields of agency – while the proposal is the masculine form of agency, the one relegated to women consists in wedding preparations. Accordingly, in the same way Debby subverted the repertoire of proposal in her wedding experience, she used the one of wedding preparation to index her subversive bridal femininity:

Extract 3.13

R: And how did you prepare the wedding?

Debby: °To be honest Martin did most preparation.° ((laugh))

R: Really?

Debby: ((laugh)) I mean, obviously, I had an impact on stuff and … But in terms of calling people, arranging the restaurant, booking the limo things like that … he did all that.

R: How did you feel about it?

Debby: I was very pleased and I'm lazy and unorganized, I mean, I can do it, I am perfectly capable of doing it, but if somebody wants to do it for me, they're more than welcome. ((laugh))

Debby's non-traditional bridal self takes shape when she talks about Martin's commitment to wedding preparations, which, following dominant wedding discourse, constructs him as taking on the traditional feminine role. That Debby consciously relates to the discourse is evident in how she marks the unconventionality of this arrangement with laughter, lower speech volume and the apologetic formulation "to be honest". This also indicates Debby's unspoken assumption that the interviewer will find what she says surprising.

Debby was not only aware of the notion of a 'traditional bride' but also of how she was interactionally constructed as such:

Extract 3.14

Debby: = and people are happy for you =

R: = So you could have felt a bit like a princess in that way…

Debby: Well, sort of, yes, because, you know, it still was a puffy dress, and, you know, people start to treat you like, you know… "Oh be careful, don't mess your hair" ((mocking)) or "your shoes"… ((mocking))

R: Why are people so focused on the bride?

Debby: Because it's just tradition, something that almost happens from being a young girl, you know…

R: Mm.

Debby: Young girls dress in pink fairy-tale outfits and, you know, I've been seeing people, like, "Oh you're so beautiful, you're a princess". ((mocking))

R Mm =

Debby: = And they do a little dancing stuff and they love it.

Recalling her wedding day, Debby brings the voices of the significant others who hailed her as the 'princess'. As at other points of the interview, she turns to mockery, most probably to disclaim the ownership of the identity that she was ascribed in that moment. Also, in the extract Debby takes the subject position that she adopted at several points in the interview when claiming her awareness of the arbitrariness of the existing gender order and lack of emotional relationship to it. Here, constructing little girls as the objects of gaze and gender socialization, Debby implies their fondness of it. This renders a clear ideological contradiction in Debby's identity work. After all, such an assumptive and impassive relationship with the matter is incongruous with how she worked at other points of the interview to maintain the subject position of a woman who finds the available model of femininity constraining and defies it.

Debby evidently positioned herself as a non-traditional bride also in the reconstruction of the wedding ceremony:

Extract 3.15

R: So what was your wedding like?

Debby: It was a Las Vegas wedding. We went for the Elvis package ((laugh)) °and everything°.

R: And what did it consist of?

Debby: It was at the … I think, °Graceland Chapel° we got picked up in a limo, to be honest it was very much like in Las Vegas, those Las Vegas weddings are, like, combo, it's like fifteen minutes' ceremony and that's it, it's like "<bang, bang, bang">This mom leaving and this mom waiting to come in, it's just constantly, but, yeah, it was lovely … We still did the little walk down the aisle. ((changes the tone into subtle and dreamy)) My mom gave me away and, you know, he ((Martin, the groom)) spoke really nice words and stuff, exchange of rings =

R: = Mm

Debby: And you know we had the Elvis wedding. ((laugh)) He sang two Elvis songs which we had picked, and then he finished and it was, like, really … My mom was dancing, he was, like, do the exchange of vows, and then he, went into a song and, like, everyone dancing, and, you know, happy, clapping and °it finished really nice°.

In the extract, Debby draws on the popular imagery of extravagant weddings. That she is orienting to widely shared images of a wedding celebration can be seen in the deictic definite pronouns (*"the* Elvis package", *"those* Las Vegas weddings", *"the* little walk"), as well as in the enumeration of loose formulations which sometimes takes on an almost telegraphic style. Though brief and seemingly not very informative ("much like in Las Vegas", "exchange of rings", "went for this Elvis package"), they are meaningful to anybody conversant with the media imagery of extravagant and celebrity weddings. Debby constructs her identity of a 'Las Vegas bride' by deploying the indexical elements of the scenery of the non-traditional wedding ("got picked up in a limo", "Las Vegas weddings are like combo"). The identity is indexed not only by the specific esthetic, which contrasts with the esthetic of the 'white wedding', but also by Debby's expressions of her rather nonchalant attitude to the event (for instance, the somewhat slack mention of the name of the venue) and by the emphasis on the speediness and care-freeness of the ceremony ("fifteen minutes' ceremony", "<bang, bang, bang> This mom leaving and this mom waiting to come in"). As in the previous extracts, it can be seen, however, that Debby to some extent submits also to the traditional bridal identity in the constructions of herself enjoying with the guests the romantic, sentimental moments ("we still did the little walk down the aisle", "exchange of rings", "he spoke really nice words").

In Extract 3.16, Debby continues the subversive positioning when she talks about her choice of the wedding dress:

Extract 3.16

R: And what was your dress like?

Debby: It was quite traditional everyone says ((laugh)), but it was green and it wasn't like a wedding dress.

R: Why?

Debby: I guess, again, just to be different. I mean, I did try on real wedding dresses but they, you know, they were nice in the mirror but I don't suit white color anyway, I'm quite pale. ((laugh))

R: Mm.

Debby: But I did want just to be different. It was a Las Vegas wedding and I wanted to try something different and because I have never really wanted to get married, I didn't have the dream of the big white dress and...I had two children. I thought if I see one that you know...maybe, but I didn't really.

R: So why didn't you have all these images of you in your wedding dress?

Debby: Maybe our culture would say that, that it's because my parents got divorced, but my sister dreams of a white wedding...I suppose it's a li:tle bit that half of it which is not a big fairy tale, you know, not necessarily a big fairy tale, you know, it kind of can end in tears and stuff =

R = Mm

Debby: I don't know really...

The extract above shows that the wedding dress was another indexical resource of Debby's identity work. In the sequence, she is orienting to the traditional notion of the bride, which is evident in how she asserts that the dress was not traditional ("It was quite traditional everyone says...but it was green and it wasn't like a wedding dress"), as well as in how she elaborates on the reasons why she wanted "something different". The culturally established symbolic role of the white wedding gown offers some potential for self-construction – Debby takes advantage of the potential somewhat iconoclastically by drawing of the spectacle of the non-traditional Las Vegas wedding.

Debby's constructions of her bridal looks demonstrate, thus, in what sense women's experience of their body is implicated in the discourse of gender. As discussed in Chapter 2, women perceive and transform their bodily appearances in relation to textually mediated images. In reference to wedding discourse this means that the choice of the dress is a social practice developed in relation to the textual and visual representations of the bride. Debby's constructions of her wedding gown bear some similarities to the constructions of 'trashing the dress' in the "Wedding file debate"; as such, they explain her involved reader positioning when she related to the article.

Still in reference to Extract 3.16, the way in which Debby narrated her wedding has much in common with the ways in which weddings were found to be constructed in the genre of real-life weddings. Although she did not overtly identify herself as a consumer of any of the wedding media, in the extract above she submits to the popular wedding discourse. Referring to commodities and services in the construction of the 'Las Vegas spectacle', Debby assigns them symbolical and identity-constructive meanings. Importantly, still in the same extract, Debby talks about her wedding from the subject position of a daughter of divorced parents. This self-disclosure sheds a new light on her skeptical relationship with the media discourses of wedding, which, after all, regurgitate the symbolic "big fairy tale" and thus make evident how isolated the discourses are from people's lived experience.

Finally, during the conversation, Debby positioned herself in yet another way that can also be regarded as illuminating the way in which she negotiated her subjectivity in the interview. In one moment, Debby quitted the subject position of a carefree bride:

Extract 3.17

R: So how did it feel to come back to everyday life?

Debby: Um, yeah, I suppose, 'cause everyone says, like, "How does it feel to be married", "How does it feel to be a married woman" ((mocking)) and I was just, like, "great". ((laugh)) I didn't know what to say, like, to be honest with you, it felt the same, I did feel sort of, I can feel with the r:ing that sort of com- that sort of u:nion, like, that type recognized by law or whatever, like, you know, but basically speaking I obviously felt pretty much the same apart from ... older. I felt a little bit older.

R: Older? Why?

Debby: I'm a married woman, I'm Mrs. I had to admit that, you know, with two children it would do, but it was the marriage that I found myself putting a nail in the coffin of my youth and ((laugh)), you know, I'm not the young girl anymore ...

R: Wow, just like that? Overnight?

Debby: Pretty much yeah! ((laugh))

In the extract above, Debby constructs herself as a woman in whom the awareness of passing time evokes distress. Bearing this in mind, it can be claimed that by positioning herself as a spontaneous and care-free bride, Debby coped with her age insecurities. Denying the ownership of the traditional bridal identity she might have worked to detach herself from the dominant femininity, which is particularly troubled by the issues of aging. In that case, the reader subjectivity Debby established, like the bridal subjectivity worked up in narrative reconstructions, may have been used strategically – to project a subversive identity deflecting from her what Debby believes to be people's perception of a married ('older') woman. Finally, both the self-disclosure in the extract above and what she above said about her parents' divorce concern the social and emotional experiences that accompany getting married and marriage but are not discussed in wedding magazines. This, therefore, is yet another way in which Debby's accounts of her lived experience enable a better understanding of the reader subjectivity that she worked up in the interview.

Concluding, a substantial part of the discussion above concerned the subject positions that did not directly concern Debby's reception of the magazine. Despite their indirect relationship with the media discourse, how the interviewee positioned herself in the accounts of bridal experience shares some similarities with her relationship with the discourse of bridal magazines. Talking about both her wedding and the prompt texts, Debby showed her reflexivity of the surrounding discourses as well as defied her compliance with the gender order that they reproduce. Nonetheless, even though Debby recognized the media discourse as oppressive, she reproduced it too. This was particularly evident in her discursive relation to the bodily self.

Interpellated to the gendered position of a bride, Debby employed some subversive strategies. Nevertheless, although her self-accounts were supposed to challenge gender binaries, Debby reinforced them because she defied her affiliation with normative femininity by drawing on the normative notion of masculinity. Consequently, the stronger she pronounced her rebellious feminine self, the more intensely she essentialized women. This was also apparent in her habitual reliance on the repertoire of being unlike other women. The use of mockery helped her to disavow a close affinity with her gender group but at the same time construct traditional femininity as a negatively valued social identity. Discourse-wise, because she drew on two mutually reinforcing discourses – one of dominant femininity and one of hegemonic masculinity – their available repertoires and meaning structures did not allow Debby to index her subjectivity otherwise than along the lines of dichotomous gender. Finally, how she defied the stereotypical femininity is interestingly related with the ways in which the femininity is used to construct the bridal subjectivity in wedding magazines.

Suki

Suki, a 29-year-old, was going to get married one year following the interview. Her family came to the UK from China. Her fiancé was also British-Chinese. After getting her university degree, she started working as a transport planner. She did not claim any religious denomination. Suki was invited to the interview for two reasons. Firstly, one of the aims of this part of research was to obtain information on how the media's ostensibly Eurocentric bridal imagery is related to by women of non-white ethnicities. Secondly, she was one of the women who claimed not to read women's magazines, and whose voices were included in the study to obtain a wider spectrum of subjectivities emergent from the reception of bridal magazines. Contrary to the consistency underlying text reception patterns, Suki established a complex bridal subjectivity in the accounts that were not directly related with the media frame. The aim of the discussion below is to demonstrate in what sense comparing these two sets of data has enriched the analysis of the interviewee's media reception.

In Extract 4.1, Suki is asked about the editor's letter (see pp. 56–59):

Extract 4.1

R: 'Celebrate your style'... How do you understand this?

Suki: Celebrate your style? Um:... probably... um:, just... you know... Do what you like and not what you think you should....

R: Mm, do you celebrate your style in anyway?

Suki: Yeah, definitely.

R: How?

Suki: Well, ... ((laugh)) I wouldn't buy something that I didn't like...

R: Um

Suki: Um:... So when I bought the wedding dress, I bought the wedding dress that I liked and not something everybody else likes.

R: And on a regular basis?

Suki: Well, I don't really follow fashion.

R: Mm

Suki: Um you know... you know when you get like, um, if you get, like, every season you get some skinny jeans or something like [that].

R: [Mm]

Suki: If I don't like them, I don't buy them and if they're uncomfortable I won't buy them either. ...

R: And does your wedding reflect your style?

Suki: Yeah, sure.

R: How?

Suki: How? Well, it's not really big and lavish, like other people's weddings, it's just something small and intimate, it's just something...

R: But going to such an exotic place must be quite expensive...

Suki: Yeah...but, um...my fiancé would rather spend money on something small that he really wants =

R: = Mm

Suki: Instead of something really big and what everybody else wants.

Initially, Suki makes no reference to consumption when she explains her understanding of what it means to 'celebrate one's style'. Elaborating on it, however, she follows the underlying idea of the article by equating personal freedom ("do what you like") with the freedom of consumer choice ("I wouldn't buy something that I didn't like"). The way Suki formulates her conception of style in the sequence might have been contingent on her interpretative involvement with the prompt text – perhaps without the text she would have defined it in another way. Still, in Althusserian terms, in the specific context Suki was hailed by the magazine's discourse. Apart from upholding its ideological code, she did not note the ultrafeminine code of the article, neither did she object to the tight concentration of commodities enumerated by its author as bridal essentials.

Like all participants, Suki was asked about the "Gossip file" (see p. 106) and the website where women are instructed how to walk in high heels:

Extract 4.2

R: Mm ... Did you pay attention to this article?

Suki: I don't think I read that ... I wouldn't walk in stilettos. ((laugh))

R: Would you go to this website?

Suki: Yeah! Maybe. Probably I would 'cause I can't walk in high heels and if I really had to walk in high-heeled shoes, then I probably would have a look.

Once she gets the main sense of the text from the headline, Suki expresses her approval of it. On the one hand, she hence tacitly accepts the discourse of the disciplined female body on which the whole idea of the article is premised. On the other hand, she claims she is not even going to wear stilettos at her wedding. In terms of the Althusserian logic of hailing, this renders extract above inconclusive – Suki accepts the obviousness of the gender discourse but she does not subscribe to it in the accounts of her lived practices of self.

Similarly, her lived bridal experience (specifically, lack of involvement in any of the media-constructed forms of body discipline) was the premise on which she constructed the uninvested reader subjectivity in Extract 4.3:

Extract 4.3

R: ((flipping through the magazine)) Okay, um, then, we have, like, a whole lot of beauty tips.

Suki: Mm.

R: Do you think brides find them useful in any way?

Suki: Um: ... ((looking at the article about perfumes)) I think when you're gonna buy a perfume, probably, I wouldn't, I don't really wear perfumes anyway.

R: = Mm

Suki: But probably I wouldn't buy a perfume especially for a wedding.

R: [Mm]

Suki: ['Cause], I mean, if you're gonna, people who wear perfumes, you know, I'm really picky about perfumes, you see.

R: Mm

Suki: So even when I do buy them I hardly wear them.

R: Mm

Suki: And I can't imagine buying a perfume just for a wedding day.

R: What about other tips?

Suki: I suppose make-up and hair are important...

R: Mm

Suki: And and hair...

R: Mm, why?

Suki: Well you want to look nice at your wedding =

R: = Mm

Suki: And the photos, you know, that you see in the future.

R: Mm, and 'the beauty countdown'...

Suki: Mm

R: Is there any other way for you to get your looks ready for the day?

Suki: Um:...um:...well, I don't know, yeah, I guess so...Maybe if I had a dress that's really fitted and then you don't wanna put on weight, so that you fit in, um, and then, um...

R: Okay. And that's pretty much everything you've been planning to do?

Suki: I suppose shave my legs before. ((laugh)) I don't know, I have never really thought about it.

R: Mm

Suki: Um, I would probably hire a hairstylist.

R: Mm

Suki: And if I didn't have a hairstylist, I would think how, about how I would cut my hair and how I would do my make-up.

Suki indexes her distance from the magazine's discourse of the bridal body by means of the conditional mood ("would") and hedging devices ("maybe", "I guess so", "I don't know", "well", "I suppose", "probably"). Her detachment from the discourse is also indexed by the generic 'you'. The pronoun constructs Suki's actions and feelings as natural and shared, nothing that should be taken as her own initiative or personal preference. Although while talking about the beautification of the bridal body, Suki constructs it as the object of gaze, in her reference to the pictures "that you see in the future" the bride is the 'beholder'. In contrast to the magazine's repertoires of commodified, disciplined bridal beauty, she does not construct the body as the object of meticulous, systematic care or specialist knowledge. Moreover, Suki does not initiate new topics at that moment. Talking about her wedding preparations, she does not go beyond the page she is looking at a given moment – these are subsequently articles about perfumes, hairstyle and make-up. Unlike other interviewees, who initiated polemical positioning, Suki does not raise (neither here nor elsewhere in the interview) the issue of the unattainable beauty standards reproduced by the media.

Suki gave no indication of being affected by the media's imperative of the perfect (bridal) body. She did not articulate at any point of the conversation dissatisfaction with her appearance. For instance, in the extract above she indeed mentions the issue of weight, but in a way unlike the interviewees who expressed their concern with the media discourse. That is, Suki seems to approach it purely pragmatically, in terms of fitting in the dress, while Debby and Mary constructed their weight insecurities in terms of 'size 10', thus the standard 'skinny' size (Cara also talked about fitting in her gown but associated it with her fiancé's gaze).

Therefore, similarly to what was found in Extract 4.2, in terms of what Althusser claimed about hailing, Suki's positioning in Extract 4.3 does not lend itself to a straightforward explanation. Lack of oppositional positioning could be considered as Suki's submission to the magazine's discourse. Yet, the discourse does not mediate Suki's accounts of her practices of self, which demonstrates how vital it is to regard media consumers as both 'subjects-in-discourse' and 'subjects of their actions' (D. Smith 1990). The interview with Suki, more than any other conducted in this study, shows the analytical value of this distinction and the uneasy relation between the two forms of subjectivity. Of course, in research interviews the relation between discourse practice and social practice can only be assessed through participants' self-accounts. Therefore, it can only be speculated whether Suki did not produce any critical resistance to the discourse of the magazine because she did not find it problematic or because she did not want to elaborate on it.

Nevertheless, lack of overtly critical engagement with media discourse may not necessarily mean that Suki was unaware of the sociocultural codes underlying the prompt texts. For example, this can be seen in the extract below, where she is asked about an advertisement exploiting the rhetoric of fairy tales:

Extract 4.4

R: Yeah, and did you pay any attention to this ad here?

Suki: Yeah!

R: So what do you make of it?

Suki: Well … it's … quite nice …

R: What do you like about it?

Suki: Um … I don't know. It doesn't make me want to have a wedding there.

R: Um, "it's a fairy-tale beginning get married in a style to which you would like to get accustomed to, a fairy-tale wedding in an exclusive and enchanting [place]"

Suki: [Um] …

R: "where dreams come true and memories are made" …

Suki: It's a bit corny.

R: Why?

W: I know they make it sound like it's a fairy tale but in reality life is not that simple. You know what I mean. It's like...

R: Um, 'cause to me it sounded really girlie and innocent =

Suki: = Mm...

R: So I was wondering what actual brides make of it...

Suki: I'm not a very good expert in myself. ((laugh))

Initially, Suki reads the text solely as an advertising piece and takes no issue with its underlying assumption that every woman dreams of a fairy-tale wedding. Later on, when a few lines of the text are read aloud by the interviewer, she recognizes the text as "a bit corny" because of its reliance on the unrealistic imagery of a fairy tale. As can be observed from the subsequent turns in the extract, this observation is elicited by the interviewer – most probably Suki makes the effort to show that she understands the dominant code of the text because she considers it as the interviewer's expectation. Still, she consistently negotiates her subject position of an ideologically uninvolved reader – she cuts the conversation saying, "I'm not a very good expert in myself". Therefore, Suki's positioning in the extract is powerful in two ways. For one thing, despite the traditional allocation of roles in research interviews, as an interviewee she negotiates the direction of the interaction. For another, she manifests her awareness of the code and rejects it as incompatible with her lifeworld discourse.

Suki continued her uninvested positioning when the issue of the magazines' ethnic bias was raised:

Extract 4.5

R: Mm...as a Chinese girl, do you feel like there should be more Chinese models in the magazines?

Suki: No, not really. It doesn't really bother me, no. No, no...

R: But in terms of, say, make-up tips...

Suki: Yeah, well, I've found since I was very young that when you look into the magazines, you know, like, women's magazines =

R: = Yeah

Suki: The make-up tips, they're not always, cause we look a bit different, we have different eyes and color maybe, so I've learnt really not to pay attention to it.

R: Mm

Suki: So I look on the Internet and I look for Asian eyes, you know, they say there's an eye make-up for Asian [eyes]

R: [Mm]

Suki: And I look at that, but, you know, these magazines, none of them are catered towards other races.

R: And it really doesn't bother you in any way?

Suki: Um, I mean probably they want to cater towards the majority of people.

R: Mm

Suki: And we are not the majority. Same way, if I went to Hong Kong and bought a magazine, the make-up tips in there would be full of Hong Kong people, Chinese people and you wouldn't get any of English people. I wouldn't, I mean, it's just a fact of life.

In the sequence, Suki is hailed into the subject position of a member of an ethnic group underrepresented in the popular media. She accepts the position by assuming the group identity of Chinese people (shifting to the plural pronominalized subject 'we'). Although from this position she could have reproached the magazine for its ethnic bias, Suki shuns engaging in an anti-racist polemic. Similarly to what was seen in Extract 4.4, Suki does not disclaim her awareness of what could potentially be regarded as problematic, but she does not use the opportunity to engage herself with critical discourse.

Nonetheless, in the same passage, having acknowledged that some parts of the magazines are useless to Chinese consumers, Suki emphasizes she has "learnt really not to pay attention to it". By constructing her indifference as a practice developed over time ("so I've learnt really not to pay attention to it"), Suki takes an agentic and powerful position in relation to the media's discriminatory discourse. Likewise, saying that she "looks for the Asian eyes" on the Internet, she does not adopt the passive subject position of someone who is not provided with necessary instructions but positions herself as a person who can find them on her own. Moreover, Suki rejects the position into which she was interpellated when she positions herself as a member of the 'majority'. Namely, she inverts the relations between Chinese and white people by pointing out that in Hong Kong similar magazines "would be full of Hong Kong people". Capping that with a note that "it's just a fact of life", Suki reinforces the position from which she consistently acknowledged her reflexivity but denied involvement in any form of critical practice. Seen in this way, how Suki dealt with the media's ethnic bias can be regarded as her 'tactic of resistance', even though it by no means resembles an overt criticism of racist media.

Suki took the subject position of an invested reader by selecting the parts of the magazine she found interesting. These were readers' letters, the honeymoon destinations section and the fashion file. The author of the letter in the prompt magazine wrote about her mother's objections to excessive wedding expenses:

Extract 4.6

R: And... "Emotional rescue"? Have you read it?

Suki: Yeah I have read that.

R: Why?

Suki: Seemed really interesting.

R: In what ways?

Suki: I think... was it the... the mother who says that her daughter is spending too much money on the wedding?

R: Mm.

Suki: And I do kind of agree with that.

R: Mm.

Suki: Because I think it's just one day and unless you've got loads and loads of money I don't see why you should spend thousands of pounds, I mean... spending 20 thousand pounds on wedding is enough to pay deposit for the house, which is a lot more useful than on a wedding.

R: Mm, and do you usually read advice columns and readers' letters?

Suki: Yeah, I read it when the letter sounds interesting. <Yeah, yeah>...

R: And do you follow the advice given there?

Suki: Yeah, sometimes.

R: Do you pay attention to who gives the advice?

Suki: No, I don't really pay attention to who they are.

R: And are such family issues, like, typi-

Suki: Yeah, I think so, yeah.

R: So are there any family issues around your wedding?

Suki: Not really... My dad... He's been really... well, he, he... When my sister got married =

R: = Mm

Suki: She was the first of our generation to get married and so there was a lot, we've got a lot of relatives, and so they came and were very particular about "Oh, you have to do this, you have to do that" =

R: = Mm

Suki: And then, and then, and so and we've got to, and now there have been a few weddings and not all of them have done those things =

R: = Yeah

Suki: And don't seem bothered anymore...

R: What would you do if your father did try to impose something on you?

Suki: Well, um, probably if he wanted to do something, he, it would be probably to have the Chinese banquet for all the relatives... But then if we did that, we couldn't get married abroad.

The sequence is unlike the ones presented so far in terms of the number of exchanges made, the length of Suki's subsequent responses as well as the extent of the interviewer's contribution. The conversation gained some impetus, probably because Suki found the reader's letter relevant to her own experience. Positioning as one of the sides in the disagreement indicates Suki's involvement in 'comparison reading' (Currie 2001), hence a discourse practice in which the textual reality and lived experience entwine (cf. also interview with Mary, p. 137). The fact that Suki read and discussed the article in more detail provides a clue about how to interpret her other, mainly uninvolved, reader positionings. As could be seen, she did not eagerly talk about particular texts in *You & Your Wedding*. In Extract 4.6, however, she demonstrates genuine interest in the advice as well as acknowledges she sometimes follows this kind of guidance. This may mean that she did not read (or did not want to discuss) other texts not due to her neglectful attitude to the interview or absolute rejection of media discourse but because they were irrelevant to her lived experience of getting married.

That Suki related to the reader's letter more personally is understandable given its topic of wedding expenses and the concern with money that she repeatedly expressed throughout the interview (for example, when talking about trashing a wedding dress, wedding expenses, the prices of women's magazines and the costs of raising children). Suki's accounts of wedding preparations were detailed and she was noticeably happy to talk about them at length. In doing so, she ascribed herself a lot of agency but never did she position as a 'project-manager superbride'. Instead, Suki built her accounts of wedding preparations from the shared position of 'we', hence constructing her fiancé as equally involved in the process:

Extract 4.7

R: Can you first tell me a bit about your wedding?

Suki: We're going to get married, we'd supposed to get married in ... 'cause my boyfriend's mother says it's unlucky to get married next year and I'd planned to get married next year =

R: = But why is it unlucky?

Suki: Chinese calendar and stuff ((laugh)), something to do with the Chinese calendar and how, I'm not sure actually, but I think she said there's only, there's no summer next year in the Chinese calendar, but I don't really know what that means, [so]

R: [But] did you take that into consideration?

Suki: Yeah, yeah.

R: Why?

Suki: I don't know. Well...

R: Ok, so about your wedding =

Suki: = My wedding, well ((excited)), we're going to get married abroad, you see, and we thought we wanted to get married in the Maldives, you see, but since the Maldives is a Muslim country, you can't actually get married there, unless you're Muslim. But they do ceremonies, you know, like a blessing, you know, vows type of thing, and so we're going to get married here. Probably just the two of us, and then next year in the spring we're going to the Maldives with our family, close family, to have a ceremony there.

R: And why did you decide to do it that way?

Suki: Um, well, um, at first we wanted, like, ((to)) do it next year, somewhere like in Mexico but we're not going to Mexico, and then, I mean, I suppose it just fitted in with what everybody wanted. I mean, I don't know, it just seemed the best way to keep everyone happy.

R: Then why not a traditional wedding?

Suki: My fiancé doesn't...The thing is that in the Chinese weddings ((laugh)) the most important bit is, like, the banquet, Chinese banquet, and that's where your parents invite everybody that they know [practically].

R: [Parents?]

Suki: Yeah, in the Chinese culture the parents are really important when you get married and so what usually happens is that the parents invite a lot of people to a Chinese restaurant for meal and it's really busy, and we both really didn't want to do that.

In Suki's identification practices, both the Chinese calendar and Chinese banquet worked indexically, as culturally specific symbols of the tradition that she did not want to follow in her wedding celebration. In Extract 4.7, Suki's dis-identification with the Chinese wedding tradition is constructed by means of epistemic stances indexing her tentative knowledge of it ("Chinese calendar *and stuff*", "I *don't* really *know* what *that* means", "I'm *not sure* actually"). Also, Suki seems to be constructing an implicit contrast between the intimacy of the wedding ceremony she has chosen (the emphasis "with our family, *close* family") and the scale of traditional Chinese weddings ("parents *invite a lot of people* in Chinese restaurant for meal and *it's really busy*", "that's where your parents *invite everybody that they know* practically"). Suki's wedding is constructed as an effect of compromise ("*it just fitted in* with what everybody wanted", "it just seemed the best way to *keep everyone happy*"). Although this consequently helps Suki to constitute a powerful subject position, there are some indications of her doubts and anxieties as to how the compromise was worked out. For instance, asked about reasons for which her fiancé and she did not want a traditional wedding, Suki initially ascribes agency only to him and comes back to the joint subject position only after providing some accounting work.

Clearly, in her constructions of wedding preparation, Suki positioned herself as a person in charge of the whole process. Yet, this positioning pattern was discontinued when she was asked about more general aspects of wedding culture. These were raised in the conversation naturally, as it progressed, when specific elements of the dominant wedding discourse were read from the magazine pages. To illustrate, at one point the interviewer referred to the notion of wedding as the 'big day':

Extract 4.8

R: Why do so many people call it the [big day]?

Suki: [Big day]...because...I guess...They are the most important days in their lives.

R: Why?

Suki: Um...because they made a commitment to spend the rest of their lives together.

R: Is that the way you see it?

Suki: Um...I guess so. Well, one of the most important days of my life.

R: So what are the other days?

Suki: Other days? Um:...I've never really thought about important days of my life. ((laugh))

R: Mm

Suki: Graduation? Um: yeah...I don't really know...

Suki's explanation of the idea of the 'big day' is unlike the accounts she provided when talking about wedding organization. Here, asked about the repertoire of wedding being the 'big day', she refers to another one – that marriage means a life-long commitment. Yet, when she is next asked about her personal attitude to this, Suki qualifies her earlier statements emphasizing that to her it is "one of the most important days" and she finds that point difficult to expand on.

In Extract 4.9, Suki employs the repertoire of tradition to explain people's attitude to marriage:

Extract 4.9

R: So where do you think people get their ideas of marriage from?

Suki: I think it's just tradition. I don't know, I think...

R: What do you mean by 'tradition'?

Suki: Um, I think when two people have been together and when they think they've gonna be together for the rest of their lives, then, you know, they would naturally consider marriage...

In the sequence, Suki basically restates the interpretative repertoire of marriage as a life-long commitment. The interpretative repertoire that "it's just tradition" is immediately followed by Suki's disclosure "I don't know", which mitigates her commitment to the repertoire. As the extracts above illustrate, in the interview Suki used both statements regularly. The repertoire of 'tradition' reappeared when she talked about things that "naturally", "eventually", "probably" happen and about events that are going to take place because "it is just tradition", etc. Apart from the hedging formulation "I don't know", Suki used parallel qualifications such as "I guess", "I've never really thought about", etc. Also, she did not elaborate on the notion of 'tradition', unlike other interviewees who usually deployed some relevant repertoires of gender socialization, such as exposing children to fairy tales, gender preferences for the selection of toys, blue and pink colors, etc. A note that needs to be made at this point is that the way Suki related to the dominant heteronormative discourse bears some resemblance to how she related to the media's racist discourse – in both cases she maintained the position of ideological neutrality by claiming acceptance of 'facts of life', the way things 'naturally' happen, etc.

Of course, it cannot be ruled out that Suki decided to get married solely for the sake of tradition. Alternatively, however, the repertoire may have worked as Suki's fallback position on which she relied when asked to elaborate on the meaning of marriage. It might have been the case that Suki said "I don't know" or "It's tradition" not because she really had no idea what to say, but because she did not want to make personal confessions. Yet, as the conversation progressed, Suki exposed more intimate facets of her bridal experience. Although not directly relevant to her media practices, they cast an interesting sidelight on her way of relating to hegemonic discourses:

Extract 4.10

R: So how do you imagine your marriage?

Suki: Same to what's right now I think...

R: Are you afraid of anything?

Suki: I wouldn't say I am afraid of anything.

R: Mm

Suki: I suppose I'm a bit scared of having kids. ((laugh))

R: Scared? Why?

Suki: It's just... I don't feel responsible in the present moment, whereas in the future I probably would probably come round to the idea, yeah. Maybe when I get bit older, I'll think "Oh, I wanna have kids" but right now I don't. Not right now.

Asked about her anxieties before getting married, Suki admits of her insecurities concerning transition to motherhood, which she constructs as culturally expected from women at a certain age. In the sequence Suki refers to time by means of *extreme case formulation* (Pomerantz 1986). The multiple articulations of time ("in the present moment", "in the future", "right now", "not right now") underscore her sense of not being ready to be a mother. Suki deployed the repertoire of 'timely' motherhood regularly when accounting for her decision to get married:

Extract 4.11

R: And have you ever considered staying single?

Suki: Um, well... I always thought I <u>will</u> get married, at some point. Have some kids =

R: = Why?

Suki: I don't know, that's what usually happens... ((laugh)) I don't [know].

R: [What] do you think it feels like to be single?

Suki: Um, I think it's just uncertainty. Don't know because, I think women have their biological clock. If you're gonna have kids, you need to have them before you're 33. And so you have to think about what you want to do in the future, and you know, when you want to get married.

R: Do you want to have kids?

Suki: At some point, yeah. I think I want to have them in the future but not now.

The topic of singleness, initiated by the researcher, does not directly lead to the one of having children at the right time of life. Hence, the proximity of the two issues in Suki's accounts is noteworthy. As can be seen in Extracts 4.10 and 4.11, the interpretative repertoire of compulsory motherhood repeatedly accompanied Suki's constructions of her personal relation to marriage. In Extract 4.11, she draws on the normative conception of a family as a formally acknowledged relationship of a woman and a man who have children. Moreover, not only does she weave the two but she also constructs this as her own belief rather than an idea that extrinsically organizes her life ("*I always thought* I <u>will</u> get married, at some point. Have some kids"). Drawing on Wetherell's concept of 'personal order' (see p. 119), it could be considered that this demonstrates Suki's internalization of the 'dominant coupledom narrative'. This argument may be regarded by some readers as overly deterministic, but such implications cannot be discounted given how regularly Suki relied on the repertoire and that she constructed it as a belief which she has always held.

Considering Suki's general positioning patterns, it can be argued that through her extensive reliance on the pre-established discourses and repertoires, Suki constructed herself as someone with no options and of little self-reflexivity, regurgitating the 'truths' imposed on her by the society and culture in which she has been raised. Nevertheless, the intensity with which she seemed to be working on the repertoire of women's natural maternal instincts can be taken as indicative of Suki's enhanced self-reflection, her attempts to understand what she believes all women feel – the willingness and readiness to bear children. In her frequent employment of the traditional discourse of femininity, Suki may not necessarily feel disempowered by its overbearing 'truths' because she has internalized it and uses its repertoires as her own. For example, in the subordinate sentence structure "I *think* women have their biological clock" (Extract 4.11) Suki frames the repertoire as her own idea. The conceptual verb constructs Suki as the author of her opinions, a person in control of her thoughts and judgments.

Importantly, Suki came back to the repertoire of compulsory motherhood at another point of the conversation. Her first accounts of the reasons why she decided to get married (presented in the extracts above) were occasioned by the media-related talk. Additionally, after the interview, as the conversation went on, Suki came back to the topic of the decision. This time she constructed the decision as related to her family. The importance of the family was signaled at other points in the interview – for example, when Suki positioned herself to them by drawing on the opposition between the Chinese banquet and the destination wedding. Extract 4.12 is part of the narrative that Suki produced after the recording was back on and it is unlike what she had said before. As will be seen from the transcription, her speech was marked with irritation, which starkly contrasted with the emotional detachment at the earlier stage of the interview:

Extract 4.12

R: So did you feel like under pressure?

Suki: Oh yeah! When you're at Christmas gatherings and then everyone says "Oh, when are you going to get married, and are you gonna have kids?", and something like that.

R: I guess it happens in many families =

Suki: = Yeah and then everyone <u>asks</u>...

R: So how did you feel back then?

Suki: You just feel that I should get married, it's just pressure that...that...

R: So what would happen if you resisted that pressure?

Suki: Nothing really, 'cause, 'cause the first time my <u>aunties</u> had asked me and that was probably, like, 2 years ago, and they asked me every time they see us again, and then they <u>asked</u> and then more recently, my dad's been asking as well. And then maybe it's because I'm nearly 30 that I should get married.

R: So how would you feel during the gatherings if you stayed single?

Suki: Oh, I'd feel probably left out, not left out but...

R: Left out 'cause your twin sister is married?

Suki: No, no, no, actually I sometimes forget that she got married. ((laugh)) And maybe sometimes I feel like I'm really young and not old enough to get married. °I don't know...°

R: So maybe it's a bit too early for you?

Suki: Well, I don't think it's early. I'm 29 now but I just don't feel 29. I think that's the problem. ((laugh))

R: Why do you call it a problem? Isn't that great to feel young?

Suki: Y:eah...But it's just the responsibility and getting to the time when I'll have to decide whether I want to have kids and things like that.

R: And how do you think your fiancé and family would react if you decided not to have kids?

Suki: I think my future husband is scared of having children as well. But, um I don't know how they would react. But then...there's always the feeling "have I made the right decision not to have children", you know, when I'm 37 or something like that I regret it and it might be too late then. I mean I just feel that probably I <u>will</u> want to have kids in the future but I just don't feel ready at all yet. It's just the responsibility of having kids.

Suki enumerates more than one reason behind her decision to get married but it is unclear which of them was the most important – the family pressure, anxiety of being "left out" (hence, the status of a single woman) or the 'biological clock'. Despite this ambiguity, the issue of age seems to be overbearing in the extract. When Suki adds, "And then maybe it's because I'm nearly 30 that I should get married", she constructs family pressure as distinct from the sense of the biological clock ticking away. Such a way of differentiating between the family pressure and her own sense-making practices could be Suki's way of denying that she has been influenced by her relatives. The repertoire of the biological clock was therefore convenient at that point because she could construct it as her own reason to get married. However, to what extent this was a reason of her own making is not obvious. The categorical, generic construction "But then...there's always the feeling 'have I made the right decision not to have children'" presents an ambiguous construction of authorship. It remains unclear and highly impressionistic whether it was an implicit form of double-voiced discourse in her positioning or whether these were Suki's own sense-making practices. Nevertheless, here they evidently indexed the identity of a person who is the subject of her actions and decisions.

Concluding, on the one hand, data gathered in this interview, confirm Hermes's (1995) note that readers find media texts far less 'meaningful' than researchers in their analyses. On the other hand, it is posited here that the disregard of media's implicit discourses may render one vulnerable to their potential agendas. Therefore, this book contends, neither individuals' overt withdrawal from the discourses nor their apparent detachment from them is a sufficient premise upon which to claim that people are not affected by the media. Individuals' (declared or apparent) rejection of or indifference to media discourses needs to be verified. As could be seen in the current examination, both can be confirmed by the analyst indirectly. Suki's withdrawal from the media discourses was evident not only in the relationship that she established with the prompt texts, but also in how she handled the magazine's advertising and gender discourses, which was consistent with her apparent lack of involvement with the body discipline promulgated by the media. In this sense, both the discourse and social practices could be regarded as Suki's 'tactics of resistance' (de Certeau 1984).

Nevertheless, the findings should not leave readers of this book overly optimistic about individuals' capabilities of subversion. Like in the relationship that she constructed to media discourse, in her self-accounts Suki seemed to apply the same 'tactic' of maintaining a non-problematic relationship with dominant discourses. More specifically, she denied their power implications by positioning in the interviews as the author of the repertoires that the discourses reproduce. This was particularly notable in her regular deployment of the interpretative repertoire of a biological clock, which, when used in reference to women, appears a hybrid of the powerful discourses of medicine and patriarchy. In the analysis, this positioning pattern was considered as Suki's way of establishing an independent subjectivity. Of course, whether the agreement with the discourse is indeed an effect of a careful and self-reflexive consideration cannot be determined; in the same way it cannot simply be argued that Suki has fallen a 'victim' of the dominant discourses. However, given how troubled and inconsistent Suki's accounts became as the interview progressed, the impression that one may get from the conversation is that the 'tactic' that seemed to work in coping with media interpellations did not prove equally effective in dealing with the symbolic power of other discourses.

6
Reading a Magazine: Discussion

The interviews were analyzed one by one to acknowledge the complex psychological reality of text reception and of the accompanying identification processes. Yet, the ways in which the interviewees negotiated their subjectivities reveal some shared patterns that need to be singled out. The patterns were observed in the majority of interviews conducted for the purpose of the study. As has been mentioned, because in this book the depth of the analysis has been favored over its breadth, it meant the difficult decision of limiting the discussion to four (out of eleven) interviews. Yet, before the discussion proceeds, it needs to be emphasized that patterns referred to below were also found in the conversations not included in this volume.

What did they mean?

Because of what Benwell (2007: 541) refers to as "unknownability of intention and reception", the determination of the interviewees' reasons for taking specific positions was highly speculative. In the discussion, the reader subject positions have often been differentiated from the subject positions that the interviewees took in their personal narratives. The distinction proved analytically useful as it enabled the identification of both continuities and contradictions between the opinions that the participants expressed about *You & Your Wedding* and what they said in the moments when the magazine was not discussed.

In a study of text reception it would not be ungrounded to expect more analysis of what readers said about specific texts and less about their own experience and general outlooks. Still, no pressure was placed on the participants to delve into the prompt texts deeper than they chose to because this would have distorted the picture of the women's

185

actual reception of the magazine. Contrary to my initial expectations that they would make a special effort to read the prompt magazine more carefully because of the sense of obligation to the researcher, the interviewees read the magazine selectively. Apart from specific articles that attracted the women's attention, their involvement with the prompt magazine indicated an ambivalent, rather unabsorbed relationship with its content. The reception patterns identified in the study thus seem to confirm Hermes's cautionary note for researchers to avoid the assumption that "texts are always significant" (Hermes 1995: 148). The results corroborated what has been established so far about individuals' consumption of lifestyle magazines (Hermes 1995; Jackson et al. 2001; Benwell 2007; Gauntlett 2008) – they are first and foremost expected to provide light entertainment, and the reading of specific texts is supposed to be a non-absorbing, in-between activity rather than an intellectual exercise requiring increased cognitive and emotional effort.

Nevertheless, the conclusion that the participants found texts in *You & Your Wedding* 'meaningless' is offered here with the adequate reflection on how misleading their accounts might have been. This is not to claim that the women were intrinsically unreliable, but to note that talk is inherently ambivalent and intentional, and this complicates mapping meaning onto the form. After all, although the women did not discuss specific texts in great detail, reading *You & Your Wedding* might have in fact given them some authentic pleasure, or might have made them think much more than they claimed in the conversations. However, to admit that they enjoyed a given article or liked a specific picture would contradict their self-image or would work against the identity they intended to project in the interview. Also, the women might have chosen not to discuss their thoughts and feelings about the magazine at length because, for example, they did not consider them worth mentioning.

The interview data need to be considered in terms of what has been argued in this volume about media texts reception being a learnt cultural activity. The consumption of glossy magazines is considered here as a 'conceptual practice' (A. M. Smith 1988), which has been socioculturally recognized as a specific practice of femininity. Along these lines, it can be considered that the generic identity of the prompt magazine, highlighted by its hyperbolic, ultrafeminine style, might have affected the participants even before they had read anything (it might have generated some socioculturally informed associations). Moreover, it has been proposed in this book that people are subjects of various discourses and hence establish multiple, idiosyncratic meaningful connections between texts. Texts, D. Smith (1990: 3) argues, are not "inert extra-temporal blobs of meaning, the fixity of which enables the reader to forget the actual back and forth on the piece of paper in front of her". Therefore, the interviewees' relationship with every text and image in the prompt magazine needs to be regarded as a result of both general preconceptions about women's magazines and of the participants' idiosyncratic experience (for example, the memory of other texts).

Accordingly, the reason why the interviewees did not talk much about texts in the prompt magazine may have been to manifest their critical attitude to the media in general, which they have developed after reading, other women's magazines. With this assertion, the book does not subscribe to Hermes's (1995: 21) line of reasoning that "the apparent meaninglessness of much media can be explained in terms of routines rather than resistance". After all, the previous textual encounters might have left the women disappointed with the media genre of women's magazines to the point at which their subsequent disengagement with the genre indicates (unmarked) resistant positioning to the media discourses of gender. Additionally, Hermes's line of argument is problematized here also because it does not seem to observe that positioning people as research participants heightens their identity concerns. Because of that, what individuals claim about their relation to media texts may be to some extent affected by their self-reflexivity.

Construction of reader subjectivity

The first pattern identified in reference to the interviewees' reader positioning was that they rarely mentioned specific articles. Apart from Mary, who initiated text-based talk quite often, as well as demonstrated other forms of reader investment, the women were mainly first asked about particular texts (in the moments when the interviewer's reference to them did not obstruct the natural flow of the conversation). References to the prompt texts occasioned by their bridal narratives were relatively infrequent in the interviews. This might imply that the relevance of the magazine to their lived experience was marginal (but see discussion below).

The participants' self-accounts that were not directly related to the prompt texts are an interesting outcome of the interviews for a number of reasons. The self-accounts involved positioning either as a media critic expressing her opinion or as an individual talking about her lived experience. They occurred either independently or in connection with the text-based talk. Sometimes the interviewees deployed narrative accounts to justify their opinions on the media texts; occasionally the narratives led to a particular text. At some points, the autobiographic talk developed from 'comparison reading', as could be seen in the interviews with Mary and Suki. Interestingly, thus, Suki constructed a relationship between her lived and the textually created experience despite a relatively low personal investment in the media texts. Moreover, it needs to be taken into consideration that 'comparison reading', especially the one indicating dis-identification, could have been constructed by the participants implicitly. (Without stating that directly, they could have been narrating their bridal experience in a relationship of difference to the textual reality set up by the magazine.)

In the majority of cases, when asked if they had read a given text, the interviewees first interpreted its gist and expressed their individual opinions about it, or moved to the latter right away. A similar pattern of reader self-presentation has been identified by Benwell (2007: 544) among readers of men's lifestyle magazines who constructed themselves as distant from the magazine, but conversant with its discourse and approving some of its values. Still, unlike Benwell's interviewees, the ones in this study did not display their affinity with the values of the bridal magazine. In fact, at some points, it seemed that exposing the trashiness and superficiality of the world recreated on the pages of the magazine gave the women subversive pleasure. The oppositional mode of reception led the participants to insights that in many respects overlapped with the results of the critical discursive investigation. Of course, in the construction of their resistance the women used their own discursive strategies and resources. For instance, relating to the text about the website where brides can learn how to gracefully walk down the aisle in stilettos, Mary and Debby did not launch politically engaged diatribes. Yet, their laughter might have indexed their responses as dismissive, unwilling or subversive.

Generally, a cross-analysis of data presented in the critical discourse examination of the interviews and bridal magazines can be considered as a note cautioning against the text-centered approaches in which meaning is elicited from the formal features of texts. If text reception consisted solely in the decoding of its inherent meanings, all participants in the study would have interpreted articles in the magazine in the same way. This did not happen. For instance, most interviewees constructed a relationship of distance from texts in *You & Your Wedding* as well as from bridal and women's magazines in general. Nevertheless, they did not relate polemically to the same articles; when they did, the critiques often differed. Additionally, reader identity work varied from open, emotionally invested contestations to implicit subversions; it thus revealed a variety of subject positions from which the participants accounted for their criticism.

Moreover, differences in text reception were found to stem from the women's lived experience. For example, some interviewees referred to the iconicity of the bride, but the specific features of the icon that won their attention were unlike. Debby, who commented on the young age of models in the magazine, later disclosed her age insecurities; Mary, who referred to the models' size, talked about her weight concerns. Even though not groundbreaking, these observations make evident the idiosyncrasy of reading and the necessity of selecting methodologies that address the complexity of media reception. It can be seen from the data that media reception cannot be explained solely in terms of readers' ideological engagement with the texts, as implied in the encoding/decoding model. After all, although this piece of research has primarily looked into the ideological implications of reader subjectivities, the data revealed the affective patterns of reader involvement, which need to be accounted for as well.

Moreover, given the complexity of the participants' positionings, the encoding/decoding model, even if applied solely to the ideological level of text reception, may be too rigid. In general, the cross-examination of the subject positions that the interviewees took to texts in *You & Your Wedding* belied the crude binary of acceptance and rejection of a given discourse. Even those interviewees who manifested a relatively high awareness of being positioned by the discourse of the magazine at some points suspended their dispositional detachment and skepticism, mainly when they responded to readers' letters and the "Wedding file debate". In Chapter 3 it was demonstrated that such texts give the implied recipient an impression that there exists a community of women who turn to the texts for advice or to share their experience with other brides. In Chapter 5 it could be seen that not only Mary (the invested reader), but also the self-professed uninvested readers (Suki and Debby) either read the texts as presenting experts' valuable advice and credible information or they identified themselves with the authors of the texts.

Another important breakdown in reader subversion was identified in the interviewees' self-accounts that were indirectly related to the prompt magazine.[1] Namely, all participants were found skeptical of real-life wedding texts – especially their authenticity and their underlying consumerist ideology. In this sense, their embodied text reception paralleled my critical discourse analysis of the magazines. Nevertheless, when talking about their own wedding experience the interviewees reproduced the major idea on which the genre is premised – that weddings should express couple's lifestyle choices and identities. They constructed their weddings as "romantic utopias" (Illouz 1997: 26) organized without excessive reliance on commodities that the magazine presented as indispensable in the construction of modern romance. However, when narrating their weddings, the women did refer to some commodities and ascribed them symbolic meanings (for example, a green wedding dress, the Mexican band). Such self-accounts, thus, are instructive for the analysis of the interviewees' reader identity work. They indicate the proper amount of distance required in the analysis of the participants' subversive positioning to media discourse. By implication, they prompt an adequately suspicious approach to data in forming any conclusions about speakers' apparent rejection of specific social practices.

Apart from Cara, all interviewees in the study took some contradictory reader subject positions. As demonstrated, the uninvested readers (Suki and Debby) first openly criticized women's and wedding magazines as trashy and deceiving but at other points of the interviews constructed some articles as interesting and credible. Mary, who recognized herself as an avid reader of the magazines, mostly took the invested reader positions, but gave many indications of identity trouble which the investment in the magazines' discourse apparently meant to her. Identified among both the invested and uninvested readers, the incongruities in their relationship with the magazine can be regarded as suggestive of the inconsistent and dynamic nature of media reception.

Finally, the identity trouble that reader investment posed to both types of readers can be considered as indicative of their rhetorical orientation to talk. As mentioned earlier in this chapter, it needs to be considered that even if the women found some articles in the magazine appealing, being wary of the social perception of both exalted femininity and thought-less consumption of the popular media, they assumed the position of defiance. Nevertheless, the book proposes that this kind of identity trouble should not be seen as accompanying only the interview context. Individuals may be reluctant to acknowledge their actual relationship with media even to themselves as they might want to think of themselves as knowledgeable enough to defend themselves against the 'brain-washing' that the media are infamous for in the popular discourse.

Clearly, the relationship between the prompt media texts and the participants' locally negotiated subjectivities was identified by means of a detailed analysis of both the written and the oral data. This research project was devised with the specific idea in mind – to account for reception processes, analysts need to have a sufficient understanding of the texts which are received, rather than focus solely on the examination of the textual, affective or ideological mechanisms of text interpretation. By not losing sight of the texts, analysts gain the opportunity of locating the processes in the embodied experience of reading. This, in turn, allows careful guesses to be made about the place of text reception in the wider context. For example, in this study the participants' loss of focus on the texts, rather than considered as an undesirable result, was taken as an indication of the subsequent steps in the analysis. It instructed me to focus on the interviewees' self-accounts and to compare them to what the women said when positioned as readers. Overall, supported by the discursive examination of the magazines, the analysis of the interview data provided some insight into the relationship of the magazines' discourse to the individuals' media and wedding practices.

Because the recruited participants were told that the study was primarily focused on wedding culture, that the wedding stories were told is understandable. But the volume of the autobiographic information provided was so considerable that it also needs to be pointed out. At the beginning of this chapter it was proposed that the difference in the volume of autobiographic and prompt-related talk was indicative of the marginal relevance of the texts to the interviewees' lived experience. Alternatively, rather than in terms of the media genre of the bridal magazine, this finding could be explained in terms of the genre of the interview. Bringing a person into the context of an interview, after all, can be considered as an invitation to autobiographic talk (see also Chapter 4). Interviews nowadays, especially ones in the media, spawn diverse forms of intersubjectivity between the interviewees, the interviewers and the implied audiences. With "life stories... everywhere" (Plummer 2001: 78), people have become intensely self-reflexive and intersubjective. In this sense, the women's talk would be more accurately explained by the arguments about the contemporary autobiographical society, or the culture of expert systems and the 'reflexive projects of the self' that valorizes introspection and communication skills.

Thus, the autobiographic information provided by the participants is also worth considering. Although it was not strictly related to the prompt texts, it definitely cast some light on the participants' relationship to the discourses that circulate not only in the media but also in the wider sociocultural circuits embracing people in their lifeworlds. As will be demonstrated below, this study indicates an uneasy relationship between the interpellations of recipients in their local encounters with media texts (for instance, when reading a magazine) and the interdiscursive interpellations in the mundane practices (by the discourses that permeate through our lifeworlds). The latter interpellations, because they are varyingly related to the media discourses, will be the object of the following part of the analysis. Therefore, in the discussion below I will seek to explore the role of the media-perpetuated discourses in the interviewees' sense- and self-making practices, that is, in the locally available constructions of their personal order(s).

Construction of gender subjectivity

Even though I sought to avoid 'leading questions', the socio-semiotic environment of the interviews was significantly gendered. Exposing the interviewees to the textual and visual representations of gender in *You & Your Wedding* meant putting them in what Sunderland and her colleagues called in their research 'gender critical points', that is to say, moments when one has to "do something about the particular gender representation" (Sunderland et al. 2002: 231). For example, the magazines' advice on perfecting one's body before the 'big day' positions an individual as both a magazine reader and a woman. Hence, accepting the whole 'big day' implicature means taking the subject position of a reader who is conversant with the magazine's discourse, and the subject position of a woman who embraces the gender discourse it represents. After all, to object to the magazine's emphasis on the bride's esthetic role and on the symbolic value of the wedding means to express disagreement with the gendered repertoires by means of which women are interpellated not only by the media.

Following this thinking, this study aimed to investigate the women's way of negotiating femininity by attending to their positioning to the media discourse of gender. The main argument developed in the first two chapters of the volume was that the media-based reproduction of knowledge is a form of symbolic power. The power consists in forging links between meanings and, consequently, fabricating subjectivities. The notion of subject associated with this perspective has been that of the subject who is unable to step outside the discursively reproduced 'regimes of truth'. As explained by Foucault (1982: 212), "[t]here are two meanings of the word subject: subject to someone else's control and dependence and to his own identity by a conscience and self-knowledge. Both meanings suggest a form of power which subjugates and makes subjected to." In other words, displaced from the position of knowing, people are unable to think, talk and act as independent subjects.

Still, the data gathered in this study complicate Foucault's notion of subjectivity. After all, the discussion in the previous chapter enumerated examples of participants' reflexive engagements with the media constructions of bridal femininity. Because of the variability and complexity of their positioning patterns, in the discussion below the interviewees' gender subjectivities are discussed in terms of *subjectivation* (Foucault 1982, 1988) and *subjectification* (Foucault 1985). *Subjectivation* implies that people are bound by pre-established identities, limiting their scope of self-construction. *Subjectification* (Foucault 1986) consists in the subversive acts of the subject, the attempts to transform the ready-made identities by defying the normative discourses of specific 'regimes of truth'. In this study, both mechanisms were identified.

Subjectification

The most popular practice of subjectification consisted in the interviewees' critiques of the media discourse of the female body. Notably, the critical analysis of bridal magazines in the previous chapter demonstrated that wedding magazines construct bridal bodies as "the objects of salvation" (Baudrillard 1998: 129). In their symbolic subversion of media discourse, the interviewees appeared to follow a similar pattern when they constructed their bodies as the sites of ideological struggle, which have "taken over that moral and ideological function from the soul" (Baudrillard 1998: 129).

The women confronted the media discourse of the female body mainly in their direct references to the media texts and the textually mediated images of the body. As for the latter, asked if they would like to have pictures of themselves similar to those in the magazine, some participants denied, others admitted they would, but next did some repair work (as could be seen in the interview with Debby). That being the object of gaze was a troubled subject position might seem surprising given the long-established tradition of considering the bride as the focus of attention and the source of spectators' esthetic pleasure. However, the acceptance of that position might have undermined the resistant subjectivities that the women might have sought to establish in the interviews. Another vital way of confronting the media's discourse of the 'perfect' bridal body was to first acknowledge one's involvement with it and then construct a strategic distance from the discourse, as could be seen in the interview with Mary when she did some mitigating work following the disclosure of body self-discipline.

Relating to texts in the magazine polemically, some of the interviewees drew on discourses that, based on the biographical information obtained from the participants, must belong to the discourse orders in which the women function on a regular basis. For instance, drawing away from the media discourse of femininity Cara extensively relied on the Catholic notion of gender. Such lifeworld discourses are considered here as part of the interviewees' intertextual, polyglossic identities. This, in turn, illustrates the role of intertextuality and hybridity in both text interpretation and the identification practices that the interpretation entails:

> People also establish their identities and their differences through the diverse ways in which they interpret texts, and more generally, incorporate them into their own practices. This can also be approached in terms of hybridity: different interpretations entail bringing different discourses to the interpretation of a text, creating in a sense a new, hybrid text which combines the text interpreted with the discourses that are brought to it in the process of reading. (Chouliaraki and Fairclough 1999: 14)

In Chapter 3, it was demonstrated that hybridity of media discourse can conceal the relationships of power. As can be seen from the interviews, interdiscursivity can be used by media consumers to resist the power. In the study the readers' lifeworld discourses allowed them a wider scope for negotiating their subjectivity in the magazine consumption. Deploying repertoires and subject positions inherent in the discourses, the interviewees belied some of the magazines' trivializing and reductive constructions of femininity and wedding experience.

For example, in the magazines a woman's life is basically divided into two periods – before and after the wedding. First, she spends long years dreaming of the day (after the proposal, as the 'wedding countdowns' suggest, time speeds up). All that can be learnt about her life after the wedding is that she lives 'happily ever after'. By contrast, Debby's and Suki's interviews revealed a more complex relationship between the moment of getting married and their experience of passing time. Cara rejected the magazines' notion of the commodified wedding with a bridal narrative mediated by the Catholic discourse. (She hence constructed it on her own terms – not from the subject position of a wedding or media consumer.) Another resource of subversive reading was double-voicing in Debby's strategic deployment of parody (yet, see discussion below for some qualifying remarks). Still another noteworthy practice of subjectification consisted in narrating one's experience of learning how to deal with dominant discourses (for example, Suki's relation to the media's race bias).

Moreover, it could be observed that one's affinity with the traditional discourse of femininity does not exclude developing a critical reflexivity to it. To illustrate, although Mary reproduced the hegemonic repertoires of gender, she acknowledged other discourses of femininity. She was able to work up an agentic subject position within the dominant gender discourse when she constructed her need to find 'the other half' as evidence of the self-reflexive practice of introspection and when she talked about getting married as a well-thought-out choice. (Whether this was indeed an expression of volition or an internalized heteronormative imperative cannot be determined by means of the methodology applied in this study.)

Clearly, thanks to their self-reflexivity and awareness of surrounding discourses, the women were able to position themselves in relation to the discourse of the magazine as independent subjects. By hybridizing disparate discourses and producing competing femininities, the interviewees presented their "potential for creating new types of subjective experiences" (Markula 2003: 102). Interpreting media texts, the women did their identity work in which they used specific subject positions, meaning structures and repertoires as available socio-discursive means of (gender) resistance. In this sense, the contestation of the discourse of *You & Your Wedding* can be considered as the participants' situated practices of subjectification.

The examples gathered to this point substantiate D. Smith's conception of the subject. As was explained in Chapter 2, Smith distinguishes between the 'subject-in-discourse' and the 'subject of one's actions'. The former – limited by the available sets of subject positions, socioculturally available interpretive repertoires and other socio-semiotic means of meaning construction – lacks agency. Yet, as a 'subject-of-her-actions', a woman is not an abstract, hypothetical subject (which has been widely assumed in the text-centered approaches to meaning) but a person who makes texts meaningful by contextualizing them in her lived experience.

The distinction proved insightful when the participants narrated their wedding experience. To illustrate, as has been mentioned, despite their censorious relationship to the magazines' consumerist discourse, all of them relied on the symbolical potential that has been vested in some commodities by popular wedding culture. Importantly, however, it needs to be noted how the dominant discourses and their meaning-making resources were organized by speakers in their talk. For instance, on the one hand, the women constructed themselves as the objects of gaze. On the other hand, the repair work that accompanied some of the constructions indicates their problematic relation to the position. Additionally, it was observed that although the interviewees claimed their emotional investment in their bridal appearance, the women had their own, more or less explicit, ways of distinguishing between their 'mundane' identities and who they *became* (or were going to *become*) on the wedding day. The constructions demonstrably showed in what sense bridal identity is a construct – negotiated and performative. This, in turn, suggests that analysts need to take notice of how differently 'media pleasure' is actualized in individuals' lived experience.

Evidently, the differentiation between the 'subject-in-discourse' and the 'subject of one's actions' is analogical with Foucault's distinction between subjectivation and subjectification. As such, this book posits, the notions of the subject can serve as analytical concepts in the studies of media reception, especially those which seek to contextualize it in the "situated in the actualities of...experiencing" (D. Smith 1990: 5). Last but not least, the patterns noted above substantiate Baxter's (2003, 2010) argument that subjectivity should be examined in terms of the possibilities of powerful positioning that are made available by the intertextual workings of discourses. The findings support the caveat she issues, that is not to "locate a group identified as silenced or oppressed as unambiguously powerless, such as female speakers within a patriarchal society" (Baxter 2002: 480). Analysts who avoid this assumption put themselves in a better position to find that (and why) "females are multiply located and cannot be dichotomously cast as powerless, disadvantaged or as victims" (Baxter 2002: 480).

Subjectivation

Subjectivation was particularly manifested in the participants' contradictory positionings. As has been proposed, the conspicuous and reductive hyperfemininity of the 'modern bride' might have led to their subversive reactions, which were particularly notable when they were directly asked about their relationship to women's magazines. During the conversations, however, the interviewees changed their subject positions and contradicted what they said at other points; incongruities were also found in the interviewees' accounts of their bridal experience.

For example, throughout the interview, Suki maintained the subject position of an ideologically uninvolved reader. She continued this uninvolved line of positioning in her self-accounts when she deployed some established interpretative repertoires without interrogating their relevance to her lived experience, or noting that they position her as powerless. Consequently, when articulating her anxieties, Suki did not talk about whether to get married and have children but repeatedly claimed that she should be ready to do it. In this sense, her reliance on the preexisting sense-making resources illustrates women's adverse location in the power-discourse nexus – how they have been "deprived of the narratives, or the texts, plots, or examples, by which they might assume power over their own lives" (Heilbrun 1988: 17). However, although reiterating the established repertoires Suki reduced her agency, it could be argued that she regained it by ascribing herself the authorship of some of them (when she constructed herself as someone who *considered* accepting them). In doing so, Suki defended herself from the potentially troubled identity of a woman who succumbed to family pressure. This, thus, bore a striking resemblance to how Mary talked about her dream of finding 'the other half'.

Cara, manifested a significant scope of agency in self-construction. In the interview she talked from the subject position of a highly self-reflexive Catholic. This allowed her to maintain a consistent line of uninvested reader positioning, even though she claimed that she had read some bridal magazines recommended by her mother. Cara relied on the Catholic discourse throughout the interview and maintained the subject position of someone who chose to subscribe to its inherent values at some point in life. Nevertheless, her constructions of personal autonomy could be considered debatable because the femininity that she enacted was constrained by the repertoires and subject positions reproducing an essentialist and patriarchal gender order, as could be seen in her constructions of spousal relations.

Debby's identity work was mediated by the discourse she apparently resisted – the hegemonic, essentialist discourse of gender. Orienting to the traditional concepts of gender, Debby indexed her resistant self as either masculine or 'non-traditionally-feminine'. It could be argued that she hence defied normative femininity. Yet, because Debby used a limited scope of subject positions and repertoires, what she basically did was relocate (and reproduce) the essentialist categories of masculinity and femininity. The recognition of her subversive positioning was, after all, contingent on the interviewer's consensual understanding of the normative concepts of masculinity and femininity. Consequently, indexing her subversive femininity by means of the interpretative repertoire of being unlike most women, Debby essentialized femininity of other women. Besides, by ascribing her intended self the antithetical qualities of traditional masculinity, she implicitly reinforced the androcentric view of femininity.

The ambiguities in Debby's and Cara's constructions of resistant subjectivity illustrate the challenge of establishing feminine subjectivity whose empowerment would be undisputable. The challenge can be explained in a way proposed by Weedon, namely, by noting the endurance of the relationship between any definition of femininity and hegemonic gender discourse. Following Weedon (1997: 83), the persistent referentiality restricts possibilities of resistance:

> even when we resist a particular subject position and the mode of subjectivity which it brings with it, we do so from the position of an alternative social definition of femininity. In patriarchal societies we cannot escape the implications of femininity. Everything we do signifies compliance or resistance to dominant norms of what it is to be a woman.

Simply, women remain anchored in the dominant gender paradigm in spite of their insubordination to its underlying discourses. Drawing on Weedon's argument, it could be argued that articulating her rejection of the media-reproduced femininity, Cara indexed her submission to another powerful (Catholic) gender discourse. By working up her subversive bridal femininity, Debby reinforced the patriarchal definition of it.

Many of the ideological dilemmas and contradictions between reader positioning and the self-accounts that were not (or were indirectly) related to the discussion of the prompt texts appeared when the women talked about body issues. Producing their resistance to the materials on beauty and fashion, all interviewees (except for Suki) criticized them as generating factitious consumer needs and forcibly argued against the unattainable beauty standards promoted in the media. Still, the media discourse of female beauty was reinstated in the women's self-accounts (for example through their reliance on the interpretative repertoire of the 'normative discontent', on which media draw when interpellating readers as consumers). Likewise, deploying the interpretative repertoire that 'it is important to look your best on your wedding day', the interviewees reproduced the magazine's notion of a picture-perfect bride who should arouse esthetic pleasure.

Interestingly enough, constructing their bridal experience as lived through the creation and exposition of an appropriate bridal appearance, the participants reinforced the link between gender, gaze and performance, that is, "imaginable and realizable gender configurations within culture" (Butler 1990: 9). However, all of the women (apart from Cara) presented concern about attractive looks as related to their own expectations rather than to the ones of their partners or other people. But, it could be argued that to make such claims a woman has to first internalize the gazing look of the other and the imperative of 'looking good'. (The male gaze could be so intrinsic to our culture that it may underpin women's body insecurities even if this is not stated explicitly.)

The emergent contradictions of power show how vague the line between subjectification and subjectivation is. The way the participants handled the media's discourse of the female body illustrates how the disciplinary, bottom-up power enhances the vulnerability of self-reflexive individuals. As proposed by Brown (1995: 19), "disciplinary power is extraordinarily effective in 'colonizing' allegedly free subjects, for example, those highly individuated, self-interested subjects produced by liberal cultures and capitalist political economies". Indeed, some of the study's findings imply that in the direct encounters with the textually mediated discourses of gender the interviewees established consistent subversive subjectivities. Yet, the subjectivities emerging from some other of their self-accounts revealed uneasy patterns of, usually unacknowledged, involvement with the surrounding, interrelated discourses of gender, consumerism, neoliberalism and popular wedding culture.

Feminist (?) standpoint(s)

Another distinction that has been included in the conceptual framework of this project is the one that standpoint feminists make between 'location' and 'standpoint'. Like the distinction between being the 'subject-in-discourse' and the 'subject of one's actions', it is related to the idea that when exposed to the external forms of control and regulation (by discourses, ideologies as well as structures and relations), people work up individual ways of handling this, ways which are situated in their lived experience.

The findings arising from the interviews indeed indicate a substantial amount of diversity in media reception. Yet, contrary to what some standpoint feminists would expect, the data did not reveal any forms of collective consciousness – either in the women's attitudes to the media or in any other experience. What the data seem to show is, in fact, subjectivity "embracing a singular, self-centred form of agency that undermines the communal aspects of feminism and its distinct social and political goals" (Genz and Brabon 2009: 168). An interesting form of individualism could be observed when the interviewees shunned ready-made constructions of femininity by means of the interpretative repertoire of being unlike other or most women. This generated a paradoxical situation in which a group of women shared a subject position although they produced it to avoid collective subjectivity.

Such a denial of belonging to women's community can be seen as symptomatic of 'engaged individualism' (Mann 1994), that is, living one's identity amidst late modern contradictions and ambiguities by working up "multiple and changing forms of individual agency" (Mann 1994: 32). This, in turn, contravenes the "second wave notions of collective struggle [that] are replaced with more individualistic assertions of ... self-rule" (Genz and Brabon 2009: 24). Finally, adding to this complexity, data gathered in this book show differences and conflicts not only between the women but also within each of them. The plurality and dynamism revealed in their positioning expose what Genz and Brabon (2009: 159) construe as the third-wave subject, which, they claim, is "always in process and accommodating multiple positionalities".

Another insight arising from the interview data is a note against the potential forms of elitism underlying the formulation of what it means for a woman to work out a powerful subjectivity while being located in a patriarchal society. Participants in the study presented diverse ways of handling the hegemonic discourses of gender. Moreover, rather than thoroughly reject them, the interviewees sometimes expressed their acceptance of these discourses. This could be regarded as casting doubt on the women's awareness of existing power structures. Still, it cannot be denied that the subjectivities that they established were in their own ways reflexive and critical. Sometimes the interviewees gave indications of identity trouble while positioning themselves along the lines of the dominant discourses of femininity (for example, as the self-disciplined objects of the male gaze). The less ambiguous, unapologetic acceptance of the position could be on the one hand regarded as the internalized docility of the subjected 'body'; on the other hand – as a personal choice to accept the existing gender order (or as a well-thought-out decision to reject the counter-hegemonic discourses of gender).

Drawing on the arguments that have been put forward above, the book proposes that the notion of what it means to be a self-reflexive woman (or media consumer), needs to be more inclusive. It is suggested that efforts are necessary to work out a way of handling the ideas so that they are not ideologically appraised. After all, the book argues, considering one's position as the position of knowing amounts to the establishment of another normative gender discourse. In relation with this proposal, this volume finds insightful Baxter's emphasis on FPDA's challenge to the traditional "polarization of subjects of study" (Baxter

2010, see also Baxter 2007), which belies the crude dichotomy of the powerful and the powerless. What it means to position oneself as 'free', 'powerful' and 'subversive', etc. is lost in the complexity and diversity of competing discourses, and analysts need to retain their awareness that, like the subjects of their research, they are also 'cultural dupes' (Modleski 1991), positioned in the midst of dominant ideologies.

Conclusion

Data gathered in this chapter make evident the heterogeneity and complexity of both media consumption and lived femininity. Of course, it could have confidently been expected that every person will read the same text in a different way and that all people have their unique gender identities. Yet, what does not seem a particularly revealing social finding generates important questions concerning discourse practices as well as the methodologies of exploring widely assumed social practices.

Overall, the data collected in this study advise against applying any rigid frames of text reception. As was seen, the interviewees' talk at times indicated an affective and personal level of engagement in the media discourse (positive or negative), and sometimes their engagement was ideological (subversive or compliant, or negotiated). Some of their references to the prompt magazine took the form of 'comparison reading'. At other times, the responses were evaluative but did not indicate the interviewee's sense of identification with the textually constructed bridal or feminine experience. Individual recipients (and individual interpretative communities likewise) may differ in numerous ways and the variability needs to be accounted for by researchers.

Moreover, the model of encoding/decoding, even though a landmark progress in reference to the earlier approaches premised on the transmission model, might not necessarily resonate with the particular study because of the genre of wedding magazines which is the object of its analysis. Seiter (1999: 20–1) finds Hall's (1996) model more applicable to examining media genres, such as news and non-fiction programs, but less so to examining the media genres that are consumed for pleasure and entertainment. Bridal magazines, as a subgenre of women's lifestyle magazines, are read not only for information but also (or mainly) for entertainment. Finally, what may render the model too categorical for the nature of data collected here is the dialogical nature of the interviews. In these intersubjective contexts, textual meanings were not simply decoded but negotiated by the participants with the (authors of) media texts and the interviewer.

Furthermore, it could be noted in the interview data that interpellation is an apt term for the exploration of the ideological implications of
media reception but its limitations become apparent once it is applied
in the empirical engagement with local discourse practices. In the interviews, the notion was applicable as long as the participants established
their subjectivities unambiguously, which usually took place in the
media-related talk (hence, in the direct encounters with gendered texts).
Still, the categorical logic of hailing did not account for the more ambiguous positionings, which were observed especially when the women
were interpellated by the discourses mediating their self-accounts.

How participants in the study organized their subject positions in relation to the media frame discussed in this volume makes evident their
ability to have critical insight into their presence in the media-saturated
culture and consumer society. Their awareness of being positioned as
women was apparent at different moments of the interviews. Apart from
the easily noticeable subject positions when they were interpellated by,
for example, the media images of gender or advertisements, their reflexivity was evident in the moments of ideological dilemmas and identity
trouble. The troubled subject positions were mainly associated with the
constructions of investment in the discourse of the prompt magazine
and of dominant (emphasized and commodified) femininities. The fact
that the women did some repair work in those moments is interpreted
in this volume as the evidence of not only their awareness of being
interpellated by media discourse, but also of their negative evaluation of
the practices related to the troubled subject positions.

How the interviewees contested dominant discourses did not yield
itself to an easy interpretation. On the one hand, the participants showed
their "playful ability to move between and amongst discourses, to move
in and out of them, to mix them, to break their spell when necessary"
(Davies 1997: 29). On the other hand, sometimes the defiance of one
repressive discourse entailed submission to another discourse that was
also in some way restrictive. This makes evident the pivotal and complex
role of intertextuality in identity processes, as well as indicates how the
processes should be approached by analysts. As explained by Kristeva,

> the participation of different texts at different levels reveals a particular
> mental activity. And analysis should not limit itself simply to iden-
> tifying texts that participate in the final text, or to identifying their
> sources, but should understand that what is being dealt with is a specific
> dynamics of the subject of the utterance, who consequently, precisely

because of this intertextuality, is not an individual in the etymological sense of the term, not an identity. (Guberman 1996: 190)

Therefore, the findings confirm the analytic applicability of the 'decentralized' approach to media reception. As could be observed, it allows identification of the 'fissures' in people's meaning-making work and indicates how they obfuscate the authorship of words uttered in a given moment.

Finally, the participants' awareness of being positioned varied in degree. How they subverted dominant discourses seemed to depend on their individual experience, which was narrated in their bridal self-accounts. Therefore, this study shows that "the ability to develop a critical awareness of the discourses of femininity depends on the individual's experiences and position within the existing power-discourse nexus" (Thorpe 2008: 217). The emphasis which the current book puts on the differences in the deconstructive readings of media texts is meant here as a linguist's note to feminist debates. In this discourse-analytic examination of readers' positioning and meaning-making no unanimous discourse of gender was found – no one, gender-specific discursive awareness, no shared socio-discursive lens through which the women read media texts. It is therefore proposed that the reflexivity of one's location within gender ideologies should be seen as more problematic than it usually is by feminist and gender analysts.

Conclusion

The central concern of this book was to pursue the relations between the media-based discourses of femininity and women's sense of gender self. The processes were approached by exploring how wedding magazines define bridal femininity and how these definitions are negotiated by readers. In this way, the analysis presented in the volume empirically interrogated the questions of the media's capacity to "[constitute] the given through utterances" (Bourdieu 1991: 170) and to hail individuals into the subject positions which validate it. Both the theoretical and methodological paradigms of this piece of research are based on multiple premises. Synthesizing different theories of discourse and power, this study took the approach of conceptual pragmatism to establish a conceptual framework for the analysis of the specific aspects of discourse that it set out to pursue. Consequently, the analytical toolkit was also complex. The complexity of both the toolkit and its theoretical premises was intended to manage the complexity of the object of the current study. Briefly, this book followed Foucault's view of the knowledge-based power and considered discourses as productive of the objects of which they speak. Media, as one of the contemporary expert systems ('knowledge specialists'), have the capacity of constructing and reinforcing the normative definitions of gender. Formulated as invitations to celebrate one's femininity or masculinity (rather than as imperatives to comply), they are likely to be embraced by media audiences as self-chosen forms of living one's identity. In this sense, media can be regarded as the 'engineers of the soul' that reassert the hegemonic paradigm of gender. To investigate the processes, this study followed the Critical Discourse Analysis (CDA) methodology of analyzing individual texts, genres and the intertextual and interdiscursive connections between them. The conceptual units of CDA were found to analytically link the processes of gender construction and commodification to texts that mediate them in the discursive practices of media production and reception. Because, despite its ostensible inspiration from Foucault, CDA has remained a critical realist paradigm, not only did it provide the major methodological frames in the book but also resonated with the book's view of the relationships between discourse and social reality.

Moreover, also in line with Foucault, the current volume did not see power as solely negative, in the way they have been considered in the Marxist paradigms mentioned in the discussion. The notion of 'interpellation' was adopted here as a conceptual unit referring to the attempts to wield authority; yet, the subject's compliance to the authority was not presumed. It was considered here that power may be creative – by effecting resistance to the power itself. For example, upon being hailed as a loyal consumer of the commodity market, one can take the position of a reader and consumer who is critically engaged with the hegemonic discourse of consumerism. Importantly, however, the relatively straightforward contexts of confrontation with power in the local encounters with media texts were not the only contexts of power that this book sought to explore. This volume was interested in pursuing the interpellative practices of the hegemonic discourses of gender in the contexts that are less directly marked by power, namely when the discourses mediate women's sense- and self-making practices. The practices were accessed in this study through talk which did not directly pertain to media discourse and which usually took the form of the narrative accounts of lived experience.

The lifeworld experience of the subject was considered here in terms of Bourdieu's notion of 'habitus' (and the parallel, discursive psychological notion of the 'personal order'). Accordingly, it was considered that within his or her field, an individual develops disposition ('habitus') that reflects and reproduces the field as a result of that individual's subjection to the field's structuring system of knowledge and values. The media's structuring influence was regarded here as more difficult to resist than other (for example, material) forms of constraint on human agency because it is less tangible. (After all, it has the symbolic power of an expert system.) Nonetheless, all this does not mean that people are incapable of creative actions. To avoid the implicit assumption of human inability to position reflexively, the current piece of research relied on Smith's distinction between the 'subject-in-discourse' and the 'subject of one's actions'. The former was meant here as related to the power enforced on the subjects by hegemonic discourses, while the latter was associated with the subjects' lived experience in which the interpellations are materialized or not. This conceptualization helped the current research project to avoid both 'embracing relativism' and taking a realist position, which resonated with the study's critical realist premises. Also in line with critical realism, this understanding of subjectivity meant acknowledging that the divide between the discursive and the embodied experience of subjectivity is indistinct. The implicitness could be seen in the intricate ways in which discourses echoed in the participants' accounts of lived experience.

This chapter will not go into detail while reviewing the findings offered in the book, as these were thoroughly discussed while summarizing the subsequent chapters. Instead, it will conclude the exploration by enumerating the major arguments arising from its findings. In the discussion below they will be drawn under the three themes that are considered here as the most relevant when investigating the formation of gender subjectivities. Accordingly, this piece of research is concluded by attending to the issues of how women are spoken about (and to) in the media, how women speak, and how to approach these two kinds of discourse practices analytically.

As regards the media's constructions of femininity, the discourse on which this study set its focus was not expected to offer particularly subversive forms of feminine subjectivity. The fact that the discourse of bridal magazines has not been extensively explored (despite the great volume of discourse studies on gender in the print media) is regarded here as an indication that this media genre has been taken for granted by researchers. Indeed, as shown in the book, compared with how other media (for example, women's magazines) appear responsive to the changing landscapes of gender, bridal magazines are by no means at the cutting edge of the media discourses of femininity.

The subject positions made available by the magazines examined do not render any resistant or transgressive bridal subjectivities. They exclude other ethnicities and sexual orientations as well as all the heterosexual femininities which do not accommodate to the patriarchal image of the white virgin bride – young, conventionally beautiful, Caucasian-looking and submissive. Therefore, the absence of pregnant, supersize, old and disabled women was underscored in the analysis as an unambiguous indication of the magazines' reductive and exclusive discourse. Another notable discourse practice, which was singled out in regard to the magazines' tampering with readers' subjectivities, was how the magazines yoke the discourses of identity and consumerism. Although the magazines' subscription to the conservative discourses of femininity was expected at the outset of the study, I was surprised at the extent to which they were connected to commodification. As could be seen, the constructions of commodified bridal femininity exemplify media encouragements for people to go 'shopping for subjectivities' (Frost 2001).

Crucially, although critical of the reductive and normative meanings which the magazines apparently circulate, this book neither disclaims women's right to celebrate their 'Cinderella' moments nor does it argue that there is a direct relation between such celebrations and women's relationship to the discourses in which the practices have their origin. The participants in the study gave indications of their sense that bridal femininity is a role to play. It was demonstrated that even though willing to assume the role, the women were also aware of, but not particularly affiliated with, the symbolic meanings that the traditional bridal femi ninity has accrued. At the same time, as the book propounds, the reality of the practices accompanying the spectacle cannot be denied. The bridal body, which is supposed to be captured by the actualizing gaze of the groom, guests and of the bride herself, is subject to the actual disciplining practices (as was indicated by the interviewees). Based on that, while the pleasure from inhabiting the media-constructed bridal body is not appraised here, the book raises the question why women choose to play the particular role, especially if they do not fully identify with it (as the interviewees claimed they did not).

In making its central argument to move away from the text-centered approaches to media discourse, the current book is perfectly aware of this being an already established postulate of feminist and gender analysts. Yet, this piece of research was conducted with the aim of proposing methodological solutions that have yet not been applied in reception studies. Based on the findings arising from the data examined, this volume presents insights that are in several ways unlike those from other studies of media reception. Interestingly, some of the insights are based on similar results. For example, as will be addressed below, the volume concludes that the differences observed between the media-fabricated 'superbride' and the bridal identities which were locally worked up by the interviewees confirm the point of conducting reception anal yses that do not lose sight of media texts. Conversely, upon observing similar discrepancies in her study of women reading popular magazines, Hermes (1995: 146) argues that if the meanings which are vested in popular media texts are so detached from the ones that the magazine texts render, it suffices to explore only the interpretations of the magazines. The disparity, I suggest, stems from how the implications of the apparently unabsorbed style of media consumption are interpreted.

For Hermes, the substantial superficiality of participants' interpretative work indicates that the influence of the media must be weaker than researchers often assume. In this book the uninvolved way of reading media texts was also observed, but it is argued that such a relationship to media discourse is not a sufficient premise to discount the analysts' concern about the influence of the media by treating it as the 'fallacy of meaningfulness'. As will be elaborated below, one of the book's central arguments is that weak emotional and cognitive involvement with media texts may either indicate people's actual detachment from media discourses (thus, no influence of the media as such) or, to the contrary, it may indicate that they have already internalized the discourses. In the latter case, the loose style of text consumption might additionally enhance individuals' vulnerability to the media, which makes them the first (but not the only) group for whom the findings provided by critical discourse analysts can be empowering.

Moreover, recipients' claims of distance from media were approached here with a dispositional mistrust. As explained, in times when people have the appropriate awareness of the media's bias and of the 'trashiness' of popular culture, the consumption thereof has become a vital form of one's cultural capital. In consequence, individuals may thus seek not to disclose many of their media pleasures. It was also posited that while people may not be willing to disclose the pleasures in the mundane (informal) contexts, the self-censoring inclination may be particularly strong in the research context. For this reason the book has postulated the importance of pursuing the recipients' involvement with discourses that are not directly related to the media but may provide an auxiliary body of data illuminating individuals' relationship to popular culture and the media.

Claiming interest in women's view of the media's representations of gender does not necessarily mean approaching them "en masse as silly housewives" (Hermes 1995: 147). This book sought to show this by applying a small-scale qualitative methodology of media reception and by asking questions that do not invite categorical thinking and therefore do not yield themselves to definite and straightforward answers. This comes at a price. The sociocultural and psychological complexity of the textual encounters demanded multiple tools of analysis, which were both theoretically and methodologically demanding. What is more, such an approach will not satisfy the readers who expect a systematic analysis of language based on substantial bodies of texts. This book sees many advantages of using the large-scale quantitative methodologies to support the qualitative studies of the situated practices of discourse. Yet, it makes a point of underscoring the strength of the small-scale, qualitative methodologies by noting the value of exploring people's individual discourse practices and bringing out their richness and complexity. This defies definite and easy answers but is indispensable to the acquisition of a better understanding of the practices.

In order to situate the discourse practices of media reception in the participants' lives, this study involved the cross-analysis of their reader and bridal subjectivities. Their subjectivities were cross-examined with regard to the distinction between the 'subject-in-discourse' and 'subject of one's actions'. The methodology of the current study was broadened with this auxiliary perspective because it was expected that the notion of hailing (as an example of the workings of symbolic power) might be found reductive when this study explores individuals' lived practices of media and gender. Indeed, in the interview data, although the participants did not acknowledge the hegemonic discourses of gender in their media-related talk, in their self-accounts they spoke from the subject positions inherent in the discourses.

The distinction between the 'subject-in-discourse' and 'subject of one's actions' was given a substantial amount of attention in the volume also because it encapsulates the ideas that were advanced in the investigation with regard to the construction of meaning in media reception. Following the 'decentralized' view of media texts, the context of media reception was understood in terms of both the immediate conditions of individuals' encounters with the text and their lived experience. It was considered that the experience which readers bring into the encounters may affect their interpretative work and that it is in the lived experience that the emergent textual meanings become embodied. Accordingly, media reception was investigated in terms of how it was embedded in the readers' accounts of their lived wedding experience, an approach premised on the following idea:

Not everything that a text says is in the text. The missing moments in the transformative process are well understood by the practitioner of the discourse of femininity. The work which is presupposed but not represented is that of the production in local historical settings of simulacra of the textually imaged idea. (D. Smith 1990: 198)

This view resonated with the study's understanding that subjects are constituted by intertextual connections between texts (and thus read from the texts more than they directly say) and that the subjects give the texts meanings by carrying them over into their lifeworld practices.

In the interviews, the participants indeed relied on intertextual connections while interpreting the prompt texts and while weaving the intertexts into their wedding auto-narratives.

Based on their autobiographic experience, each of the women established her individual relationship to the 'iconic bride'. In doing so, the interviewees related to the bride's symbolic features in ways that indicated that the women assumed the interviewer's familiarity with the icon. Namely, their own bridal narratives were loosely based on the popular discourse of bridal beauty. Constructing the narratives, the participants used socioculturally shared meanings and intertextual connections between the socioculturally available bridal texts and images. Moreover, the discourse which the participants mentioned in their narratives had apparently been embodied in their lived experience, for instance in the choices of wedding gowns, in which the women drew on the indexical qualities of the dress (for instance the dislike of the 'puffy' shape indexing the attitude to the 'big white weddings').

The intertextuality of the bridal self-narratives revealed an undeniably complex relationship between the frame of media discourse and the subjectivities emerging from the autobiographic accounts. For example, the participants used the magazines' discourse of commodification while contextualizing its repertoires of the commodified wedding in the accounts of their bridal experience, as a result of which the repertoires were given individual meanings and roles. It was observed that neither of the repertoires seemed to have as strong commodifying appeal as might be assumed based on the analysis of the magazines' forceful neoliberal rhetoric. However, the interviewees' denial of their acceptance of the media discourses of gender was not taken at face value. Allowing for the women's identity concerns and rhetorical orientation to the interaction, the study traced their deployment of gender discourses throughout the whole context, not only when media were referred to directly.

Furthermore, approaching women as the 'subjects of their actions' was meant to acknowledge their subjectivity as media consumers and as the subjects of the study. In line with Baxter's (2002: 831) idea to pursue the goal of "locating...and analyzing discursive contexts where silenced or marginalized voices may be struggling to be heard", this research project sought to create a context where women's voices can be heard next to the voices of an academic researcher and of the media. Of course, while this book does not find genuine the media's interest in the women's voices and in their lived experience, my own, analyst's interest in them would have been by all means sincere even if no reader-inclusive methodology had been applied in this study. Yet, as was explained in Chapter 2, the current project was guided by D. Smith's (1990) concern with women's experience of being abstracted and objectified in the discourses of public life, one of which is, after all, the academic discourse. The interviewees did not sound particularly concerned about being silenced by the discourses. Nevertheless, one of the aims of this investigation was to marry its academic identity with its social agenda, and address the implications of media discourse for women without assuming their naivety (as it seems to be done in many media).

Clearly, the mere interest in the local sites of media reception does not suffice to authenticate the researcher's intentions to revoke the patronizing attitude to the subjects of the study. This raises the question of the methodology of investigating the receptive site of media discourse. The one employed in this research project sought to explore the recipients' entanglement in the network of discourses on which they were expected to rely in their interpretation of media texts. For this purpose, media reception was explored by means of the methodology of Critical Discursive Psychology (CDP). While this study does not claim success in that respect, the underlying goal was to retain the reflexivity of its own standpoint when adopting an approach to media reception that entails some import of the analyst's sociocultural knowledge into research process. Therefore, effort was made to investigate media reception in a way in which ideological codes of gender are recognized both in the interviewees' talk and in the analysis thereof, and it is specified how the researcher's standpoint informs her interpretation of specific parts of the talk. In spite of that, it was acknowledged that with their own parameters, the methodologies applied must have to some extent shaped the view they rendered. Yet, similar limits on the parameters of other methodologies need to be admitted as well.

By putting side by side the discourses of media, academic research and lifeworld experience, apart from questioning the notion of a 'media dupe', I sought to avoid the position of an 'academic dupe' who makes socially engaged forays into language convinced that the 'masses out there' need the analyst's edifying work. In the analysis, in the moments when it was not only the media discourse but also the critical, academic discourse that were collated with the lifeworld discourses, not all of my conclusions from the critical examination of the magazines were confirmed by the interviewees, which led me to confront my own 'standpoint' (that of a researcher and a woman). This made me realize how much caution such a research goal requires from the analyst in the discussion of discourse data so that the declared intention of paying heed to the women's agency in sense- and self-making is not vitiated by the undue reliance on one's own standpoint. Therefore, in the data discussion, the interviewees' reflexivity of their lifeworld practices was acknowledged and so were the ideological disparities between the individuals and me.

In consequence, ideology critique in this exploration gained a double axis – such that the study was reflexive of the media ideology of gender and of the analyst's feminist position. Accounting for one's ideological disposition while interpreting media is a common practice in CDA-informed inquiries. By claiming its ideological premises, the current study acknowledged the potential distance that an ideologically positioned research may put between the analyst and the participants. Still, by making the distance the object of a self-reflexive discussion, the book sought to minimize it, an effort inspired by Smith's feminist sociology. Importantly, Smith is concerned about the way in which women have been marginalized by the masculinist scientific discourse. In this volume, the concern was extrapolated and the goal was to avoid the exclusionary feminist academic lens which would make some of the interviewees' self-reflexive practices fall outside the book's understanding of self-reflexivity and contestation. By adopting what Jørgensen and Phillips (2002: 181) call "modified ideology critique", I sought to reduce the asymmetries between my position of a researcher and the positions of the people involved in the study. Stating this, I am aware that this piece of research is still asymmetrical, but it gains from the 'double' ideology critique the advantage of providing a self-reflexive feminist critique.

Such a mode of investigation, this book suggests, is valuable in that it occasions and facilitates the review of one's research agenda and approach to discourse data. Emphatically, however, this is not to deny the need for and the value of the critical approaches to media discourses of gender whose methodologies are less inclusive. This book was not preoccupied with proposing a subjective appraisal of the ways in which specific researchers of media discourse have triangulated their approach to data. Without negating any of the individual frameworks which were deployed here as the constituents of one complex frame of analysis, the current investigation hopes to show how they can inform one another within a single study and therefore enhance its empirical and analytical capabilities. For example, it was demonstrated in this research project that an extended, CDA-based inquiry of specific discourse(s) may intensify the analyst's awareness of the discourses that are at work in talk that is subject to a CDP-based scrutiny.[1]

Premised on three frameworks of discourse analysis (CDA, FPDA and CDP), this piece of research may be frowned upon for its methodological inclusiveness. Also, some of the practitioners of the frameworks may reproach the investigation for claiming its endorsement of 'their' approaches while employing methods or advancing ideas that they do not acknowledge. Yet, these two potential lines of critique are subverted here. For one thing, the models of discourse weaved into the study share the critical perspective. For another, unlike CDP (whose analytical tools were applied), neither CDA nor Feminist Poststructuralist Discourse Analysis (FPDA) impose any specific methods of language analysis. Although CDA has been criticized for lack of methodological rigor, and Baxter (2010: 133) finds it also one of FPDA's limitations, this book has considered it as one of the main advantages of the models. As argued in the volume, analysts' autonomy in the choice of methodological solutions, apart from making their approach to data more precise, allows the examination of the data from multiple perspectives.

The interview data clearly show that a close analysis of media reception complicates the popular notion of the media's 'effect' on individuals. The critical investigation of the bridal magazines revealed a discourse operating with subtle meaning-constructive resources (such as hybrids, recontextualization, color modality), but its basic message was found admittedly uncomplicated – to become Cinderella is a "girlhood fantasy, a democratic right, and *the* central preoccupation of the wedding" (Otnes and Pleck 2003: 54). Still, the critical analysis of women's relationships to the discourse did not render comparably unequivocal outcomes. This book thus finds the CDP- and FPDA-based research to complement the CDA examination of media discourse by flagging shifts and discontinuities in the recipients' engagements with the discourse. Parallel with the analysis of media texts in its focus on the intertextual and interdiscursive mechanisms of meaning-making, the investigation of media reception demonstrated that the same meaning-making processes which lead to the construction of fixed and hegemonic subject positions in media texts, allow individuals to engage with the texts in dynamic and more ambiguous (sometimes subversive) ways.

Namely, the participants' brief attachments to different discourses generated not only variability but also contradictions in their media reception. Oscillating between the media and lifeworld discourses, they took contradictory subject positions and grappled with ideological dilemmas. The interviewees distanced themselves from the discourse of bridal magazines, but they did so inconsistently; also, despite their critique of the discourse, some of them notably relied on its meaning-making resources. In this sense, they were found entangled in the complex, implicit relations of symbolic power – in the very way that

CDA analysts consider people to be. After all, the most conspicuous construction of the magazines' discourse – the fairy-tale bride manipulated by the wedding market – was readily recognized and subverted by the interviewees. Still, other forms of the media's discursive appeal affected their sense- and self-making practices in the ways that none of them seemed to realize. This was particularly noticeable in the accounts that were not directly related to the prompt texts.

Overall, it was demonstrated that media recipients can either embrace the hegemonic discourses of gender or escape the rigidity of the media-fabricated subjectivities. Consequently, neither can media reception be examined independently from the situated context of media practice, nor can it be understood as the experience of one collective subjectivity. In the study the magazines were found to address women as if they shared one feminine subjectivity. Nevertheless, the interviewees' reader and gender identities were locally grounded in their individual, lifeworld experience, rather than indicated the women's sense of being part of a group subject to the same forms of media's symbolic power. In fact, the interviewees worked up their own positions from which they (either explicitly or implicitly) denied their like-mindedness with other women.

Clearly, this piece of research did not explore the processes of media production and reception by measuring the manipulative 'efficacy' of media language, nor did it approach them as responsible for the fabrication of formatted gender identities. As emphasized in the Introduction, it was intent on compelling an informed reflection about the role of discourse in how people talk and think about gender (rather than who they become following exposure to the media). Also importantly, the inquiry did not claim its purpose of generating the 'explanatory critique' in the sense in which it was problematized in this book. Nevertheless, although the study did not aim to explain people what reductive and depreciative representations of femininity media perpetuate, it does argue in favor of 'interventionist' research. As mentioned above, the participants' discernible awareness of the media discourse notwithstanding, they were found in many ways vulnerable to it. This, the book posits, suggests the necessity of underscoring the problematic nature of media discourse so that the idea of 'active audience' (Fiske 1987) is not overestimated.

The belief in the reader's agency and reflexivity is not the only premise from which to question the point of conducting principled, critical inquiries into the media representations of gender. The systematic analyses of the dominant gender discourses could also be criticized for how they undermine their declared pursuit of contravening the obviousness of the discourses. After all, it could be argued, they do so by starting from the idea that the discourses exist, which assumption reinforces the validity of the discourses (Sunderland 2004: 208).

Still, the findings arising from this piece of research imply that even the discourses about which it could be assumed there is not much more to learn require a constant scrutiny and, if necessary, critique. Even the long-established gender discourses undergo the process of a continual transformation. In Chapter 3, the study indicated how the traditional discourses of femininity merge with the emergent discourse of commodification and the neoliberal rhetoric of a resourceful and self-managerial approach to life. Making this process explicit, this book posits, does not lead analysts to reinforce it. Bridal magazines apparently exemplify the pressures that are loaded on their readers in terms of their marital status, appearance and involvement with consumption, as well as follow media's general practice of marginalizing the minority and non-hegemonic feminine subjectivities. Such disturbing media practices are often covert – it is impossible to expose and then question them without first assuming their presence.

As regards the private forms of contesting hegemonic ideologies of gender, it was found that the participants (directly and indirectly) rejected some of the media-reproduced ideologies, and that the media-perpetuated discourses did not always inhibit their articulation of self-reflexive or subversive feminine subjectivities. In that regard, it proved applicable to combine the CDA-minded pursuit of covert power relations with FPDA's belief in women's "agency to resist, challenge and potentially overturn discursive practices that conventionally position them as powerless" (Baxter 2002: 840). Still, inasmuch as it is vital to approach media recipients with this belief, it is also essential not to let them be overly assured of their control over the socioculturally available discourses of gender. As mentioned in the discussion above, the interviewees did not express a particularly harsh critique of how they are spoken about in the media. However, their impassive relationship to the media was not explained in terms of their ignorance of what is said in the media. In fact, the women gave clear indications of being able to recognize the magazines' consumerist agenda and the gender codes circulating in their textual and visual discourses. Therefore, the apparent indifference that the women at the same time usually demonstrated might have been caused by their implicit belief in the ability of rejecting and rationalizing the discourses that they do not agree with – if the media's ideologies are so blatantly obvious and easy to refute, any 'moral panic' on the recipients' part is unnecessary.

Nonetheless, it has been underscored in the discussion that although the participants apparently developed a strong sense of being free subjects, they gave indications of being in fact colonized by dominant discourses perpetuated in the media. Despite the interviewees' involvement in the self-reflexive and subversive discourse practices, the established discourses on which they relied in the practices were found to significantly "inhibit the possibilities for a kinetic interplay of diverse voices, perspectives, accounts and narratives" (Baxter 2002: 831). By attending to the intertextuality of media and lifeworld discourses, this study demonstrates that even in the case of manifest intertextuality, the polyglossic capabilities of language obscure the authorship of texts and cast doubt on the speakers' possibilities of self-determination.

In conclusion, although this piece of research is not based on a large body of interview data, the sample of talk examined shows that media pleasures can be taken with different amounts of reflexivity about the forms of subjectivity that they involve. This allows the book to advocate non-elitist approaches to popular media that can lead to informed, but neither hermetically academic nor highbrow, debates about the media's place in social life. With this in mind, the idea of academic 'intervention' in media discourse practices proposed here is that of a "transformative quest" (Baxter 2010: 131). Rather than suggesting any institutionalized forms of struggle and contestation, this book considers as more viable individual, bottom-up practices of subverting powerful discourses. For example, because the interviewees revealed undeniable, but inconsistent contestatory practices, their awareness of the covert mechanisms of power could be made more profound. The intensified awareness of the media-reproduced ideologies like the ones revealed in this piece of research might help individuals to work out their own ways of handling the "micropolitics of everyday life" (Baker 2000: 99). Indeed, suggesting to people why and how they could involve themselves with reflexive critique has still much of a top-down approach. Therefore, it was strongly emphasized in the discussion that in the academic 'intervention' in media discourse individuals need to be granted their right to retain their own standpoints. This will allow them to subvert those discourses of gender that they find oppressive or inferiorizing, not the ones that are found as such by researchers.

Notes

1 Discourse and Power

1. While CDA makes a specific distinction between discourse and language, many researchers in other disciplines (some of them quoted in this volume) refer to what 'discourse' means for CDA by means of the concept of 'language'. In fact, even linguists affiliated with CDA sometimes use these two concepts interchangeably (see for example Scollon 2001).

2. Bourdieu considered habitus primarily in terms of social groups and defined it as a "system of practice-generating schemes" (Bourdieu 1992: 172) that is internalized by a social class. The class distinctions are not, however, what this book involves itself with because it considers that 'class' would not have a particularly strong explanatory power in the specific context of the study. Accordingly, rather than as an ideology internalized by classes, habitus is understood here as ideology embodied in individuals. This, hence, is the way in which the relations between structure and agency have been conceptualized by Giddens. Nevertheless, although the class-based dispositions are not explored here, neither is Giddens' focus on the individual agent fully embraced here because it may lead the exploration away from its focus on the gender-specific social location. Thus, in Chapter 2, this book will incorporate the notions of 'location' and 'standpoint' which will be more theoretically relevant to the study.

3. See also Fairclough (1996: 49–50) for his distinction between "interpretation-1" and "interpretation-2".

4. For an extended discussion of triangulation in linguistics see Litosseliti (2010: 34–6).

5. The concept of ISA's is introduced here as a descriptive unit to articulate the book's view of dispersed power. This book, however, distances itself from Althusser's Marxist understanding of ideology as a distortion of the 'real' social relations. This realist claim does not resonate with the study's critical realist premises, which consider that the material and the discursive practices have the same ontological status.

6. Like ISA's, the notion of hailing/interpellation is extrapolated here from Althusser's theory to refer to discursively mediated practices of power. However, this book does not endorse Althusser's notion of the subject as the notion implies an overly deterministic view of positioning.

7. Foucault's concept of the 'regimes of truth' can be related with his theory of biopower (1980), that is, power which is enacted implicitly – both through the discursive production of various historically and geographically specific 'truths' and through disciplinary practices. This form of power operates bottom up – it regulates social life by having people embrace the 'truths' and reproduce them in their daily practices.

8. For a related observation see also Lazar's (2002) examination of the discourse of 'other-centeredness' in Singaporean national advertising, where she finds

that feminine identity is attained in the course of heterosexual relationships including courtship, marriage and motherhood.

9. Although in the analysis of interview data I will refer to 'self-reflexivity', the concept is not directly translated into the analysis from Giddens' theory. It is meant here as the qualities of talk that indicate interviewees' introspective practices and mindfulness of their location in specific conditions of living. Giddens' concept of a self-reflexive individual implies a cognitivist view of identity which this study does not take. The cognitivist view is rejected in the current exploration to propose that identity is socioculturally contingent and that people's ability to control their 'reflexive projects of the self' should not be overrated (in the same way the power of hegemonic discourses should not be overestimated).

2 Women as Subjects of Discourse

1. That most participants in the study basically endorsed the dominant discourses of gender and sexuality could be safely assumed given that all of them (with one exception) were in heterosexual relationships.
2. For examples of the internal dynamic of language see Bakhtin's concept of the struggle between centrifugal and centripetal discourses (see pp. 11–12), and to the notion of 'bids for meaning closures' see Laclau and Mouffe (see pp. 25–26).
3. Clearly, despite its emphasis on the mediated nature of discourse data, and its reliance on the toolkit of discursive psychology, this study does not follow the idea proposed by its major adherents to 'embrace relativism' (Edwards et al. 1995). Instead, when accounting for the participants' lived experience, this book affords the experience and the spoken texts mediating it the same ontological status. Otherwise, this investigation would not be able to take a critical position in relation to the dominant discourses of gender (see Parker 1992, 1998; Willig 1999).
4. This book highlights the developments in audience and reception studies that it considers relevant to its objective of study. For an overview of the major themes and methods that have been proposed within this ever-expanding field see Alasuutari (1999), Ross and Nightingale (2003), Ruddock (2001), Schroder et al. (2003), and Stokes ([2002] 2013: 170–200).
5. For a discussion that concerns gender and media reception specifically, see van Zoonen (1994: 105–26).
6. For an interesting overview of the feminist literature on media and audience pleasures, see Gills (2006: 13–19).

3 Bridal Femininity in Wedding Magazines

1. The research data include the following issues: *You & Your Wedding* (7–8/2009, 11–12/2009), *Cosmopolitan Bride* (6–7/2009, 12–1/2010), *Wedding Ideas* (53, 54, 55, 56, 57, 58/2008), *Brides* (7–8/2009), *Brides. Wedding Planner* (2008) and *Perfect Wedding* (4/2008). So as to include the most available publications, the magazines in the sample were bought in newsagents in

Manchester and Newcastle (the cities where the subsequent interviews were conducted).
2. All emphases added in the quotations from the magazines come from the author of the book.
3. For example, in their analysis of two issues of women's glossies, Eggins and Iedema (1997: 180) recognize lack of an editor's letter in one of them as indicative of "a lesser concern to establish contact and solidarity with readers".
4. To illustrate, Leap (1994) found 'women's language' ironically echoed in gay discourse. As a symbol of 'ideal femininity', it has been a resource for performing femininity by transsexuals (Stevens 1990; Glass 1992). Other studies depict it as a pervasive model of gender-appropriate language in linguistic socialization, popular culture as well as everyday and professional communication (Coates 1997; Cameron 1995, 2003; Crawford 1995; K. Hall 1995; Talbot 2003; Holmes and Schnurr 2006).
5. See also Frisby and Engstrom (2006).
6. For extended discussion, see Currie's (1993) exploration of 'modern traditional' weddings in Canada and Walter's (2010) conception of 'new traditionalism'.
7. For instance, in her investigation of the American wedding culture, Ingraham (2008: 128) reports that the average share of advertisements in a single issue of *Bride* is 80 percent.
8. The same process is also referred to as *appropriation* (Sunderland 2004: 30).

4   Reading a Magazine: Methodological Considerations

1. In discourse analysis 'accounting work' is approached as a discursive practice in which social and psychological phenomena are talked about and, as a result "versions of a moral order" are locally produced (Baker 1997: 133). This provides analysts with information about the role of language in individuals' sense- and self-making practices (for examples see Hepburn and Wiggins 2007).
2. The analytical toolkit chosen for the exploration of interview data consists of tools that are commonly associated with discursive psychology. The distinctly critical position from which the second stage of exploration is conducted makes it continuous with the first part of the project in terms of the socially and ideologically engaged standpoints that they represent.
3. Manchester and Newcastle are large cities with industrial backgrounds in the north of England. With an estimated population of 512,000, Manchester is an ethnically and religiously diverse area. The majority of its inhabitants are white British and Christian, and it has a considerable Asian population. Once a leading center for manufacturing, the city's economy is now largely based on the services industry. Newcastle upon Tyne is a city with an estimated population of around 259,000, largely white British and Christian. Formerly known for its coal mining and manufacturing industries, it is now recognized for its focus on commerce, technology and culture.
4. The participants in the study were recruited by means of chain sampling. The first members of the sample were found through personal acquaintance networks – they were mainly women from the local neighborhood in Manchester where I lived during my stay in the UK. One of the interviewees, Cara, lived in Newcastle

and she volunteered to take part in the interview after we met at my friend's wedding, which we both attended. The other group were colleagues at a civil service agency – they were contacted through Stephanie, another girl whom I met at the wedding and who was also one of the interviewees.

5. The remaining interviewees were:

Jennifer
45-year-old, held a Higher National Diploma in hotel management, worked as a HR manager in the civil service, got married in 1989 and had one son. She claimed she did not particularly like women's magazines; in the interview, she was particularly critical about their infantile representations of women. She said she considered herself as a feminist.

Clara
22-year-old, with a BA in history, she worked as an administration assistant in the civil service in Manchester. She was in a three-year-long heterosexual relationship but did not want to get married yet. Clara claimed she liked women's magazines, but in the interview she made a distinction between fashion magazines (which she was fond of) and lifestyle magazines (which she did not like).

Sue
43-year old, an administration worker, mother to an 18-year-old daughter and a 16-year-old son. She claimed she had read wedding magazines when she was getting married in 1988. In the interview, she compared them to the prompt magazine and often talked about her daughter as a future bride and wife.

Anne
22-year-old personal assistant in the civil service, at the time of the interview she was studying to qualify as a solicitor. She was in a long-term homosexual relationship and did not yet plan to get married. She said she did not like women's magazines for the "girly" stereotypes that they reinforce.

Stephanie
34-year-old, a civil service worker, in a five-year heterosexual relationship; Stephanie was engaged but did not know the wedding date yet. At work she was responsible for community engagement in the city's immigrant districts (raising people's awareness of hate crimes, domestic violence, homophobia, sexism, etc.). Stephanie claimed to read women's magazines occasionally. As a British African-Caribbean, she expressed resentment about their ethnic bias. She was also critical of their prejudice against homosexual couples.

Elisabeth
26-year-old, married in 2009, thus one year before the interview. After receiving an MA in theology, she decided to withdraw from what she called a 'traditional' career pattern to be able to engage in the life of her church community. She worked for a social justice charity for which she organized music and dance classes. She claimed she had read bridal magazines before her wedding but her attitude to women's magazines in general was ambivalent in the interview.

Caroline
27-year-old, got married in 2008. She received a doctoral degree in education studies and was looking for a full-time job in a primary school. She belonged to the same church community as Elisabeth and talked a lot

about her faith. She presented it as the reason for her critical view of the media and women's magazines.

6. Giving the reasons for which the specific four interviews were discussed in the book, I explained that for lack of space not all interviews could be presented, and that the others were not selected for the discussion because the interviewees talked about less immediate wedding experience. However, as can be seen from the information in endnote 4, Elisabeth and Caroline had been married for one year at the time of the interviews, as had Debby. However, their interviews are not discussed in the volume because due to their involvement in a church community they bore many similarities to Cara, for whom the experience of getting married was more immediate (her wedding took place one week after the interview).

7. For another analysis of the interviews see Glapka (2012).

5 Reading a Magazine: The Interviews

1. The names of all interviewees have been changed.

2. R = researcher. All interviews were collected and transcribed by the author of the book. Therefore, 'researcher' is used interchangeably with 'interviewer'.

3. In the analyses of the reception of television programs, this form of relating one's subjective experience to media texts is referred to as a 'referential mode' of viewing (Liebes and Katz 1990; H. Wood 2005).

4. For an in-depth analysis of women's constructions of singleness and coupledom see Reynolds (2007).

6 Reading a Magazine: Discussion

1. For a similar finding, see Banaji's (2006) analysis of adolescents' reception of Hindi movies which shows how the interviewees' comments of the on-screen behaviors contradicted their claims of the off-screen systems of values.

Conclusion

1. See also Jørgensen and Phillips (2002: 167–71) for an example of an analysis where the same piece of data is approached by means of CDA-based methods and methods deployed in discursive psychology.

Bibliography

Abell, Jackie, Elizabeth H. Stokoe and Michael Billig. 2004. "Narrative and the discursive (re)construction of events", in: Molly Andrews, Shelley Day Sclater, Corinne Squire and Amal Treacher (eds), *The uses of narrative: Explorations in sociology, psychology and cultural studies*. New Brunswick and London: Transaction Publishers, 180–92.

Adorno, Theodore W. 1974. *Minima moralia*. London: New Left Books.

Alasuutari, Pertti (ed.) 1999. *Rethinking the media audience. The new agenda*. London: Sage.

Althusser, Louis. 1971. "Ideology and ideological state apparatuses", in: Louis Althusser (ed.), *Lenin and philosophy and other essays*. New York: Monthly Review Press, 121–76.

Althusser, Louis. 1984. *Essays in intertextuality*. Verso: London.

Annandale, Ellen and Anne Hammarström. 2010. "Constructing the 'gender-specific body': A critical discourse analysis of publications in the field of gender-specific medicine", *Health*, 15, 6: 571–87.

Ang, Ien. 1996. *Living room wars: Rethinking media audiences for a postmodern world*. London: Routledge.

Ang, Ien. 1988. "Feminist desire and feminist pleasure: On Janice Radway's *Reading the romance*: Women, patriarchy and popular literature", *Camera Obscura*, 16: 134–76.

Antaki, Charles and Sue Widdicombe (eds). 1998. *Identities in talk*. London: Sage.

Archer, Margaret, Roy Bhaskar Andrew Collier, Tony Lawson and Allan Norrie (eds). 1998. *Critical realism: Essential readings*. London: Routledge.

Archer, Margaret. 1995. *Realist social theory: The morphogenetic approach*. Cambridge: Cambridge University Press.

Arnott, Margaret. 2010. "Education and nationalism: The discourse of education policy in Scotland", *Discourse*, 31, 3: 335–50.

Atkinson, Paul and Sara Delamont. 2006. "Rescuing narrative from qualitative research", *Narrative Inquiry*, 16: 164–72.

Atkinson, Paul and David Silverman. 1997. "Kundera's immortality: The interview society and the invention of the self", *Qualitative Inquiry*, 3: 304–25.

Baker, Carolyn D. 1997. "Membership categorization and interview accounts", in: David Silverman (ed.), *Qualitative research: Theory, method and practice*. London: Sage.

Baker, Carolyn. D. 2000. "Locating culture in action: Membership categorisation in texts and talk", in: Alison Lee and Cate Poynton (eds), *Culture and text: Discourse and methodology in social research and cultural studies*. London: Routledge, 777–95.

Bakhtin, Mikhail. [1935] 1981. "Discourse in the novel", in: Michael Holquist (ed.), *The dialogic imagination*. (Translated by Caryl Emerson and Michael Holquist.) Austin: University of Texas Press, 259–422.

Bakhtin, Mikhail. [1953] 1986. "The problem of speech genres", in: Caryl Emerson and Michael Holquist (eds), *Speech genres and other late essays*. (Translated by Vern M. McGee.) Austin: University of Texas Press, 60–102.

Bakhtin, Mikhail. 1973. *Problems of Dostoyevsky's poetics.* (Translated by Caryl Emerson.) New York: Ardis.

Balsamo, Anne Marie. 1996. *Technologies of the gendered body: Reading cyborg women.* Durham: Duke University Press.

Bamberg, Michael. 2006. "Stories: Big or small. Why do we care?", *Narrative Inquiry*, 16, 1: 139–47.

Banaji, Shakuntala. 2006. *Reading "Bollywood": The young audience and Hindi film.* Basingstoke: Palgrave Macmillan.

Bardin, Laurence. 1977. *L'Analyse de contenu.* Paris: PUF.

Barrett, Michèle. 1991. *The politics of truth: From Marx to Foucault.* Cambridge: Polity Press.

Barthes, Roland. 1986. *The rustle of language.* Oxford: Blackwell.

Bartky. Sandra. 1990. *Feminism and domination: Studies in the phenomenology of oppression.* New York/London: Routledge.

Baudrillard, Jean. 1998. *The consumer society: Myth and structures.* (Translated by Chris Turner.) London: Sage.

Baudrillard, Jean. 1988. "Simulacra and simulations", in: Mark Poster (ed.), *Selected writings.* Cambridge: Polity Press, 166–84.

Bauer, Martin W. and George Gaskell. 2000. *Qualitative researching with text, image and sound.* London: Sage.

Bauman, Zygmunt. 1989. *Legislators and interpreters.* Cambridge: Polity Press.

Bauman, Zygmunt. 2004. *Identity.* Cambridge: Polity Press.

Baumeister, Roy F. 1986. *Identity. Cultural change and struggle for self.* New York: Oxford University Press.

Baxter, Judith. 2010. "Discourse-analytic approaches to text and talk", in: Lia Litosseliti (ed.) *Research methods in linguistics.* London: Continuum, 117–37.

Baxter, Judith. 2008. "Feminist Post-structuralist Discourse Analysis: A new theoretical and methodological approach?" in: Jane Sunderland et al. (eds), *Theoretical and Methodological Approaches to Gender and Language Study.* Basingstoke: Palgrave, 243–55.

Baxter, Judith. 2007. "Post-structuralist analysis of classroom discourse", in: Marilyn Martin-Jones and Anne-Marie de Mejia (eds), *Encyclopaedia of language and education: Discourse and education.* Vol. 3. New York: Springer, 69–80.

Baxter, Judith. 2003. *Positioning gender in discourse: A feminist methodology.* Basingstoke: Palgrave Macmillan.

Baxter, Judith. 2002. "Competing discourses in the classroom: A Post-structuralist discourse analysis of girls' and boys' speech in public contexts", *Discourse and Society*, 13, 6: 827–42.

Beck, Ulrich. 1992. *Risk society: Towards a new modernity.* London: Sage.

Beck, Ulrich and Elisabeth Beck-Gernsheim. 1995. *The normal chaos of love.* Wiley-Blackwell.

Belk, Russell, Gliz Ger and Soren Askegaard. 1996. "Metaphors of consumer desire", in: Kim Corfman and John Lynch (eds), *Advances in consumer research.* Vol. 23. Provo, Utah: Association for Consumer Research, 368–73.

Bem, Sandra. 1993. *The lenses of gender. Transforming the debate on sexual identity.* New Haven: Yale University.

Bennett, Lance and Robert Entman (eds). 2001. *Mediated politics.* Cambridge: Cambridge University Press.

Benwell, Bethan. 2009. "'A pathetic and racist and awful character': Ethnomethodological approaches to the reception of diasporic fiction", *Language and Literature*, 18, 3: 300–15.

Benwell, Bethan. 2007. "Readers' responses to the use of irony in men's magazines", *Journalism Studies* 8, 4: 539–49.

Benwell, Bethan. 2005. "'Lucky this is anonymous!' Men's magazines and ethnographies of reading: A textual culture approach", *Discourse and Society*, 16, 2: 147–72.

Benwell, Bethan. 2003. "Introduction: Masculinity and men's lifestyle magazines", in: Bethan Benwell (ed.), *Masculinity and men's lifestyle magazines*. Oxford: Blackwell: 6–29.

Benwell, Bethan, James Procter and Gemma Robinson (eds). 2012. *Postcolonial audiences: Readers, viewers and reception*. New York: Routledge.

Benwell, Bethan and Elizabeth Stokoe. 2006. *Discourse and identity*. Edinburgh: Edinburgh University Press.

Bergvall, Victoria, Janet Bing and Alice Freed (eds). 1996. *Rethinking language and gender research: Theory and practice*. London: Longman.

Bernstein, Basil. 1996. *Pedagogy, symbolic control and identity*. London: Taylor & Francis.

Bhaskar, Roy. 1986. *Scientific realism and human emancipation*. London: Verso.

Billig, Michael, Susan Condor, Derek Edwards, Michael Gane, David Middleton and Alan Radley. 1988. *Ideological dilemmas: A social psychology of everyday thinking*. London: Sage.

Blommaert, Jan. 2005. *Discourse: A critical introduction*. Cambridge: Cambridge University Press.

Blommaert, Jan and Chris Bulcaen. 2000. "Critical Discourse Analysis", *Annual Review of Anthropology*, 29: 447–66.

Boden, Sharon. 2007. "Consuming pleasure on the wedding day: The lived experience of being a bride", in: Lydia Martens and Emma Casey (eds), *Gender and consumption: Material culture and the commercialisation of everyday life*. Hampshire UK: Ashgate Press, 109–22.

Boden, Sharon. 2003. *Consumerism, romance and the wedding experience*. New York: Palgrave MacMillan.

Boden, Sharon. 2001. "'Superbrides': Wedding consumer culture and the construction of bridal identity", *Sociological Research Online*, 6, 1, (http://www.socresonline.org.uk/6/1/boden.html) (access date March 13, 2009).

Bordo, Susan. 1999. *The male body: A new look at men in public and in private*. New York: Farrar, Straus and Giroux.

Bordo, Susan. 1993. *Unbearable weight: Feminism, western culture, and the body*. California: University of California Press.

Bourdieu, Pierre. 1992. *Distinction: A social critique of the judgement of taste*. London: Routledge.

Bourdieu, Pierre. 1991. *Language and symbolic power*. (Translated by Gino Raymond and Mathew Adamson.) Cambridge: Polity Press.

Bourdieu, Pierre. 1990. *The logic of practice*. Stanford, CA: Stanford University Press.

Bourdieu, Pierre. 1979. "Symbolic power", *Critique of Anthropology*, 13, 14: 77–85.

Bourdieu, Pierre. 1977. *Outline of a theory of practice*. Cambridge: Cambridge University Press.

Bourdieu, Pierre and Jean-Claude Passeron. 1977. *Reproduction in education, society and culture*. London: Sage.

Bourdleu, Pierre and Louis J. D. Wacquant. 1992. *An invitation to reflexive sociology*. Chicago: Chicago University Press.

Brown, Gillian and Stephen Levinson. 1987. *Universals in language use: Politeness phenomena*. Cambridge: Polity Press.

Brown, Wendy. 1995. *States of injury: Power and freedom in late modernity*. Princeton: Princeton University Press.

Brunsdon, Charlotte. 2005. "Feminism, postfeminism, Martha, Martha and Nigella", *Cinema Journal*, 44, 2: 110–16.

Brunsdon, Charlotte. 1993. "Identity in feminist TV criticism", *Media, Culture and Society*, 15: 309–20.

Bucholtz, Mary and Kira Hall. 2005. "Identity and interaction: A sociocultural linguistic approach", *Discourse Studies*, 7, 4–5: 585–614.

Bulcroft, Kris, Richard Bulcroft, Linda Smeins and Helen Cranage. 1997. "The social construction of the North American honeymoon, 1880–1995", *Journal of Family History*, 22, 4: 462–90.

Burr, Vivien. 1995. *An introduction to social constructionism*. London: Routledge.

Butler, Judith. 1997. *The psychic life of power: Theories in subjection*. New York: Routledge.

Butler, Judith. 1994. "Gender as performance: An interview with Judith Butler", *Radical Philosophy*, 67: 32–9.

Butler, Judith. 1993. *Bodies that matter: On the discursive limits of "sex"*. London: Routledge.

Butler, Judith. 1990. *Gender trouble: Feminism and the subversion of identity*. New York: Routledge.

Caldas-Coulthard, Carmen Rosa. 1996. "'Women who pay for sex. And enjoy it': Transgression versus morality in women's magazines", in: Carmen Rosa Caldas-Coulthard and Malcolm Coulthard (eds), *Texts and practices: Readings in critical discourse analysis*. London: Routledge, 250–70.

Caldas-Coulthard, Carmen Rosa. 1993. "From discourse analysis to critical discourse analysis: The differential representation of women and men speaking in written news", in: John M. Sinclair, Michael Hoey and Gwyneth Fox (eds), *Techniques of description: Spoken and written discourse*. London: Routledge, 196–208.

Calhoun, Craig. 1995. *Critical social theory: Culture, history, and the challenge of difference*. Oxford: Blackwell.

Calhoun, Craig, Edward Li Puma and Moishe Postone (eds). 1993. *Bourdieu. Critical perspectives*. Cambridge: Polity Press.

Cameron, Deborah. 2005. "Language, gender, and sexuality: Current issues and new directions", *Applied Linguistics*, 26, 4: 482–502.

Cameron, Deborah. 2003. "Gender and language ideologies", in: Janet Holmes and Miriam Meyerhoff (eds), *Handbook of language and gender*. Oxford: Basil Blackwell, 447–67.

Cameron, Deborah. 1998. "Gender, language and discourse: A review essay". *Signs*, 1: 945–73.

Cameron, Deborah. 1995. *Verbal hygiene*. London: Routledge.

Carabine, Jean. [2001] 2009. "Unmarried motherhood 1830–1990: A genealogical analysis", in: Margaret Wetherell, Stephanie Taylor and Simeon J. Yates (eds). *Discourse as data: A guide for analysis*. London: Sage, 267–310.

Carey, James. 1989. *Communication as culture: Essays on media and society*. London: Routledge.

Chaney, David. 1996. *Lifestyles*. London: Routledge.

Chen, Yumin. 2010. "Contestable reality: A multi-level view on modality in multimodal pedagogic context", in: Ahmar Mahboob and Naomi Knight (eds), *Appliable linguistics*. Continuum: 221–33.

Chiapello, Eve and Norman Fairclough. 2002. "Understanding the new management ideology: A transdisciplinary contribution from critical discourse analysis and new sociology of capitalism", *Discourse Society*, 13, 2: 185–208.

Chinwe, R. Ezeifeka and Nneka N. Osakwe. 2013. "Gender representation in the 1999 Nigerian constitution: A critical discourse analysis for socio-political equity", *Discourse & Society*, 24, 6: 687–700.

Chouliaraki, Lilie. 2002. "'The contingency of universality': Some thoughts on discourse and realism", *Social Semiotics*, 12, 1: 83–114.

Chouliaraki, Lilie and Norman Fairclough. 1999. *Discourse in late modernity. Rethinking critical discourse analysis*. Edinburgh: Edinburgh University Press.

Cicourel, Aaron V. 1969. *Method and measurement in sociology*. New York: The Free Press.

Coates, Jennifer. 1997. "Competing discourses of femininity", in: Helga Kotthoff and Ruth Wodak (eds), *Communicating gender in context*. Amsterdam: John Benjamins, 285–314.

Connell, R.W. 1995. *Masculinities*. Cambridge: Polity Press.

Connell, R.W. 1987. *Gender and power: Society, the person, and sexual politics*. Cambridge: Polity Press.

Corner, John. 1991. "Meaning, genre and context", in: James Curran and Michael Gurevitch (eds), *Mass Media and Society*. London: Edward Arnold, 267–84.

Couldry, Nick. 2000. *The place of media power: Pilgrims and witnesses of the media age*. London: Routledge.

Crawford, Mary. 1995. *Talking difference: On gender and language*. London: Sage.

Currie, Dawn. 2001. "Dear Abby. Advice pages as a site for the operation of power", *Feminist Theory*, 2, 3: 259–81.

Currie, Dawn. 1999. *Girl talk: Adolescent magazines and their readers*. Toronto: University of Toronto Press.

Currie, Dawn. 1997. "Decoding femininity: Advertisements and their teenage readers", *Gender and Society*, 11, 4: 453–77.

Currie, Dawn. 1993. "'Here comes the bride': The making of a 'modern traditional' wedding in Western culture", *Journal of Comparative Family Studies*, 24, 3: 403–21.

Currie, Dawn, Kelly M. Deirdre and Shauna Pomerantz. 2007. "Listening to girls: Discursive positioning and the construction of self", *International Journal of Qualitative Studies in Education*, 20, 4: 377–400.

Davies, Bronwyn. 1997. "Constructing and deconstructing masculinities through critical literacy", *Gender and Education*, 9, 1: 9–30.

Davies, Bronwyn. 1991. "The concept of agency: A feminist poststructuralism analysis", *Social Analysis*, 30: 42–53.

Davies, Bronwyn and Rom Harré. 1999. "Positioning and personhood", in: Rom Harré and Luk van Langenhøve (eds), *Positioning theory*. Oxford: Blackwell, 32–52.

Davies, Bronwyn and Rom Harré. [2001] 2009. "Positioning: The discursive production of selves", in: Margaret Wetherell, Stephanie Taylor and Simeon J. Yates (eds), *Discourse theory and practice*. London: The Open University, 261–71.

de Certeau, Michel. 1984. *The practice of everyday life*. (Translated by Steven Randall.) Berkeley: University of California Press.

de Lauretis, Teresa. 1989. *Alice doesn't: Feminism, semiotics, cinema*. Bloomington: Indiana University Press.

Downing, John and Charles Husband. 2005. *Representing "race": Racisms, ethnicities and media*. London: Sage.

Drew, Paul. 1998. "Complaints about transgressions and misconduct", *Research and Social Interaction*, 31: 295–325.

Eckert, Penelope and Sally McConnell-Ginet. 2003. *Language and gender*. Cambridge: Cambridge University Press.

Edwards, Derek. 1995. "Sacks and psychology", *Theory and Psychology*, 5, 4: 579–96.

Edwards, Derek, Malcolm Ashmore and Jonathan Potter. 1995. "Death and furniture: The rhetoric, politics and theology of bottom line arguments against relativism", *History of the Human Sciences*, 8, 2: 25–49.

Eggins, Suzanne. [2004] 2007. *An introduction to systemic functional linguistics*. London: Continuum.

Eggins, Suzanne and Rick Iedema. 1997. "Difference without diversity: Semantic orientation and ideology in competing women's magazines", in: Ruth Wodak (ed.), *Gender and discourse*. London: Sage, 165–96.

Emerson, Caryl and Michael Holquist (eds). 1986. *Speech genres and other late essays*. (Translated by Vern M. McGee.) Austin: University of Texas Press.

Engstrom, Erika. 2012. *The bride factory: Mass media portrayals of women and weddings*. New York: Peter Lang.

Eriksson Barajas, Katarina and Karin Aronsson. 2009. "Avid versus struggling readers: Co-construed pupil identities in school booktalk", *Language and Literature*, 18, 3: 281–99.

Fairclough, Norman. 2005a. "Critical Discourse Analysis in transdisciplinary research", in: Ruth Wodak and Paul Chilton (eds), *A new agenda in (Critical) Discourse Analysis*. Amsterdam: John Benjamins, 53–70.

Fairclough, Norman. 2005b. "Peripheral vision: Discourse analysis in organization studies: The case for critical realism", *Organization Studies*, 26, 6: 915–39.

Fairclough, Norman. [2001] 2009. "The discourse of New Labour: Critical discourse analysis", in: Margaret Wetherell, Stephanie Taylor and Simeon J. Yates (eds), *Discourse as data. A guide for analysis*. London: The Open University, 229–66.

Fairclough, Norman. 1996. "A reply to Henry Widdowson's 'Discourse Analysis: A Critical View'", *Language and Literature*, 5, 1: 49–56.

Fairclough, Norman. 1995a. *Critical discourse analysis: The critical study of language*. London: Longman.

Fairclough, Norman. 1995b. *Media discourse*. London: Edward Arnold.

Fairclough, Norman. 1994. "Critical discourse analysis and marketisation of public discourse: The universities", *Discourse and Society*, 4, 2: 133–68.

Fairclough, Norman. 1992. *Discourse and social change*. Cambridge: Polity Press.

Fairclough, Norman. 1989. *Language and power*. London: Longman.

Fairclough, Norman, Jane Mulderrig and Ruth Wodak. 2011. "Critical discourse analysis", in: Theo van Dijk (ed.), *Discourse studies: A multidisciplinary introduction*. London: Sage, 357–78

Fairclough, Norman and Anna Mauranen. 1997. "The conversationalization of political discourse: A comparative view" in: Jan Blommaert and Chris Bulcaen (eds), *Political linguistics*. Amsterdam: John Benjamins, 89–119.

Featherstone, Mike. 1991. *Consumer culture and postmodernism*. London: Sage.

Finch, Janet and Penny Summerfield. 1991. "Social reconstruction and the emergence of companionate marriage, 1945–59", in: David Clark (ed.), *Marriage, domestic life and social change*. London: Routledge, 7–32.

Fish, Stanley. 1980. *Is there a text in this class? The authority of interpretative communities*. Cambridge, MA: Harvard University Press.

Fiske, John. 1987. *Television culture*. London and New York: Routledge.

Fiske, John. 1986. "Television: Polysemy and popularity", *Critical Studies in Mass Communication*, 3: 391–408.

Flanagan, Eugene. 2010. "Death penalty discourses, the printed media, and the UK public sphere: A critical analysis", *Critical Discourse Studies*, 7, 3: 177–90.

Foucault, Michel. 1989. *Foucault live (Interviews 1966–84)*. (Edited by Sylvere Lortinger.) New York: Semiotext.

Foucault, Michel. 1988. "Technologies of the self", in: Luther H. Martin, Huck Gutman and Patrick H. Hutton (eds), *Technologies of the self: A seminar with Michel Foucault*. Amherst: University of Massachusetts Press, 16–49.

Foucault, Michel. 1986. *The care of the self: The history of sexuality*. Vol. 3. New York: Pantheon.

Foucault, Michel. 1985. *The use of pleasure: The history of sexuality*. Vol. 2. London: Penguin Books.

Foucault, Michel. 1982. "The subject and power", in: Hubert Dreyfus and Paul Rainbow (eds), *Beyond structuralism and hermeneutics*. Brighton: Harvester, 208–26.

Foucault, Michel. 1981. *The history of sexuality*. Vol. 1: *An introduction*. Harmondsworth: Pelican.

Foucault, Michel. 1980. *Power/knowledge: Selected interviews and other writings 1972–1977*. (Edited by Colin Gordon.) Brighton: Harvester.

Foucault, Michel. 1977. *Discipline and punish: The birth of the prison*. New York: Pantheon Books.

Foucault, Michel. 1972. *The archaeology of knowledge*. London: Tavistock.

Foucault, Michel. [1966] 2001. *The order of things: The archaeology of human sciences*. London Routledge.

Frazer, Elizabeth. 1987. "Teenage girls reading *Jackie*", *Media, Culture and Society*, 9, 4: 407–25.

Frisby, Cynthia M. and Erika Engstrom. 2006. "Always a bridesmaid and never a bride: Portrayals of women of color as brides in bridal magazines", *Media Report to Women*, 1–4.

Frost, Liz. 2001. *Young women and the body: A feminist sociology*. New York: Palgrave Macmillan.

Gal, Susan. 1995. "Language, gender and power: An anthropological review", in: Kira Hall and Mary Bucholtz (eds), *Gender articulated: Language and the socially constructed self*. London: Routledge, 169–82.

Ganahl, Dennis J., Thomas J. Prinsen and Sarah Berker Netzley. 2003. "A content analysis of prime time commercials: A contextual framework of gender representation", *Sex Roles*, 49, 9–10: 545–51.

Garfinkel, Harold and Harvey Sacks. 1970. "On formal structures of practical actions", in: John C. McKinney and Edward A. Tiryakin (eds), *Theoretical sociology*. New York: Appleton Century Crofts, 338–66.

Gauntlett, David. 2008. *Media, gender and identity*. London: Routledge.

Genz, Stéphanie and Benjamin A. Brabon. 2009. *Postfeminism. Cultural texts and theories*. Edinburgh: Edinburgh University Press.

Gergen, Kenneth. 1994a. *Realities and relationships: Soundings in social construction*. Cambridge, MA: Harvard University Press.

Gibson, James J. 1979. *The ecological approach to visual perception*. Boston: Houghton Mifflin.

Giddens, Anthony. 1984. *The constitution of society: Outline of the theory of structuration*. Cambridge: Polity Press.

Giddens, Anthony. 1992. *Transformation of intimacy*. Cambridge: Polity Press.

Giddens, Anthony. 1991. *Modernity and self-identity: Self and society in the late modern age*. Stanford, CA: Stanford University Press.

Gilbert, Nigel and Michael Mulkay. 1984. *Opening Pandora's box: A sociological analysis of scientists' discourse*. Cambridge: Cambridge University Press.

Gills, Rosalind. 2006. *Gender and the media*. Oxford: Polity Press.

Glapka, Ewa. 2012. "Stories of bridal and feminine experience: Production of gendered narratives in the context of media reception", in *Poznań Studies in Contemporary Linguistics*, 48, 1: 127–48.

Glass, Lillian. 1992. *He says, she says: Closing the communication gap between the sexes*. New York: Putman.

Goffman, Erving. 1959. *Presentation of self in everyday life*. London: Penguin.

Goldman Robert, Deborah Heath and Sharon L. Smith. 1991. "Commodity feminism", *Critical Studies in Mass Communication*, 8, 3: 333–51.

Gouveia Carlos A. M. 2003. "Critical Discourse Analysis and the development of the new science", in: Gilbert Weiss and Ruth Wodak (eds), *Critical Discourse Analysis: Theory and interdisciplinarity*. Basingstoke: Palgrave Macmillan, 47–62.

Graddol, David and Oliver Boyd-Barrett (eds). 1994. *Media and texts: Authors and readers*. Clarendon: Multilingual Matters.

Gramsci, Antonio. 1971. *Selections from the prison notebooks of Antonio Gramsci*. (Edited and translated by Q. Hoare and G. Nowell Smith.) London: Lawrence Wishart.

Gray, Ann. 1992. *Video playtime: The gendering of a leisure technology*. London: Routledge.

Greer, Germaine. 1999. *The whole woman*. London: Doubleday.

Grimshaw, Jean. 1999. "Working out with Merleau-Ponty", in: Jean Grimshaw and Jane Arthurs (eds), *Women's bodies: Discipline and transgression*. London: Cassell, 91–116.

Grodin, Debra and Thomas Lindlof (eds). 1996. *Constructing the self in a mediated world*. London: Sage.

Guberman, Ross Mitchell (ed.). 1996. *Julia Kristeva. Interviews*. New York: Columbia University Press.

Haack, Susan. 1998. *Manifesto of a passionate moderate*. Chicago: University of Chicago Press.

Habermas, Jürgen. 1989. *The structural transformation of the public sphere.* (Translated by T. Burger.) Cambridge: Polity Press.

Hall, Geoff. 2009. "Texts, readers – and real readers", *Language and Literature*, 18, 3: 331–7

Hall, Kira. 1995. "Lip service on the fantasy lines", in: Kira Hall and Mary Bucholtz (eds), *Gender articulated: Language and the socially constructed self.* London: Routledge, 183–216.

Hall, Stuart. 1992. "The West and the rest", in: Stuart Hall and Bram Gieben (eds), *Formations of modernity.* Cambridge: Polity Press/The Open University, 275–320.

Hall, Stuart. [1980] 1996. "Encoding/decoding", in: Stuart Hall, Dorothy Hobson, Andrew Lowe and Paul Willis (eds), *Culture, media, language: Working papers in cultural studies, 1972–1979.* London: Routledge, 128–38.

Halliday, Michael Alexander Kirkwood. 1978. *Language as social semiotic: The social interpretation of language and meaning.* London: Edward Arnold.

Hammersley Martyn. 1997. "On the foundations of critical discourse analysis", *Language and Communication*, 17, 3: 237–48.

Haraway, Donna. [1993] 1999. "A cyborg manifesto", in: Simon During (ed.), *The cultural studies reader.* London: Routledge, 271–91.

Haraway, Donna. 1991. *Simians, cyborgs, and women.* London: Free Association Books.

Haraway, Donna. 1988. "Situated knowledges: The science question in feminism and the privilege of partial perspective", *Feminist Studies*, 14, 3: 575–99.

Harding, Sandra. 1991. *Whose science? Whose knowledge? Thinking from women's lives.* Milton Keynes: Open University Press.

Hargreaves, Jenny and Ian MacDonald. 2000. "Cultural studies and the sociology of sport", in: Jay Coakley and Eric Dunning (eds), *Handbook of sport studies.* London: Sage, 48–60.

Hartstock, Nancy. 1983. "The feminist standpoint", in: Sandra Harding and Merrill B. Hintikka (eds), *Discovering reality.* Dordrecht: Reidel Publishing Company, 283–310.

Heilbrun, Carolyn G. 1988. *Writing a woman's life.* New York: Norton. Heritage.

Hekman, Susan. 1997. "Truth and method: Feminist standpoint theory revisited", *Signs*, 22, 2: 341–65.

Hepburn, Alexa and Sally Wiggins. 2007. *Discursive research in practice: New approaches to psychology and interaction.* Cambridge: Cambridge University Press.

Hepp, Andreas, Friedrich Krotz and Shaun Moores (eds). 2008. *Network, connectivity and flow: Key concepts for media and cultural studies.* New York: Hampton Press.

Heritage, John. 1984. *Garfinkel and ethnomethodology.* Cambridge: Polity Press.

Hermes, Joke. 1995. *Reading women's magazines: An analysis of everyday media use.* Cambridge: Polity Press.

Hodge, Robert and Gunther R. Kress. 1996. *Language as ideology.* London: Routledge.

Hodge, Robert and Gunther R. Kress. 1988. *Social semiotics.* Cambridge: Polity Press.

Holmes, Janet and Stephanie Schnurr. 2006. "'Doing femininity' at work: More than just relational practice", *Journal of Sociolinguistics*, 10, 1: 31–51.

Horkheimer, Max and Theodor W. Adorno. [1972] 1993. *The dialectic of Enlightenment.* (Translated by John Cumming.) New York: Continuum.

Howard, Vicki. 2003. "A 'real man's ring': Gender and the invention of tradition", *Journal of Social History*, 36: 837–56.

Husband, Charles. 2000. "Media and the public sphere in multi ethnic socie-ties", in: Simon Cottle (ed.), *Ethnic minorities and the media*. Buckingham: Open University Press, 199–214.

Hutchby, Ian and Robin Woofit. 1998. *Conversation analysis: Principles, practices and applications*. Cambridge: Polity Press.

Iedema, Rick and Ruth Wodak. 1999. "Introduction: Organizational discourses and practices", *Discourse and Society*, 10: 5–19.

Illouz, Eva. 1997. *Consuming the romantic utopia: Love and the cultural contradictions of capitalism*. Berkeley: University of California Press.

Ingraham, Chrys. 2008. *White weddings: Romancing heterosexuality in popular culture*. London: Routledge.

Intemann, Kristen. 2010. "25 years of feminist empiricism and standpoint theory: Where are we now?", *Hypatia*, 25, 4: 778–96.

Iser, Wolfgang. 1978. *The act of reading: A theory of aesthetic reception*. London: Johns Hopkins University Press.

Ivanic, Roz. 1998. *Writing and identity: The discoursal construction of identity in academic writing*. Amsterdam: John Benjamins.

Jackson, Peter, Nick Stevenson and Kate Brooks. 2001. *Making sense of men's maga-zines*. Cambridge: Polity Press.

Järvinen, Margaretha. 2000. "The biographical illusion: Constructing meaning in qualitative interviews", *Qualitative Inquiry*, 6, 3: 379–91.

Jauss, Hans R. 1982. *Toward an aesthetic of reception*. (Translated by Timothy Bahti.) Minneapolis: University of Minnesota Press.

Jaworski, Adam and Nikolas Coupland (eds). 1999. *The discourse reader*. London: Routledge.

Jeffries, Lesley. 2007. *Textual construction of the female body. A critical discourse approach*. Basingstoke: Palgrave Macmillan.

Jones, Alison. 1993. "Becoming a 'girl': Post-structuralist suggestions for educa-tional research", *Gender and Education*, 5: 157–66.

Jones, Meredith. 2008. *Skintight: An anatomy of cosmetic surgery*. Oxford: Berg.

Jäger, Siegfried. 2001. "Discourse and knowledge: Theoretical and methodological aspects of a critical discourse and dispositive analysis", in: Ruth Wodak and Michael Meyer (eds), *Methods of Critical Discourse Analysis*. London: Sage, 32–62.

Jørgensen, Marianne and Louise Phillips. 2002. *Discourse analysis as theory and method*. London, Sage.

Kalmijn, Matthijs. 2004. "Marriage rituals as reinforcers of role transitions: An analysis of weddings in the Netherlands", *Journal of Marriage and Family*, 66: 582–94.

Kellner, Douglas. 1989. *Critical theory, Marxism and modernity*. Cambridge: Polity Press.

Koller, Veronica. 2008. "'Not just a colour': Pink as a gender and sexuality marker in visual communication", *Visual Communication*, 7, 4: 395–423.

Korobov, Neill and Michael Bamberg. 2004. "Positioning a 'mature' self in inter-active practices: How adolescent males negotiate 'physical attraction' in group talk", *British Journal of Developmental Psychology*, 22: 471–92.

Kress, Gunther R. 2001. "Sociolinguistics and social semiotics", in: Paul Cobley (ed.), *The Routledge companion to semiotics and linguistics*. London: Routledge, 66–82.

Kress, Gunther R. and Theo van Leeuwen. 2002. "Colour as a semiotic mode: Notes for a grammar of colour", *Visual Communication*, 1, 3: 343–68.

Kress, Gunther R. and Theo van Leeuwen. 2001. *Multimodal discourse: The modes and media of contemporary communication*. London: Edward Arnold.

Kress, Gunther and Theo van Leeuwen [1996] 2006. *Reading images: The grammar of visual design*. London: Routledge.

Krzyżanowski, Michał. 2010. *The discursive construction of European identities: A multilevel approach to discourse and identity in the transforming European Union*. Frankfurt am Main: Peter Lang Verlag.

Laclau, Ernesto and Chantal Mouffe. 1985. *Hegemony and socialist strategy*. London: Verso.

Lakoff, Robin. 1975. *Language and woman's place*. Oxford: Oxford University Press.

Lazar, Michelle. 2006. "'Discover the power of femininity!' Analyzing global 'power femininity' in local advertising", *Feminist Media Studies*, 6, 4: 505–17.

Lazar, Michelle M. (ed.). 2005. *Feminist critical discourse analysis: Gender, power and ideology in discourse*. Basingstoke: Palgrave Macmillan.

Lazar, Michelle. 2002. "Consuming personal relationships: The achievement of feminine self-identity through other-centeredness", in: Lia Litosseliti and Jane Sunderland (eds), *Gender identity and discourse analysis*. Amsterdam: John Benjamins, 111–28.

Leap, William. 1994. "Can there be gay discourse without gay language?", in: Mary Bucholtz, Anita C. Liang, Laurel A. Sutton and Caitlin Hines (eds), *Cultural performances*. Berkeley: Berkeley Women and Language Group, 399–404.

Lee, Alison. 1997. "Questioning the critical: Linguistics, literacy and pedagogy", in: Sandy Muspratt, Allan Luke and Peter Freebody (eds), *Constructing critical literacies: Teaching and learning textual practice*. Cresskill, NJ: Hampton Press, 409–32.

Leech, Geoffrey. 1966. *English in advertising*. London: Longman.

Lemke, Jay L. 2003. *Multimedia genres for science education and scientific literacy*. (http://academic.brooklyn.cuny.edu/education/jlemke/webs/nasa/Davis-NASA.html) (access date October 13, 2003)

Lewis, Charles. 1998. "Working the ritual: Professional wedding photography and the American middle class", *Journal of Communication Inquiry*, 22, 72–92.

Liebes, Tamar and Elihu Katz. 1990. *The export of meaning: Cross-cultural readings of Dallas*. New York: Oxford University Press.

Lim, Leonel. 2014. "Ideology, rationality and reproduction in education: A critical discourse analysis", *Discourse*, 35, 1: 61–76.

Link, Jürgen. 1983. "Was ist und was bringt Diskurstaktik", *kultuRRevolution*, 2: 60–6.

Litosseliti, Lia (ed.). 2010. *Research methods in linguistics*. London: Continuum.

Litosseliti, Lia and Jane Sunderland (eds). 2002. *Gender identity and discourse analysis*. Amsterdam: John Benjamins.

Livingstone, Sonia. 1994. "Watching talk: Engagement and gender in the audience discussion programme", *Media, Culture and Society*, 16, 3: 429–48.

Long, Elizabeth. 2003. *Book clubs: Women and the uses of reading in everyday life*. Chicago: Chicago University Press.

Lyotard, Jean F. 1984. *The postmodern condition: A report on knowledge*. Manchester: Manchester University Press.

MacCabe, Colin. 1985. *Theoretical essays: Film, linguistics, literature*. Manchester: Manchester University Press.

Macdonald, Myra. 2003: *Exploring media discourse*. London: Edward Arnold.

Machin, David and Joanna Thornborrow. 2003. "Branding and discourse: The case of *Cosmopolitan*", *Discourse and Society*, 14, 4: 453–71.

Mann, Patricia. 1994. *Micro-politics: Agency in postfeminist era*. Minneapolis: University of Minnesota Press.

Marcuse, Herbert. 1968. *One dimensional man*. London: Sphere.

Markula, Pirkko. 2003. "The technologies of the self: Sport, feminism, and Foucault", *Sociology of Sport Journal*, 20: 87–107.

Marling, Raili. 2010. "The intimidating other: Feminist critical discourse analysis of the representation of feminism in Estonian print media", *NORA – Nordic Journal of Feminist and Gender Research*, 18, 1: 7–19.

Martin, James R. 1994. "Macro-genres: The ecology of the page", *Network*, 21: 29–52.

Maybin, Janet. [2001] 2009. "Language, struggle and voice: The Bakhtin/Volosinov writings", in: Margaret Wetherell, Stephanie Taylor and Simeon J. Yates (eds), *Discourse theory and practice*. London: The Open University, 64–71.

McKee, Robert. 1999. *Story*. London: Methuen.

McNay, Lois. 2000. *Gender agency: Reconfiguring the subject in feminist and social theory*. Cambridge: Polity Press.

McRobbie, Angela. 1981. "*Jackie* magazine: Romantic individualism and the teenage girl", in: Angela McRobbie (ed.), *Feminism and youth culture*. New York: Routledge, 67–117.

Marx, Karl. [1852] 2000. "The Eighteenth Brumaire of Louis Bonaparte", in: David McLellan (ed.), *Karl Marx: Selected Works*. Oxford: Oxford University Press.

Miller, Daniel and Don Slater. 2000. *The Internet: An ethnographic approach*. Oxford: Berg.

Miller, Jodie and Barry Glassner. 1997. "'The inside and the outside': Finding realities in interviews", in: David Silverman (ed.), *Qualitative research: Theory, method and practice*, London: Sage, 99–112.

Mills, Sarah. 1995. *Feminist stylistics*. London: Routledge.

Mishler, Elliot G. 1999. *Storylines: Craftartists' narratives of identity*. Cambridge, MA: Harvard University Press.

Modleski, Tania. 1991. *Feminism without women*. New York: Routledge.

Montemurro, Beth. 2002. "You go 'cause you have to': The bridal shower as a ritual of obligation", *Symbolic Interaction*, 25: 67–92.

Montemurro, Beth. 2005. "Add men, don't stir: Reproducing traditional gender roles in modern wedding showers", *Journal of Contemporary Ethnography*, 34: 6–35.

Moores, Shaun. 1990. "Texts, readers and contexts of reading: Developments on the study of audience", *Media, Culture and Society*, 12, 1: 9–29.

Morley, David. 1986. *Family television*. London: Comedia.

Morley, David and Charlotte Brunsdon. 1999. *The 'Nationwide' television studies*. London: Routledge.

Mouzelis, Nicos. 2007. Habitus and reflexivity: Restructuring Bourdieu's theory of practice", *Sociological Research Online*, 12, 6 (http://www.socresonline.org.uk) (access date February 10, 2014).

Mouzelis, Nicos. 1995. *Sociological theory: What went wrong? Diagnosis and remedies*. London: Routledge.

Mulvey, Laura. 1988. "Visual pleasure and narrative cinema", in: Constance Penley (ed.), *Feminism and film theory*. New York: Routledge.

Nash, Meredith. 2012. "Brides n' bumps", *Feminist Media Studies*, 4: 1–20.

Negra, Diane. 2009. *What a girl wants?: Fantasizing the reclamation of self in post-feminism*. New York: Routledge.

Neighbors, Lori A. and Jeffery Sobal. 2008. "Weight and weddings: Women's weight ideals and weight management behaviors for their wedding day", *Appetite*, 50: 550–4.

Ochs, Elinor. 1992. "Indexing gender", in: Alessandro Duranti and Charles Goodwin (eds), *Rethinking context. Language as an interactive phenomenon*. Cambridge: Cambridge University Press, 335–58.

Otnes, Cele and Elizabeth H. Pleck. 2003. *Cinderella dreams. The allure of the lavish wedding*. Berkeley: University of California Press.

Parker, Ian. 1992. *Discourse dynamics: Critical analysis for social and individual psychology*. London: Routledge.

Parker, Ian. 2002. *Critical discursive psychology*. London: Palgrave.

Parker, Ian (ed.). 1998. *Social constructionism, discourse and realism*. London: Sage.

Pennycook, Alistair. 1994. "Incommensurable discourses?", *Applied Linguistics* 15, 2: 115–38.

Pinnick, Casandra, Noretta Koertge and Robert F. Almeder (eds). 2003. *Scrutinizing feminist epistemology*. New Brunswick, NJ: Rutgers University Press.

Pipher, Mary. 1994. *Reviving Ophelia: Saving the selves of adolescent girls*. New York: Ballantine Books.

Plummer, Ken. 2001. *Documents of life 2: An invitation to critical humanism*. London: Sage.

Pomerantz, Anita. 1986. "Extreme case formulations: A way of legitimizing claims", *Human Studies*, 9, 2–3: 219–29.

Potter, Jonathan. 1996. *Representing reality. Discourse, rhetoric and social construction*. London: Sage.

Poynton, Cate. 1993. "Grammar, language and the social: Poststructuralism and systemic-functional linguistics", *Social Semiotics*, 3, 1: 1–21.

Prichard, Ivanka and Marika Tiggemann. 2008. "An examination of pre-wedding body image concerns in brides and bridesmaids", *Body Image*, 5: 395–8.

Pringle, Richard. 2005. "Masculinities, sport, and power: A critical comparison of Gramscian and Foucauldian inspired theoretical tools", *Journal of Sport and Social Issues*, 29: 256–78.

Radway, Janice. 1984. *Reading the romance*. North Carolina: University of North Carolina Press.

Reynolds, Jill. 2007. *The single woman: A discursive investigation*. London: Routledge.

Reynolds, Jill, Margaret Wetherell and Stephanie Taylor. 2007. "Choice and chance: Negotiating agency in narratives of singleness", *The Sociological Review*, 55, 2: 331–51.

Reynolds, Jill and Stephanie Taylor. 2005. "Narrating singleness: Life stories and deficit identities", *Narrative Inquiry*, 15, 2: 197–215.

Rich, Adrienne. 1980. "Compulsory sexuality and lesbian existence", *Signs*, 5, 4: 631–60.

Rose, Gillian. 2001. *Visual methodologies*. London: Sage.

Ross, Karen. 2001. "White media, black audience: Diversity and dissonance on British television", in: Karen Ross and Peter Playdon (eds), *Black marks: Minority ethnic audiences and media*. Aldershot: Ashgate, 3–14.

Ross, Karen and Virginia Nightingale. 2003. *Media and audiences: New perspectives*. Maidenhead: Open University Press.

Ruddock, Andy. 2001. *Understanding audiences: Theory and method*. London: Sage.

Sacks, Harvey. 1984. "Notes on methodology", in: Maxwell J. Atkinson and John Heritage (eds), *Structures of social action: Studies in conversation analysis*. Cambridge: Cambridge University Press, 21–7.

Sacks, Harvey, Emanuel A. Schegloff and Gail Jefferson. 1978. "A simplest systematics for the organization of turn-taking in conversation", in: Jim Schenkein (ed.), *Studies in the organization of conversational interaction*. New York: Academic Press, 7–55.

Sarangi, Srikant and Stefaan Slembrouck. 1996. *Language, bureaucracy and social control*. London: Longman.

Sayer, Andrew. 2000. *Realism and social science*. London: Sage.

Schegloff, Emanuel. A. 1998. "Text and context paper", *Discourse and Society*, 3: 4–37.

Schegloff, Emanuel. A. 1996. "Issues of relevance for discourse analysis: Contingency in action, interaction and co-participant context", in: Eduard H. Hovy and Donia R. Scott (eds), *Computational and conversational discourse: Burning issues – an interdisciplinary account*. Heidelberg: Springer, 3–38.

Schroder, Kim, Kirsten Drotner, Stephen Kline and Catherine Murray. 2003. *Researching audiences*. London: Arnold.

Schweingruber, David, Sine Anahita and Nancy Berns. 2004. "'Popping the question' when the answer is known: The engagement proposal as performance", *Sociological Focus*, 37: 143–61.

Scollon, Ron. 2001. "Action and text: Towards an integrated understanding of the place of text in social (inter)action, mediated discourse analysis and the problem of social action", in: Ruth Wodak and Michael Meyer (eds), *Methods of Critical Discourse Analysis*. London: Sage, 139–83.

Scollon, Ron. 1995. *Mediated discourse as social interaction*. London: Longman.

Scollon, Ron and Suzie Wong Scollon. 2003. *Discourses in place: Language in the material world*. London: Routledge.

Scollon, Suzanne. 2003. "Political and somatic alignment: Habitus, ideology and social practice", in: Gilbert Weiss and Ruth Wodak (eds), *Critical Discourse Analysis – theory and interdisciplinarity*. London: Palgrave, 167–99.

Seiter, Ellen. 1999. *Television and new media audiences*. Oxford: Clarendon Press.

Semino, Elena and Culpeper, Jonathan. 2002. *Cognitive stylistics: Language and cognition in text analysis*. Amsterdam/Philadelphia: John Benjamins.

Sgroi, Renee. 2006. "Consuming the Reality TV Wedding", *Ethnologies*, 28, 2: 113–31.

Shakespeare, Pamela. 1998. *Aspects of confused speech: A study of verbal interaction between confused and normal speakers*. London: Lawrence Erlbaum.

Shapiro, Michael. [2001] 2009. "Textualizing global politics", in: Margaret Wetherell, Stephanie Taylor and Simeon J. Yates (eds), *Discourse theory and practice*, London: The Open University, 318–23.

Shirazi, Farid. 2013. "Social media and the social movements in the Middle East and North Africa: A critical discourse analysis", *Information, Technology & People*, 26, 1: 28–49

Shotter, John and Kenneth Gergen (eds). 1989. *Texts of identity*. London: Sage.

Silverstein, Michael. 1985. "Language and the culture of gender: At the intersection of structure, usage, and ideology", in: Elizabeth Mertz and Richard J. Parmentier (eds), *Semiotic mediation: Sociocultural and psychological perspectives*. Orlando, FL: Academic Press, 219–59.

Simpson, Alyson. 1997. "'It's a game!': The construction of gendered subjectivity", in: Ruth Wodak (ed.), *Gender and discourse*. London: Sage, 197–224.

Sinclair, John and Stuart Cunningham. 2001. "Diasporas and the media", in: Stuart Cunningham and John Sinclair (eds), *Floating lives: The media and Asian diasporas*. Lanham, Boulder, New York, Oxford: Rowman & Littlefield, 1–26.

Smith, Anne Marie. 1998. *Laclau and Mouffe. The radical democratic imaginary*. London: Routledge.

Smith, Dorothy. 1992. "Sociology from women's experience. A reaffirmation", *Sociological Theory*, 10, 1: 88–98.

Smith, Dorothy. 1990. *Texts, fact and femininity: Exploring relations of ruling*. London: Routledge.

Smith, Dorothy. 1988. *The everyday world as problematic: A feminist sociology*. Toronto: University of Toronto Press.

Smith, Dorothy. 1974. "Women's perspective as a radical critique of sociology", *Sociological Inquiry*, 44, 1: 7–13.

Smith, Paul. 1988. *Discerning the subject*. Minneapolis: University of Minnesota Press.

Sparkes, Andrew C. 1992. "The paradigms debate: An extended review and a celebration of difference", in: Andrew C. Sparkes (ed.), *Research in physical education and sport: Exploring alternative vision*. London: Falmer, 9–60.

Speer, Susan A. and John Potter. 2000. "The management of heterosexist talk: Conversational resources and prejudiced claims", in: Paul McIlvenny (ed.), *Talking gender and sexuality*. Amsterdam: John Benjamins, 151–80.

Stevens, Jennifer Anne. 1990. *From masculine to feminine and all points in between: A practical guide for transvestites, cross-dressers, transgenderists, transsexuals, and others who choose to develop a more feminine image...and for the curious and concerned*. Cambridge, MA: Different Path Press.

Stevenson, Nick, Peter Jackson and Kate Brooks. 2000. "The politics of 'new' men's lifestyle magazines", *European Journal of Cultural Studies*, 3, 3: 369–88.

Stockwell, Peter. 2002. *Cognitive poetics: An introduction*. London: Routledge.

Stokoe, Elizabeth. 2000. "Toward a conversation analytic to gender and discourse", *Feminism and Psychology*, 10, 4: 552–63.

Stokes, Jane. [2002] 2013. *How to do media and cultural studies*. London: Sage.

Sunderland, Jane. 2004. *Gendered discourses*. London: Palgrave.

Sunderland, Jane, Maire Cowley, Fauziah Abdul Rahim, Christina Leontzakou and Julie Shattuck. 2002. "From representation towards discursive practices: Gender in the foreign language textbook revisited", in: Lia Litosseliti and Jane Sunderland (eds), *Gender identity and discourse analysis*. Amsterdam: John Benjamins, 223–55.

Talbot, Mary. 1995. "A synthetic sisterhood: False friends in a teenage magazine", in: Kira Hall and Mary Bucholtz (eds), *Gender articulated: Language and socially constructed self*. London: Routledge, 143–65.

Talbot, Mary. 2010. *Language, intertextuality and subjectivity: Voices in the construction of consumer femininity*. Saarbrücken: Lambert Academic Publishing.

Talbot, Mary. 2007. *Media discourse. Representation and interaction*. Edinburgh: Edinburgh University Press.

Talbot, Mary. 2003. "Gender stereotypes: reproduction and challenge", in: Janet Holmes and Miriam Meyerhoff (eds), *The handbook of language and gender*. Oxford: Blackwell, 468–86.

Taylor, Stephanie. 2005a. "Identity trouble and place of residence in women's life narratives", in: Nancy Kelly, David Robinson, Caroline Horrocks and Brian Roberts (eds), *Narrative, memory and everyday life*. Huddersfield: The University of Huddersfield Press, 97–106.

Taylor, Stephanie. 2005b. "Identity trouble and opportunity in women's narratives of residence", *Auto/Biography*, 13: 249–65.

Taylor, Stephanie. 2005c. "Self-narration as rehearsal: A discursive approach to the narrative formation of identity", *Narrative Inquiry*, 15: 45–50.

Taylor, Stephanie. [2001] 2009. "Evaluating and applying discourse analytic research", in: Margaret Wetherell, Stephanie Taylor and Simeon J. Yates (eds), *Discourse as data. A guide for analysis*. London: Sage, 311–30.

Taylor, Stephanie. 2001. "Places I remember: Women's talk about residence and other relationships to place", *Auto/Biography*, 9: 33–40.

Taylor, Stephanie and Karen Littleton. 2006. "Biographies in talk: A narrative-discursive approach", *Qualitative Sociology Review*, 2, 1: 22–38.

Thomas, Lyn. 1995. "In love with Inspector Morse: Feminist subculture and quality television", *Feminist Review*, 51: 1–25.

Thompson, John. 1990. *Ideology and modern culture: Critical social theory of mass communication*. Stanford, CA: Stanford University Press.

Thorne, Barrie. 1993. *Gender play: Girls and boys in school*. New Brunswick, NJ: Rutgers University Press.

Thorpe, Holly. 2008. "Foucault, technologies of self, and the media: Discourses of femininity in snowboarding culture", *Journal of Sport and Social Issues*, 32, 2: 199–229.

Tiggemann, Marika and Jessica E. Lynch. 2001. "Body image across the life span in adult women: The role of self-objectification", *Developmental Psychology*, 2, 37: 243–53.

Tuchman, Gaye. 1978. "Introduction: The symbolic annihilation of women by the mass media", in: Gaye Tuchman, Arlene K. Daniels and James Benét (eds), *Heart and home: Images of women in the mass media*. New York: Oxford University Press, 3–38.

van Dijk, Theo. [2001] 2009. "Principles of critical discourse analysis", in: Margaret Wetherell, Stephanie Taylor and Simeon J. Yates (eds), *Discourse as data. A guide for analysis*. London: Sage, 300–17.

van Dijk, Theo (ed.). 1997. *Discourse studies: A multidisciplinary introduction – discourse as social interaction*. Vol. 2. London: Sage.

van Dijk, Theo. 1993. "Principles of Critical Discourse Analysis", *Discourse and Society*, 4, 2: 249–83.

van Leeuwen, Theo. 2008. *Discourse and practice. New tools for Critical Discourse Analysis*. Oxford: Oxford University Press.

van Leeuwen, Theo. 2005a. *Introducing social semiotics*. London: Routledge.

van Leeuwen, Theo. 2005b. "Three models of interdisciplinarity", in: Ruth Wodak and Paul Chilton (eds), *A new agenda in (critical) discourse analysis: Theory, methodology, and interdisciplinary*. Amsterdam: John Benjamins, 3–18.

van Leeuwen, Theo. 1996. "The representation of social actors", in: Carmen Rosa Caldas-Coulthard and Malcolm Coulthard (eds), *Texts and practices: Readings in critical discourse analysis*. London: Routledge, 32–70.

van Leeuwen, Theo and Ruth Wodak. 1999. "Legitimizing immigration control: A discourse-historical analysis", *Discourse Studies*, 1: 83–118.

van Zoonen, Liesbet. 1994. *Feminist media studies*. London: Sage.

Vološinov, Valentin Nikolaevich. [1929] 1973. *Marxism and the philosophy of language*. (Translated by Ladislav Matejka and I. R. Titunik.) New York: Seminar Press.

Walkerdine, Valerie. 1990. *Schoolgirl fictions*. London: Verso.

Walsh, Clare. 2001. *Gender and discourse: Language and power in politics, the church and organizations*. London: Longman.

Walter, Natasha. 2010. *Living dolls: The return of sexism*. London: Virago.

Weatherall, Anne. 2002. *Gender, language and discourse*. New York: Routledge

Weedon, Chris. 1999. *Feminism, theory and the politics of difference*. Oxford: Blackwell.

Weedon, Chris. 1997. *Feminist practice and poststructuralist theory*. Oxford: Blackwell.

Weiss, Gilbert and Wodak, Ruth. 2003. "Introduction: Theory, interdisciplinarity and critical discourse analysis", in: Gilbert Weiss and Ruth Wodak (eds), *Critical Discourse Analysis: Theory and interdisciplinarity*. Basingstoke: Palgrave Macmillan, 1–32.

Werth, Paul. 1999. *Text worlds: Representing conceptual space in discourse*. New York: Longman.

West, Candace. 1998. "Not just doctor's orders: Directive-response sequences in patients' visits to women and men physicians", Jenny Cheshire and Peter Trudgill (eds), *The sociolinguistics reader: Gender and discourse*. London: Edward Arnold, 99–126.

West, Candace. 2002. "Peeling an onion: A critical comment on 'competing discourses'", *Discourse and Society*, 13, 6: 843–51.

Westcott, Helen L. and Karen Littleton. 2004. "Interviewing children: Context, competence and joint meaning making", in: Sheila M. Greene and Diane M. Hogan (eds), *Researching children's experience: Approaches and methods*. London: Sage.

Wetherell, Margaret. 2007. "A step too far: Discursive psychology, linguistic ethnography and questions of identity", *Journal of Sociolinguistics* 11, 5: 661–81.

Wetherell, Margaret. 2003. "Paranoia, ambivalence and discursive practices: Concepts of position and positioning in psychoanalysis and discursive psychology", in: Rom Harré and Fathali Moghaddam (eds), *The self and others: Positioning individuals and groups in personal, political, and cultural contexts*. Westport: Praegar, 99–120.

Wetherell, Margaret. 1998. "Positioning and interpretative repertoires: Conversation analysis and post-structuralism in dialogue", *Discourse and Society*, 9, 387–412.

Wetherell, Margaret. 1995. "Romantic discourse and feminist analysis: Interrogating investment, power and desire", in: Celia Kitzinger and Sue Wilkinson (eds), *Feminism and discourse: Psychological perspectives*. London: Sage, 128–44.

Wetherell, Margaret and Nigel Edley. 1999. "Negotiating hegemonic masculinity: Imaginary positions and psycho-discursive practices", *Feminism and Psychology*, 9, 3: 335–56.

Wetherell, Margaret and Nigel Edley. 1998. "Gender practices: Steps in the analysis of men and masculinities", in: Karen Henwood, Christine Griffin and Ann Phoenix (eds), *Standpoints and differences: Essays in the practice of feminist psychology*. London: Sage, 156–73.

White, Michele. 2011. "The dirt on 'trash the dress' resistance: Photographers, brides, and the mess of post-wedding imaging sessions", *Critical Studies in Media Communication*, 29, 2: 113–31.

Widdowson, Henry. 2004. *Text, context, pretext: Critical issues in discourse analysis*. Malden: Blackwell.

Wilding, Raelene. 2003. "Romantic love and 'getting married': Narratives of the wedding in and out of cinema texts", *Journal of Sociology*, 39, 373–89.

Willemen, Paul. 1978. "Notes on subjectivity: On reading Edward Branigan's 'Subjectivity under siege'", *Screen*, 19, 1: 41–70.

Willig, Carla. 2007. "Reflections on the use of a phenomenological method", *Qualitative Research in Psychology*, 4: 209–25.

Willig, Carla. 1999. "Beyond appearances: a critical realist approach to social constructionist work in psychology", in: David Nightingale and John Cromby (eds), *Psychology and social constructionism: A critical analysis of theory and practice*. Buckingham: Open University Press, 37–51.

Winch, Alison and Anna Webster. 2012. "Here comes the brand: Wedding media and the management of transformation", *Journal of Media and Cultural Studies*, 26, 1: 51–9.

Winship, Janice. 1987. *Inside women's magazines*. London: Pandora.

Winslade, John M. 2005. "Utilising discursive positioning in counseling", *British Journal of Guidance and Counselling*, 33, 3: 351–64.

Wodak, Ruth. 2008. "Introduction: Discourse studies – important concepts and terms", in: Ruth Wodak and Michał Krzyżanowski (eds), *Qualitative discourse analysis in social research*. Basingstoke: Palgrave Macmillan, 1–29.

Wodak, Ruth. 2001a. "The discourse-historical approach", in: Ruth Wodak and Michael Meyer (eds), *Methods of Critical Discourse Analysis*. London: Sage, 63–94.

Wodak, Ruth. 2001b. "What CDA is about – a summary of its history, important concepts and its developments", in: Ruth Wodak and Michael Meyer (eds), *Methods of Critical Discourse Analysis*. London: Sage, 1–14.

Wodak, Ruth. 1997. "Introduction", in: Ruth Wodak (ed.), *Gender and discourse*. London: Sage, 1–20.

Wodak, Ruth and Brigitta Busch. 2004. "Approaches to media texts", in: John H. Downing (ed.), *The Sage handbook of media studies*. Thousand Oaks: Sage, 105–22.

Wolff, Erwin. 1971. "Der intendierte Leser", *Poetica*, 4: 141–66.

Wood, Helen. 2006. "The mediated conversational floor: An interactive approach to audience reception analysis", *Media, Culture and Society*, 29, 1: 75–103.

Wood, Helen. 2005. "Texting the subject: Women, television, and modern self-reflexivity", *The Communication Review*, 8: 115–35.

Wood, Julia T. 2009. *Gendered lives: Communication, gender, and culture*. Belmont, CA: Wadsworth Cengage Learning.

Wylie, Alison. 2004. "Why standpoint matters", in: Sandra Harding (ed.), *The feminist standpoint theory reader*. New York: Routledge, 339–51.

Index

CPSIA information can be obtained at www.ICGtesting.com
Printed in the USA
LVOW07*1317051215

465456LV00010B/370/P